nd then we proceeded to the first Cross highway on the S. West side of said
Mile of Commons which beginning a little Northwesterly of [illegible]
Whitneys Dwelling House and runs across s.d Lotts [illegible]
to Norwalk line and we measured off the [illegible]
true square the same as we found them to be [illegible]
the upright highway so called upon each line of s.d [illegible]
erected Monuments at the extent of each lot [illegible] of s.d
Cross highways by setting a Stone well in the ground & laying a
heap of Stones about the same to divide between adjoining lotts
and between s.d Lotts and s.d Upright highways and measured off
the width of them in the same manner and bounded them in the
same successive order as they are above set down from s.d Mile
of Commons to Norwalk Line — and then we proceeded to the
Second Cross highway which begins a little Northeastward of
the Dwelling House where Edmond Ogden dec.d lately lived, and
beginning next the mile of Commons We erected & fixed bounds
and Monuments between each long lott and between them
and the s.d Upright highways upon Each line of s.d Second
Cross highway in the same manner successive order & for the
same purposes as those erected upon the lines of the first Cross
highway from s.d Mile of Commons to Norwalk line and then
we proceeded to the third Cross Highway which runs across s.d
lotts by the Lyons and being next the west side of the s.d
Mile of Commons we erected & fix'd bounds & Monuments
between each long lot and between them & s.d Upright high-
-ways on Each line of s.d Cross highway in the same manner
successive order & for the like purposes as those erected upon
the lines of the aforesaid Cross highways from s.d Mile of
Commons to Norwalk Line only it so hapned that on the
lines of s.d third Cross highway bounds could not be erected
and fix'd between Osborns & Perrys long lotts on the lines
of s.d Cross highway as it fell nigh the Middle of Saugatuck
River - therefore we erected & fix'd the bounds about Seven Rods

Weston

Weston

the forging of a Connecticut town

Thomas J. Farnham

published for the
WESTON HISTORICAL SOCIETY
by
PHOENIX PUBLISHING
Canaan, New Hampshire

Farnham, Thomas J.
Weston.

Includes index.
1. Weston, Conn.—History. I. Title.
F104.W38F37 974.6'9 79-14521
ISBN 0-914016-59-8

Printed in the United States of America
by Courier Printing Company
Binding by New Hampshire Bindery
Design by A. L. Morris

Dedicated to
Lucy MacCauley Forrest
Whose bequest to the Weston Historical Society
helped make possible this History of Weston
and to
Cleora Dunn Coley
For the generous use of the Barn Museum
and the future gift of her
property in memory of her late husband
James Sturgis Coley

CONTENTS

For Jon, Chris, and Julie

PREFACE

During the Great Depression, Margaret Lylburn wrote a series of articles about Weston for the Bridgeport *Post-Telegram*. One of the articles concerned Frank Banks, a Weston farmer who had witnessed eighty years of the town's history. When asked if he recalled anything of particular interest ever happening in Weston, Banks replied, "No, I can't say as I do remember anything exciting ever happening around here." He went on to describe his life and that of the town as "quiet" and "pleasant." Like the rest of Weston's population in the nineteenth and early twentieth centuries, his was a life of "just farming, clamming, and fishing, and tending to my own business," he said.

Viewed in terms of momentous events, Weston has made little "history." No great battles were ever fought in Weston. No great discoveries were ever made there. Until recently, Weston's citizens were a conspicuously anonymous group. The direction of American history has not been dramatically altered by what did or did not happen in Weston.

But this does not mean that Weston has not had a rich and—at times, at least—a fascinating history. Its history is unlike that of Benjamin Franklin's Philadelphia or even of Roger Sherman's New Haven. It is the history, for the most part, of very ordinary people. And herein lies the wealth and the enchantment of its past. What makes the history of Weston—or, for that matter, the history of any other small community—fascinating is the fact that on this same terrain once lived other men and women, men and women much like ourselves, as full of their own thoughts and emotions as we are, as swayed by their own passions as we are. But now those earlier generations have departed, just as the present generation will one day depart. It is the passing of one generation after another, a fact that is both absolutely certain and absolutely familiar, that brings drama to the most ordinary lives and that brings an almost sublime sense to the history of Weston.

The present work is a history of the community that was and is Weston; it is an attempt to describe how that community came into being, what it was at different times, and how it changed from what it had been in the past to what it is today. In describing this community, I have viewed it as an entity in itself and more than the sum total of its institutions. I have been unwilling to believe that combining a history of public education in the town, with a history of zoning regulation, with a history of law enforcement, with a history of institutional religion, et cetera, et cetera, would make a history of Weston. Rather, I have seen changing ideas about education and zoning and law enforcement and religion as manifestations of the community's spirit and concerns at different times. More important than the details of public-school administration are the opinions of the community about what formal education is supposed to accomplish. The focus throughout will be on the community as a whole, and the community, as I have seen it, is made up of people more than institutions, of ideas and attitudes and opinions more than committees or boards or clubs.

The question that is asked over and over in this book is the question of what the people of Weston wanted their community to be—given, of course, the limits that nature and the broader society places upon it. Did the people of Weston want a democratic society? Did they want a mobile society? Did they want to be an agricultural or an industrial community? What part did they want to assign to religion or the family or governmental authority in their society?

From these sorts of questions will, I hope, emerge the essence of life in this small community. Once, not very long ago, Weston was a much different place from what it is now. What was it like in that world that is no more? How was that world similar to and different from the world of Weston today?

This work is intended for general readers, not for scholars. It is presented in a narrative form. While I wish my scholarship to satisfy modern students of social history in general and of New England towns in particular, I hope as fervently that I have used modern scholarly techniques to inform and not to impress my readers. Throughout, I have intended to write a history of Weston that will be historically accurate and readable. I have never intended to compile a history of my own labors. Therefore, scholarly apparatus has been kept to a minimum. All quotations are footnoted; general references to my sources of information will, I hope, guide those who are interested in learning more about a particular topic without intruding upon the patience of those whose interest extends no further than this narrative.

At one time, Weston and Easton were one town. So, obviously, while discussing the years from 1787 to 1845, I cannot dissociate Weston from its neighbor to the east. But recognizing this, I have attempted to write a history of the community that is the ancestor of the present Weston. Even when Weston and Easton were one town, called Weston, they were not one community. To pretend that they were would do injury to the history of both. The fact that this marriage of convenience lasted for nearly sixty years does not make it more than it was, a marriage of convenience.

In quoting from the seventeenth- and eighteenth-century documents, I have refused, as much as possible, to tinker with spelling and punctuation. Even the spellings of proper names were often phonetic at best, and I have not attempted to make them uniform. Neither have I burdened these quotations with *sics*. I have consistently altered "ye" or "yt" to "the" and "that," and I have changed the ff used to form a capital to the single *F*. I have also retained all dates as they appeared in the original documents, except that I have assumed that the year began on January 1 rather than on March 25, as it did for the period prior to 1752. Thus I have changed a double date such as January 25, 1705/6 to read January 25, 1706.

Of the many people who have helped with my work on Weston, several deserve special mention. Professor Rollin G. Osterweis of Yale University originally aroused my interest in the subject. Librarians at Southern Connecticut State College, the Connecticut State Library, the Fairfield Historical Society, the New Canaan Historical Society, the New Haven Colony Historical Society, Yale University, and the Connecticut Historical Society made my work not only possible but pleasurable. Claire Bennett of the Connecticut Room at Southern Connecticut State College was a paragon among paragons. Mrs. Cleora Coley, Raymond Fitch, Mrs. Ruth Fox, Arthur J. Hoe, Robert Lambden, Miss Ruth Lockwood, Anson Morton, and Mrs. Gertrude Walker all shared their memories of Weston with me. I hope that I have treated their remembrances fairly, for their willingness to help was greatly appreciated. Jonathan Farnham gathered and analyzed data from the censuses of the nineteenth century. Donald Yacovone examined probate court records in my behalf. Carol Culmo typed the entire manuscript. Gwen V. Davis helped me through the rough spots, of which there were many.

Louis Bregy, MacLennan Farrell, Betty Hill, and W. Scott Hill of the Weston Historical Society made a contribution to the creation of this book which only they and I can understand. My deepest gratitude to MacLennan Farrell for his painstaking and conscientious copy editing of the manuscript. Their names deserve to be both inscribed on the title page and remembered by those interested in Weston's past.

Thomas J. Farnham

December 6, 1978

Weston

FAIRFIELD, THE PARENT SETTLEMENT
1637 / 1684

"From the sea a days walke into the country"

Although it would be 1787 before Weston would formally become a town, the events that eventually converged in the creation of that community had their origins when the colony of Connecticut itself was just beginning to take seed along the banks of the Connecticut River. May 1, 1637, seems as good a date as any to begin.

On that date—when the river settlements of Windsor, Hartford, and Wethersfield were barely a year old—the General Court at Hartford declared war against the Pequot Indians, a tribe so fierce that its name meant "destroyers of men." The decision for war had come only after great provocation. Trouble had begun several years earlier. Even before the arrival of the settlers of Connecticut, a clash between Dutch traders and the Pequots had resulted in the death of Wopigwooit, chief of the Pequots. The Pequots swore revenge against any whites who might invade their lands, and in 1633 carried out their pledge of violence by killing eight or ten Englishmen, members of a trading party led by John Stone, a Virginian. Stone and his men had made the mistake of stopping to hunt in the area around the mouth of the Connecticut River.

The years 1634 and 1635 passed without serious incidents between the Pequots and the whites. In fact, during these years the Pequots, who found their position of dominance among Connecticut Indians being challenged, sought the friendship and support of the English at Massachusetts Bay. It was also during these years that stories of the natural assets of the Connecticut River valley began to drift back to the settlements of Massachusetts Bay and men in that colony began to talk seriously of migrating to the fertile valley.

But during the following year, as immigrants from the Bay colony were establishing towns like Windsor, more trouble occurred between Indians and whites in Connecticut. During the summer of 1636, a party of Block Island Indians killed John Oldham, a trader operating in the area of Long Island Sound. When the Pequots granted refuge to Oldham's murderers, they found themselves the object of an expedition sent by Massachusetts Bay to seek the murderers of Oldham, Stone, and the other Englishmen. The expedition failed to confront the Pequots in battle but did manage, in August, 1636, to destroy large quantities of Pequot property, in particular canoes, corn, and dwellings.

The English attack convinced the Pequots that there never could be peace between red men and white men. The whites had to be driven from their land, they decided, and during the winter of 1636-1637, they began a series of attacks on the English fort at Saybrook. Lion Gardiner, the commander of the outpost, had warned the Massachusetts Bay raiders during August, 1636, that, "You have come to raise a nest of hornets about our ears. . . ."[1*] Throughout the following winter, Gardiner paid for the audacity of the Bay colony soldiers.

On April 23, 1637, the event occurred that would eventually bring the Connecticut General Court to declare war on the Pequots. On that date, a party of Pequots paddled up the Connecticut to Wethersfield, where they came upon a small work party busy cleaning brush from a meadow near the river. Without warning, the Indians struck, killing three women and six men and taking two girls hostage. The Indians then retreated to their canoes and headed downriver. When they reached the fort at Saybrook, they brazenly raised poles from which flew the shirts of their Wethersfield victims.

Connecticut's General Court made preparations for war. It called

---

*Numbered notes to each chapter appear at the end of the chapter.

upon Hartford to provide forty-two men, Windsor thirty, and Wethersfield eighteen. Of these men, fourteen from Hartford and six from Windsor were to be in armor. Captain John Mason was the expedition's leader. Later, in early June, the General Court would attach forty additional men to the expedition. Even more important was the decision by Uncas, chief of the Mohegans, to join forces with Mason and his men. Uncas, a bitter enemy of Sassacus, chief of the Pequots, hoped that by aiding the English he could overthrow Sassacus and declare himself chief of the Pequots. Uncas brought with him eighty warriors.

On May 15, the expedition left Hartford, the English sailing "in one pink, one pinnace, and one shallop," the Indians paddling their swifter and more suitable canoes.

Upon reaching Saybrook, Mason learned that the Pequots were numerous and prepared to meet any attack the English could muster. Therefore, he decided to attack the Pequot strongholds from the rear. There were two Pequot forts, several miles apart, at Mystic. Mason and his men managed to strike the first without rousing the enemy within. The straw-roofed dwellings were a tempting target for Mason's firebrands; and while the flames spread, Mason ordered his men to allow no one to escape the holocaust. He later reported that the Indians "were taken in their own Snare, and we through Mercy escaped And thus in *little more than one Hour's space* was their impregnable *Fort* with themselves utterly Destroyed, to the Number of *six* or *seven Hundred,* as some of themselves confessed. There were only *seven* taken *Captive* & about *seven escaped.*"[2]

Mason had no time for celebration, however, for he knew that Sassacus, with three hundred warriors from the second fort, would soon be seeking revenge. Good fortune allowed him to avoid a full-scale battle with Sassacus and to return safely with his men to Saybrook.

The surviving Pequots and their leader, after rejecting the idea of carrying the war to the English settlements, decided to flee Connecticut and to seek refuge in the Hudson River valley, the area from which they had migrated only a few years before.

Mason's force, in the meantime, had returned to Hartford, there to receive the praise and gratitude of the colonists they had defended. About two weeks after the expedition's return, news came from Long Island Sound that a small fleet had arrived there from Massachusetts with one hundred and twenty soldiers led by Captain Israel Stoughton; these men were ready to carry on the war against the Pequots.

The Connecticut General Court quickly decided that John Haynes and Roger Ludlow should depart with Captain Mason and forty men to meet with the Massachusetts leader to consider further actions against the Pequots. At the end of June, 1637, Mason, Stoughton, Haynes, and Ludlow agreed that a joint force of Connecticut and Massachusetts men should pursue and destroy the remaining Pequot warriors.

Mason, because of his exploits against the Pequots, would become Connecticut's first military hero. But Roger Ludlow, rather than Mason, was the expedition's most important member. For it was Ludlow who would recognize the potential value of the southwestern Connecticut shoreline, who would one day bring English settlers to the area that would become Fairfield, and who would place Fairfield within the domain of the Connecticut colony.

The man who was to found Fairfield had been born in Dinton, Wiltshire, England, in 1590. He was the son of a West Country gentry family that had become prominent during the reign of Henry VIII. He attended Balliol College, Oxford, and later studied law at the Inner Temple. A Puritan and an officer of the Massachusetts Bay Company, he took passage in March, 1630, on the *Mary and John* bound out of Plymouth, England, for Massachusetts Bay. There he became one of the founders of Dorchester and was among the most active men in the colony. In 1634, he became deputy-governor of that colony.

It was during the following year that Ludlow decided that his interest would best be served by moving from the Bay colony to the Connecticut River valley. He was unhappy with Massachusetts Bay's leadership generally, and in particular with the fact that he had been overlooked as a possible candidate for governor. Tales about the great natural wealth of the Connecticut River valley had also excited him. In the spring of 1636, Ludlow led a party of Dorchester settlers out of Massachusetts Bay and into the valley of the Connecticut. He had been, before his departure, one of the eight men delegated by the Massachusetts Bay Colony to provide the framework of government for the Connecticut plantations. The Massachusetts Bay General Court had authorized these eight to carry on judicial duties and to issue executive decrees. His role in the Pequot expedition was thus in keeping with the significant role that Ludlow played generally in the life of Connecticut.[3]

When Ludlow, Mason, and the other members of the expedition finally caught up with the Pequots, the Indians had made their way to Uncoway, the area that would eventually become Fairfield. The necessity of hunting for food and the slowness of their children had delayed the flight of the Pequots. When the Indians realized how close their pursuers were, they took cover in a large swamp in what is now that part of Fairfield known as Southport. Before either side resorted to military devices, the English convinced two hundred Pequots, mostly old men and women and children, to surrender. But the Pequot warriors refused even to consider surrender and tried to break through the English lines that encircled them. Sixty or seventy did manage to escape, among them Sassacus, the Pequot chieftain. But one hundred and eighty others fell into their pursuers' hands, thus ending forever their threat to the Connecticut colony. A few weeks later, as a token of friendship and esteem, the Mohawks, eager to become allies of the English, sent the head of Sassacus to the colonial leaders in Hartford.

In terms of Weston's history, the defeat of the Pequots was less important than the impression that Uncoway and the neighboring coastline made upon Roger Ludlow. Ludlow was so pleased with what he saw that he returned to Hartford determined to move again, this time to the shores of Long Island Sound. Massachusetts Bay had drawn him from England; the Connecticut valley had drawn him from Massachusetts Bay; now he was ready to forsake the Connecticut valley for Uncoway, soon to be known as Fairfield.

Two years after the defeat of the Pequots at Southport, Ludlow obtained permission from the Connecticut General Court to move to Pequonnock, which is today the western section of Stratford. But Ludlow was unwilling to settle in Stratford; he was determined to return to Uncoway. So without any authority from the General Court, he established a plantation in that area. Upon hearing of his disobedience, the General Court summoned Ludlow. The date of October 10, 1639, was set by the Court to hear his explanation. Ludlow contended that he was eager to see that the coastal area of southwestern Connecticut was kept from the grasping hands of the Dutch in New Netherlands and from the equally avaricious hands of the English colonists who had settled New Haven. The General Court decided to reprimand Ludlow lightly and to confirm the legality of his settlement at Fairfield.

Certainly, Ludlow lost none of the prestige he held in the colony as a result of his disobedience. He already had demonstrated his importance to the colony by acting as the principal draftsman of the Fundamental Orders, the basis of government in Connecticut until the Charter of 1662. In 1646, the General Court* requested that he prepare a body of laws for the colony. The result was "Ludlow's Code," also known as the Code of 1650. For the fifteen years following the establishment of Fairfield, Ludlow served as a magistrate of Connecticut, and between 1651 and 1653, he was a commissioner of the United Colonies of New England.

In 1654, he abruptly returned to England. His departure might have been prompted either by Connecticut's refusal to support his scheme for an expedition against the Dutch in New Netherlands or by an offer from the Puritan regime in England of an important civil post. Whatever the reason for his decision to leave, the quick-tempered and gruff Ludlow appeared next in Dublin, sitting as a member of the commission to hear claims and to confiscate Royalists' lands in Ireland. He continued to serve the Puritan government until 1660, when the Stuarts returned to the throne in England. As late as 1664, he was still a resident of Dublin.

Even before he received the sanction of the General Court to establish a new plantation at Fairfield, Ludlow had begun the process of acquiring land from the Indians. In the spring of 1639, he signed a treaty with the Pequonnock Indians for the transfer of part of their territory, and in February, 1640, he purchased land from the Norwalk Indians. The Norwalk Indians agreed, "for and in consideration of eight fathom of wampum, sixe coates, tenn hatchets, tenn hoes, tenn knifes, tenn sissors, tenn jewse-harpes, tenn fathom Tobachoe, three kettles of sixe hands about, tenn looking glasses," to sell to Ludlow all the land between the middle of the Norwalk River and the middle of the Saugatuck and "from the sea a days walke into the country." Because of the vagueness of this deed—did it mean, for example, the middle of the mouth of the Norwalk to the middle of the mouth of the Saugatuck?—one would be hard-pressed to determine precisely what the English bought. Certainly it may have included part of what is today Weston. In all probability, the first purchase—that made of the Pequonnocks in 1639—failed to include any of what became western Fairfield. But the limits of the 1639 deed are unknown, for all copies of the treaty were lost during the seventeenth century.[4]

Because of the confusion caused by Ludlow's loss of the 1639 deed,

*The General Court gave way to the General Assembly in 1662.

the townsmen* of Fairfield decided, in 1656, to renegotiate the Pequonnock sale. On March 20 of that year, the Pequonnocks agreed that Fairfield owned all the land upon which it was built "from the Creeke at the Tidemill of Fairfield, South Westward [which] is called Sasqua" and "all that tract of land which they call Unceway (which is from the above said Creek Eastward into the bounds between Fairfield & Stratford) from the sea, to run into the Country seven or eight miles. . . ." This involved land close to but probably not including any of modern Weston; but, again, the bounds of this purchase are less than clear. The Indians who signed the treaty were Umpeter Nosset, Nemrod, Matamuck, Anthonye, and Washau.

Several of these same Indians also put their mark to an agreement of March 20, 1661. It transferred "all that tract of land commonly called Sasqua, bounded on the north-east with the land called Uncaway, on the south-west with the land at Maximus† . . . & this tract of land is to run from the sea strait up into the country six miles at the least . . ." The agreement allowed the Indians "the liberty of hunting in the woods" but stated that they were "to set noe traps within the six mile." It also provided that if the Indians wanted, at some time in the future, "land to plant on, the town of Fairfield is to allow them some land to plant on for their livelyhood. . . ." This land adjoined that purchased from the Pequonnocks in 1656 and would include, one would think, parts of southern Weston. But the Indians, on April 11, 1661, attested that the Sasqua lands extended only "up into the Country into Aspatuck river," thus excluding any of what is now Weston. The Indians also acknowledged receipt of "thirteen Coats, 2 yards apiece, & the rest in Wampum, which is all that Uncoway Englishmen were to pay them for the Sasqua land. . . ."

Fairfield bought another tract of land from the Indians five years later. If none of the earlier purchases included Weston, this one certainly did. It included most of Easton and Redding, as well. The negotiations for this land were completed by the autumn of 1670; for on September 10 of that year, the town meeting decided that "wheras thos that the Towne appointed have in behalf of the Towne bought the last six miles of the Indians of the Towne Commons and they having agreed that the Towne shall give them 36 pounds for it," it would designate John Burr to purchase that amount of "Trucking

---

*The townsmen were the precursors of the selectmen.

†Machamux was the Indian name for Green's Farms.

cloth" at ten shillings a yard. The meeting agreed to pay Burr for it in winter wheat at five shillings a bushel or Indian corn at two shillings a bushel. "Every particular man may pay which he pleas To be payd at or before the last of January," the meeting agreed. Apparently the townspeople were slow to pay, for on January 14, 1670, the town ordered "that there shall be forthwith a rate [tax] made upon the Inhabetants of the town . . . for the satisfaction of the Indian purchased now to be concluded and [the tax is] to be brought to obediah gilbert who is apointed to receive it: to be payd in peass within a fortnight after this date." A deed dated January 19, 1671, formalized the agreement between Fairfield and the Indians. Although the deed was signed by neither the Indians nor the English, it was duly recorded in Book B of the town records.[5]

The inhabitants of Fairfield, now believing that their title to the town lands was clear, began to prepare for the division of these newly acquired lands. But the process of division had barely begun when an Indian known as John Wampus, alias John White, laid claim to part of the town lands, including part of present Weston. Wampus was married to an Indian woman, Anne Praske, daughter of Romanock, chief sachem of the Aspetuck and Sasquannock Indians. At the conclusion of the Pequot War, troops from Massachusetts Bay had taken Anne, along with other Indian women and children of the Aspetuck and Sasqua villages, back to Massachusetts as spoils of war. Warriors from these villages had aided and abetted the Pequots in their futile effort to escape. For a time, Anne had lived as a slave in Boston in the home of Joshua Hughes, but Hughes eventually granted her freedom, and she then married Wampus. On September 11, 1661, Romanock deeded to his absent daughter a parcel of land in Aspetuck. Wampus, as her husband, claimed title to this land.

In pursuit of his claim, the Indian traveled from Boston to Fairfield. Once he arrived, he proceeded to the town clerk, William Hill, and asked to see the land records that related to the lands of Aspetuck. Hill said that although he had the deeds in his possession, he was unwilling to allow Wampus to examine them. The deeds, he said, were ancient and difficult to read. Before he would allow Wampus to see them, he insisted that Wampus go to Nathan Gold, one of the townsmen, and obtain his permission to examine the documents.

Wampus refused to be denied. He sought out Gold, but Gold agreed with Hill that Wampus had no right to examine the deeds. Wampus persisted. He brought the matter to the attention of all the townsmen, who met to deal with this issue at the home of Nathaniel Burr. The townsmen decided not only to deny the Indian the right to see the land records, but they also refused to allow him to survey the parcel that he claimed as his. When the Indian refused to accept this decision, the magistrates ordered him imprisoned and then banished from the town.

But Wampus was nothing if not persistent. He decided that if he could obtain no satisfaction in Fairfield, he would go to England and pursue his claim there. On March 28, 1679, the Lords of the Council heard his petition and responded to it by writing to the governor and magistrates of Connecticut. The Lords noted that Wampus had claimed "that by the evill practices of Major Nathan Gould [Gold] and other Inhabitants of Fairfeild, he is not only kept out of his just rights, but was also imprisoned by them in May last, when he went to demand possession of his Estate. . . ." Wampus also asserted that Connecticut consistently subjected Indians to "great hardships and miserys." The Lords ordered that Wampus and all peaceful Indians be given justice and that in the future the leaders of Connecticut "proceed in such manner as his Majesty's subjects may not be forced to undertake so long & dangerous Voyages for obteyning Justice, which his Majesty expects shalbe speedily & impartially administered upon them upon the Place." But the Lords' decision did Wampus little good. By the time it was rendered, he had died.[6]

Back in Connecticut, though, attorney Richard Thayer of Milford, whom Wampus had employed to help him pursue his case, continued the fight. He addressed a letter to Governor William Leete. Dated July 25, 1681, the letter informed the governor that Thayer had attempted to collect evidence concerning the matter in Fairfield but had been denied access to the relevant documents by the townsmen. He requested that the governor intervene in his behalf.

The governor and his assistants replied the following day. They expressed their willingness to support all lawful efforts to gather evidence and to pursue the truth, "but for to suffer strangers to draw lines within townships without order or consent of the town, we think not safe to encourage." Thayer was temporarily stymied.[7]

The whole incident had frightened the Fairfield leaders so badly that they had decided to obtain from the local Indian leaders a general deed for all the lands they had purchased. On October 30, 1680, some thirty sachems gathered in Fairfield to settle once and for all the question of the ownership of town lands. The deed that was drafted reaffirmed the old deeds of March 20, 1656; March 20, 1661; and January 19, 1671. The Indians received looking glasses, kettles, and coats in return for a small square of turf into which they had thrust a twig. The turf and twig signified the town's ownership of all the lands enclosed in its boundaries, including the "meadows, uplands, Creekes, Rivers and ponds of Aspetuck." The Indians obtained the right to fish and hunt, as well as to gather firewood, on all unfenced lands in the town. They also acknowledged that they had abandoned forever all claims to the Fairfield lands and confirmed the legality of the earlier deeds.[8]

Still, Richard Thayer had not forsaken Wampus's claim. He persisted in the matter by bringing suit against Peter Clapham and Isaac Frost, two of the persons to whom the town of Fairfield had granted the lands claimed by Wampus. In 1684, the case was brought before a jury of twelve men, four from New Haven, two from Derby, five from Milford, and one from Stratford. Before the actual trial began, the Fairfield town meeting voted that if Clapham and Frost "will Take direction from the Townsmen in the defence of the case, then the necessary Charge arising in the defence of the said case shall be defrayed out of the Towne Treasurie."[9]

Testimony concerned not only Aspetuck but the question of the ownership of Sasqua and Uncoway, as well. The English claimed that they had paid the Indians for the lands and that they also held title to the lands as a result of their victory over the Pequots and their allies in 1637. The Indians who testified during the trial confirmed the settlers' contention that Fairfield owned the land both by the terms of their purchases and by their defeat of the Pequots. The Aspetuck and Sasqua villagers acknowledged that they had assisted the Pequots in their flight. They stated that they had forsaken their claim to part of their land as a result of their involvement, brief though it was, in the war.

In addition, the jury learned that neither Wampus nor his wife had taken possession of the land in question for a period of twenty years from the date of the transfer of title. According to Connecticut law, the couple's failure forfeited their right to the land, regardless of the legality of the original Romanock deed. Thus, the executors of Wampus's estate lost their case. The willingness of local Indians to support the case of Fairfield, as well as the technicalities involved in the failure of either Wampus or Anne to take over the land, made the executor's appeal less than convincing.[10]

For the subsequent history of both Fairfield and Weston, the importance of *Wampus* v. *Frost and Clapham* was that it signaled the end of questions over the ownership of town lands. The Indian claims had been liquidated. No longer would these questions be issues for the people of Fairfield. When the town of Weston was born, it came into being with a clear title to its lands. To Roger Ludlow and his successors the founders of Weston would be grateful for this important inheritance.

NOTES TO CHAPTER 1

1. Quoted in Howard Bradstreet, *The Story of the War with the Pequots* (New Haven, 1933), p. 9. Bradstreet's story is brief and readable. The best account of the war is found in Alden T. Vaughan, *New England Frontier: Puritans and Indians, 1620-1675* (Boston, 1965).

2. John Mason, *Brief History of the Pequot War* (Boston, 1736), p. 9.

3. Ludlow's career is described in J.M. Taylor, *Roger Ludlow, the Colonial Lawmaker* (New York, 1900).

4. A copy of this deed is found in Edwin Hall, *The Ancient Historical Records of Norwalk* (New York, 1847), p. 30.

5. The deeds of 1656 and 1661 are included in Elizabeth Hubbell Schenck, *The History of Fairfield,* 2 volumes (New York, 1889), I, 93-94, 108-109. The 1671 deed is in Fairfield Town Records, Land Records, Book B. The references to the Fairfield town meeting are in Fairfield Town Records, Town Meeting Minutes, I, 46, 47, 51, 52.

6. *Public Records of the Colony of Connecticut,* I, 281-282.

7. The correspondence between Leete and Thayer is in Connecticut Archives, Towns and Lands, First Series, Volume I, Connecticut State Library.

8. Schenck, I, 330-332.

9. Fairfield Town Records, Town Meeting Minutes, I, 154.

10. The details of the suit filed in behalf of Wampus's estate have been gleaned from the "Trumbull Papers," *Collections of the Massachusetts Historical Society,* Fifth Series, IX, 93, 110, 127-138.

THE INDIANS AND THE LAND

Paugussetts and Siwanogs in the majestic virgin forest

The Indians from whom Ludlow and his successors bought Fairfield represented two of the sixteen Indian tribes that lived in Connecticut at the time Europeans began exploring the area. The first of these was the Paugussetts, one of the largest tribes in Connecticut. Their territory extended along Long Island Sound from what is today Orange on the east to the Norwalk River on the west. These Indians inhabited the present towns of Bridgewater, Roxbury, Woodbury, Middlebury, and Waterbury, but there was no precise northern boundary to their territory. Connecticut Indians generally avoided what is today Litchfield County because the Mohawks, who lived in New York, claimed northwestern Connecticut as their hunting territory. Connecticut Indians had no enthusiasm for challenging the claim of the fierce Mohawks.

The Paugussett tribe consisted of five clans; these were the Wipawaugs, Unkowas, Potatucks, Pomeraugs, and Naugatucks. All of the members of the tribe, regardless of clan, referred to themselves as Paugussetts, and they were really one people. In fact, members of the same clan were forbidden to marry. This meant that the various

One of Weston's most scenic areas, the glen at Valley Forge, as it appeared in 1902, with Gould's gristmill beyond the footbridge at upper right

clans were closely related, for there was constant marriage between clans and within the tribe. The whites, after their arrival in Connecticut, came to refer to the Indians in terms of the location of an individual village. Thus the whites referred to those Indians who lived in what is today Weston and Easton as the Aspetucks. The so-called Aspetucks were not even a clan, much less a tribe. These Indians were members of the Unkowa clan of the Paugussett tribe. Likewise, the Saugatuck Indians were neither a tribe nor a clan. The name Saugatuck was attributed to the members of a particular village by the whites. Both "Saugatuck" and "Aspetuck" are Paugussett words, Saugatuck meaning "outlet of the tidal stream" and Aspetuck meaning "river originating at the high place."

The ancestors of the Paugussetts had lived in the area for many centuries, having first come to this part of Connecticut some five thousand years before the arrival of Europeans. Archeological research at the Mother Grouse Shelter and the Eckart-Neubauer Rockshelter in Easton and in the Lucius Pond Ordway Preserve in Weston has uncovered quartz points from the Middle Archaic Period, a period which ended three thousand years before the arrival of whites in the region. The Indians who first lived in the Weston area were seminomadic; they traveled in small groups, following a particular annual circuit in search of seasonal sources of food. The long history of the Indians in the Fairfield area is further confirmed by enormous piles of shells left along the shore by countless generations of Indian shellfish fanciers.

The other Indian tribe in the Fairfield-Weston area was the Siwanog tribe, a name given to them by the Dutch of New Netherlands. These Indians were not a distinct tribe, as the Paugussetts were. They also had a much less well-defined territory than did the Paugussetts. In general, the Siwanogs occupied that part of Connecticut that extended from the New York line as far east as the Norwalk River. Their territory went from Long Island Sound on the south as far north as the present town of Wilton. Unfortunately for the Indians, this area was also claimed by the Dutch, and it was the Dutch who forced many of the Siwanogs out of what is now southwestern Connecticut and up into the area that would eventually become Ridgefield and Weston.

The reason the Siwanogs cannot in justice be called a unique tribe is that they were really under the control of the Wappinger Confederacy, an Indian group whose headquarters were then located east of the Hudson River in the general vicinity of Poughkeepsie, New York. But the Siwanogs left their mark on the Fairfield area by the place names that have persisted from the days when they wandered the region. "Sasca," for example, is a Siwanog word meaning "muddy river," and "Norwalk" meant "at the point of land" in their language.

When Roger Ludlow first came to Fairfield, Connecticut's Indian population was small, probably numbering no more than six to seven thousand. To state this statistic in more comprehensible terms, fewer Indians then lived in all of Connecticut than individuals now live in the town of Weston. The native population had been considerably larger at the beginning of the seventeenth century, but in 1616-1617, a devastating plague had killed literally thousands of Indians. Of those six or seven thousand Indians who had survived the plague, most lived along the coast, where food was easily obtained. The total Indian population of what is now Weston and Easton could hardly have numbered more than a few dozen souls, and probably these few spent only part of each year in Weston or Easton. During the spring and summer months, life was much easier along the coast; it made sense for the Indians to reside there and to return to the interior during hunting season and after the storms of autumn and winter made the coast less desirable.

Unfortunately, the Indians of Connecticut have left little evidence of the way they lived. Obviously, the Indians, who had no written language, left no written records. The investigations of archeologists in Connecticut have turned up thousands of individual Indian items and fragments of items, but the resulting picture of Indian culture is still itself only a fragment. The work of archeologists has really only uncovered enough to tantalize those who would like to know more about Connecticut during the centuries before the white man arrived.

The Indians who lived in the Weston area, like their counterparts in other areas of Connecticut, were more than just gatherers or hunters or fishers. Apparently, around A.D. 1000 an important change occurred in the lives of Connecticut Indians. It appears that before this time they had been basically gatherers and hunters, but then they learned the techniques of agriculture. So, the Indians that Ludlow and his associates first encountered in the Fairfield area were horticulturists. In fact, the principal items in their diet at the time of the arrival of Europeans were a variety of vegetables. Besides vegetables, fish and shellfish were most important to them. The meat of mammals and birds was of less importance.

Of the various vegetables that the Indians grew, corn, or maize, was clearly the most important. It was the basic ingredient in their diet, and the red men consumed it in a variety of forms. They ate it as porridge and in the form of unleavened cakes. As we do today, they ate it on the cob, either roasted or boiled. They also had learned to pop corn and consumed it in this manner. The Indians mixed corn with beans and cooked the combination in an earthen pot; the result was succotash, a dish that we traditionally think of as Indian. Less well remembered are some of the other ways they combined corn and other foods. They liked to mix it with fish or with ground nuts. These combinations were as favored as were concoctions of corn and artichokes or corn and dense flour made from ground nuts. The Connecticut Indians also, of course, turned maize into corn meal. To guarantee a supply of this basic staple for the winter months, Indians dried corn in the sun and then buried the dehydrated food in large pits, to be recovered when cold weather came. They used a similar technique with fish.

Most of the actual farming was done by the women of the village. Although a man might be willing to lend his strength to the accomplishment of a particular task, the drudgery was the squaws'. Their agricultural tools were of the crudest variety, few being anything more than conveniently formed sticks that the Indian women might modify in some very simple fashion.

When the Connecticut Indians began to farm, they did not completely forsake older forms of food collection such as simple gathering. What they managed to grow was supplemented by dietary delights they found in the forests and along the coast. Chestnuts, walnuts, currants, blackberries, strawberries, and plums added diversity to what they ate. One of the attractions of Weston for Indians was undoubtedly the large stands of chestnuts. Walnuts and blackberries also flourished in these inland areas.

Indian men used a variety of devices to catch fish. At different seasons and at different places, they might resort to nets or harpoons or hooks. They fished in both the waters of Long Island Sound and the fresh waters of inland ponds and streams. Sturgeon was a great favorite of the Indians, but bass, bluefish, bream, carp, catfish, cod, haddock, hake, halibut, pickerel, pike, and salmon were all happy catches for Connecticut aborigines. The work of collecting shellfish, like farming, was work for women, who regularly enlisted the assistance of their children.

Most of the mammal meat consumed by the Indians of the Weston area was provided by the white-tailed deer. These animals were sometimes killed with bow and arrow but were as often caught in traps. The hunting season was during the fall and winter, when the snow helped the Indians to track the deer and when possibly deep snow slowed the hoofed animals but not men on snowshoes. Bear was also a favorite winter quarry. It, too, might be killed with bow and arrow or trapped, but the Indians were also prone to kill the animals as they hibernated. Both the pelt and the meat of the bear were used by the Indians. They killed otter and beaver, but exclusively for their pelts. The Indians hunted the beaver by breaking into their lodges and killing the startled animals there. They also preyed on a variety of wild fowl. On the bays and marshes of Long Island Sound and on the ponds and rivers of the inland areas, they found geese and ducks. The fields and forests provided doves, quail, turkey, and partridge. Undoubtedly, during the autumn and winter hunting season, more Indians would take up residence in the inland Weston area than at any other time of the year, but even then its population was hardly large.

Because the Indians of Connecticut moved about as much as they did, their homes were lightly constructed and designed to be easily dismantled and reassembled. The various tribes generally remained within their tribal territories, but within these territories they were never reluctant to move. The Indian homes stood close to one another, but the Indians kept a central area open for ceremonial occasions and for the conduct of business. The houses were made of poles inserted in the ground, bent together at the top and then fastened to form an irregular ridge. These dwellings, usually twenty to forty feet in length, were covered with bark. The inhabitants used reeds and rushes to thatch the roofs. It was roofs of this construction that burned so furiously when Captain Mason put the torch to the Pequot fort at Mystic. Some villages, like the Pequot fort, were enclosed by a fortification of young tree trunks ten or twelve feet high. There is no reason to believe that the Aspetuck village would have been so fortified.

The items found within the dwellings were simple. The Indians made much use of crude hardwood bowls. More attractive and every bit as useful were Indian baskets precisely constructed and artistically decorated. Bowls and pots of baked earth were essential for cooking such Indian favorites as corn and artichokes. The spoons used by the Indians were carved of wood and were as crude as their companion pieces, the hardwood bowls. The only articles of furniture to be found in the Indian homes were light bedsteads that were covered with skins of bear, beaver, and otter.

The religion of the Paugussetts and the other Connecticut Indians lacked any real systematic dogma. They believed in one great, invisible god, a beneficent god, the source of all the good that they enjoyed. They also recognized a devil who was the source of all evil. This being brought the plagues that they periodically suffered; it was the source of all natural calamities, both great and small. In addition to these two powerful forces, a whole series of lesser deities existed whose range of control was limited to some specific aspect of life or of nature. According to the Indians, the soul was immortal, but they had no concept of resurrection in the sense that Christians have.

The Paugussetts and the Siwanogs were peaceful Indians. They never constituted a threat to seventeenth-century Fairfield and certainly never were a problem for eighteenth-century Weston. In fact, as whites began to move out from the center of Fairfield and from Green's Farms to Weston, the Indians largely withdrew from Weston. Most of the Paugussetts either moved to New York State to confederate with the Iroquois or to Kent to join the Scatacooks. The area that would eventually become Weston had never supported a large Indian population, and by the time settlement actually began to appear in the area, the Indian population had all but disappeared. Occasionally, Indians would be found in the Weston area until well into the nineteenth century, but these individuals were isolated curiosities,

The ledges of Ambler Gorge, in the Lucius Pond Ordway Preserve – 1,600 acres forever set aside for scientific research and aesthetic appreciation

men and women bearing little resemblance to their proud ancestors who had originally peopled this land and then lost it to the whites.[1]

That part of Fairfield that the Indians sold to Ludlow and his fellow settlers and which eventually came to be Weston had provided the Indians with a variety of resources, from flat bottomland on which to grow their maize, to tall chestnuts from which to gather a rich annual harvest, to bear and deer to enliven a diet of corn and beans. What the Indians sought from the land was unlike what the English would seek. But the natural environment of Weston was varied enough to satisfy many of the needs of these two diverse cultures.

When Ludlow and his successors bought the various tracts of land that eventually made up Fairfield, and part of which would eventually comprise Weston, they had never seen most of their purchase. Certainly this is true of that area that is now Weston. Few white feet would tread on Weston's soil before the end of the seventeenth century. Only during the eighteenth century would the English finally discover what they had bought.

What they did purchase was, like the rest of the earth's surface, the product of hundreds of millions of years of geologic development. Five hundred to six hundred million years ago, Weston was part of a huge trough. Various forms of rock, many of them sedimentary, formed the crust of the trough. Then, during the Paleozoic era, this trough went through incredible geologic changes. The surface of the earth was folded and lifted and shattered by great earthquakes, earthquakes that shook the entire New England area. Simultaneously, vast amounts of heat were released from the center of the earth. The result of all this concentrated activity was a change in the basic structure of the rock that had been in the Weston region, a change brought about by the combined agencies of heat and pressure. The shales, sandstones, and graywackes that had been so plentiful in the area became schists, quartzites, and gneisses. The rock which is now characteristic of the region developed during this period.

As a consequence, Weston lies within what is known as the Hartland Formation, which is actually a complex assortment of crystalline rocks. These consist of mica, quartzite, schists, and gneisses. This formation in Weston is associated with granites and with the granite gneisses of the so-called Harrison type. These rocks of the Middle Paleozoic age are the most extensive rock formations found in Weston. They are the basis of the extremely variable and folded terrain that characterizes the town.

But certainly Weston's geological history did not end with the Paleozoic age. The great mountains formed during the Paleozoic era began to erode during the Mesozoic era; and they continued to erode so that at the end of that era, about 130 million years ago, the mountains had been reduced to nearly a plain. It was approximately forty million years ago, during the Cenozoic period, that Connecticut felt the effects of the Tertiary uplift. Much of the surface of what is now Connecticut was elevated by this upheaval. The western part of the state experienced the greatest uplift, with the northwest area feeling even greater effects than did the Weston region. The elevation was followed by a period of violent erosion as racing rivers cut deep ravines into the crystalline rock that had been formed so many millions of years ago during the Paleozoic era. This fluvial etching brought a beauty and character to the landscape that had been unknown during the centuries when the area had been a plain. In the process, more and more of the Paleozoic base of Weston was exposed.

Much more recently, between twenty and thirty thousand years ago, the great Ice Age descended upon Weston. This was during the Pleistocene period. As the climate began to cool, a great sheet of ice began to descend over the northern part of North America. The ice came like a great, inundating mass. It moved forward so slowly that its progress was almost imperceptible. It pushed forward until it reached a climate that was too warm to allow it to continue. Here the ice stopped. In the northeastern part of the United States, the ice extended to a point south of Long Island; all of Connecticut was covered. At Weston, the ice was at least 1,700 feet deep.

In Weston, the glacial modification was relatively minor. The ice grooved and polished the slopes facing the ice; that is: the northern and northwestern slopes. It plucked and quarried those slopes that faced away from the advancing ice, the southern and southeastern slopes. The glaciers also removed and redistributed the rock and soil that happened to be in its path. In its wake it left a thin layer of stony till, one to ten feet in depth on ridges and higher slopes and ten to fifty feet deep on lower slopes and valleys.

Since the departure of the last glaciers, about twelve or fifteen thousand years ago, the action of streams and erosion on the sides of slopes has modified much of the glacial cover by removing the till from higher areas. But during this same period Weston's soils have not been significantly altered by either erosion or climate. The cover left by the glaciers and the rock beneath are both resistant to soil-making processes created by the particular environment in Weston. Furthermore, the forests and grass, which covered Weston until the arrival of Ludlow and his companions, discouraged erosion. The only significant exception to this general rule was the formation of muck and peat swamps that has taken place since the retreat of the ice. Those descendants, both real and figurative, of Ludlow and his followers who settled in Weston have done more to change Weston's topography in the last 350 years than nature did in the previous ten thousand years.

From a physiographic point of view, what the English colonists purchased when they obtained Weston was a part of the Appalachian Highlands known as the Western Connecticut Highlands. It was an area characterized by variable topography and underlain by a variety of hard, metamorphic, crystalline rocks. This fact meant, among other things, that much of Weston was too steep either for the construction of homes or for the cultivation of crops. As beautiful as the terrain was, it was not what the settlers of the eighteenth century would have selected if they had had the power to select.[2]

The first white residents of Weston would be farmers. While the topography of their new home was of concern to them, they were just as interested in the soil that covered the rock beneath. If they might have delighted in the natural beauty of Weston's landscape, they were less than enthusiastic about the soils they found. A great part of the surface cover of Weston was made up of a group of soils identified by modern agronomists as Hollis soils. Derived from glacial till, these soils are a mixture of sands and silts overlying gneissic and granite rocks. This soil is rarely more than twenty inches in depth and is interspersed with outcroppings of base rock covering from ten to fifty percent of the surface. This type of soil is obviously more desirable than Rockland, which is also to be found extensively in Weston and which has bedrock exposures in over fifty percent of the surface. Hollis and Rockland soils are located primarily in that part of Weston that is between the East Branch of the Saugatuck River and the Georgetown Road, extending along a line running east and slightly south from where that road enters Redding to the point where Steep Hill Road intersects Davis Hill Road—clearly a large section of the town. Other areas where these soils are found are between Kettle Creek Road and Good Hill Road and between Old Easton Turnpike and the Easton Road.

Leicester and Whitman soils are thicker than Hollis soils, but these soils are hardly a farmer's delight. They are also derived from glacial till and are characteristically composed of silty sands and appear as rocky, sandy loam. Easily compressed into hardpan, these soils are poorly drained. They are found in the vicinity of the Weston and Georgetown Roads and as far east as Good Hill Road in the southern part of the town. Though not ideal, these surface materials are infinitely preferable to the peat and muck soil to be found in the wetlands scattered throughout Weston.

The best soil that Weston had to offer the farmers who came in the eighteenth century was Narragansett soil. This was a well-drained and stony silt loam, usually found in depths of more than forty inches. Derived from meltwaters from glaciers and deposited along river valleys, this soil is found along both branches of the Saugatuck.[3]

If the Weston area offered the settlers little in terms of rich soil, it did offer other valuable resources. The land was covered by a virgin forest of deciduous trees, of oaks, maples, basses, whitewoods, walnuts, butternuts, and especially chestnuts. To view the forests of Weston today is by no means to know what these forests were like in the seventeenth or eighteenth centuries. Today, the forests are made up of a complex array of vegetation types. Oaks dominate the uplands and red maples the wetlands. Mixed hardwoods predominate in other areas. But today in Weston, few trees are older than one hundred years. In the seventeenth century, trees that were hundreds of years old were common. Today, the chestnut is gone, destroyed by the blight that hit this noble variety at the beginning of the twentieth century. But more destructive to Weston's forests than nature were the farmers, the lumbermen, and the charcoal makers, all of whom were yet to come. They would leave behind them a pathetic substitute for the majestic forests that Weston's first settlers found. But with the land as poor as it was, no one could be surprised that the settlers began quickly to harvest the wealth of their forests.

The Indians had treasured Weston's forests for the game that lived in them. While the English settlers would take advantage of the area's wildlife, they were more interested in farming than in hunting. And just as the forests were regarded as an obstacle to overcome before crops could be planted, so, too, the settlers considered the wildlife to be as much a nuisance as a benefit. They ate fish from the rivers and game birds from the forests. Wild turkey, partridge, quail, and doves were favorites. So, also, was venison. But most mammals—bear, fox, mink, bobcat, raccoon, and wolf—were regarded as little more than pests, something that served no useful function and so should be eliminated.[4]

Along with the plant life and the wildlife, the topography and the soils, the Englishmen who purchased Weston from the Indians inherited the region's climate. The climate, just as certainly as the soil, would determine what crops could be grown and, therefore, how the people would live.

Weston's climate is not vastly different today from what it was in the eighteenth century, when weather records were first kept in Connecticut. One can also assume that it was not vastly different during the seventeenth century. Today, Weston has a moist, cool climate. It receives forty-six inches of precipitation a year; this precipitation is evenly distributed throughout the year. It has an average annual temperature of 49° and an average growing season without a killing frost of 170 days. Rarely is there a killing frost after April 15 or before October 15.

Indian shelter under the ledges west of Godfrey Pond in craggy area of Devil's Den

Over the years since weather records were first kept, there have been long-term fluctuations in temperature and, correspondingly, in snowfall. Between 1790 and 1810, for example, the weather was warmer than normal, but between 1811 and 1875, it was colder. Between 1876 and 1880, it was again warmer, and between 1881 and 1905, it was slightly colder. Since 1905, the weather has been markedly warmer. These fluctuations in temperature could as easily be caused by a hot summer as by a warm winter or by a cool summer as by a cold winter. The winters between 1811 and 1873 were very definitely colder than normal. Stories told by old-timers of winters that were desperately cold and of snow that was piled higher than the houses are fun to hear but bear little relation to reality. In the famous blizzard of March 11-14, 1888, forty inches of snow fell in Weston. High winds blew the snow into great drifts, but there is no reason to believe that such storms were common in Weston's earlier days. Unless an old-timer can recall the years before 1875 (and in 1978 few can) he cannot in truth tell of horrendous cold and mountains of snow. In fact, of all the benefits that Weston's physical environment had to offer, perhaps none was more valuable than its relatively mild climate. If Weston's topography and soils had been equally hospitable to Englishmen, Weston's history might have been greatly different.[5]

NOTES TO CHAPTER 2

1. For information about the original human inhabitants of the Weston area, I have relied upon John W. DeForest, *History of the Indians of Connecticut* (Hartford, 1853); *The Indians of Connecticut* (New Haven, 1936) and *Connecticut circa 1625: Its Indian Trails, Villages, and Sachemdons* (Hartford, 1934), both by Mathias Spiess; Frank G. Speck, *Native Tribes and Dialects of Connecticut* (Washington, 1928); Kenneth H. Kinner, "Archaeological Investigations: Lucius Pond Ordway Preserve—Devil's Den," *The Nature Conservancy* (Washington, 1971); and Helen Partridge, *Easton, Its History* (Easton, 1972).

2. Aspects of Weston's geologic history are described in Thomas A. Cook, *Geology of Connecticut* (Hartford, 1933); William N. Rice, *The Physical Geography and Geology of Connecticut* (Hartford, 1930); Carlos Carranza, "Geology and Geologic History: Lucius Pond Ordway Preserve—Devil's Den," *The Nature Conservancy* (Arlington, Virginia, 1971); Dominski/Oakrock Associates, *The Weston Environmental Resources Manual* (Weston, 1977).

3. *The Weston Environmental Resources Manual*, mentioned in the note above, contains information about Weston's soils, as does David B. Thompson, "Soil Survey: Lucius Pond Ordway Preserve—Devil's Den," *The Nature Conservancy* (Arlington, Virginia, 1971).

4. Information about Weston's flora and fauna may be found in John C. Pease and John A. Niles, *A Gazetteer of the States of Connecticut and Rhode-Island* (Hartford, 1819) and in Phillip Barske, "Wildlife Survey: Lucius Pond Ordway Preserve—Devil's Den," *The Nature Conservancy* (Arlington, Virginia, 1971).

5. Joseph Milton Kirk discussed this aspect of the physical environment in his work, *The Weather and Climate of Connecticut* (Hartford, 1939). The Bridgeport Hydraulic Company has been collecting weather data since 1894.

THE DIVISION OF NORTHWESTERN FAIRFIELD 1639 / 1682

"To every man his proportion of land"

It was many years after Roger Ludlow's arrival in Fairfield that Englishmen came to realize all the advantages and disadvantages of Weston's physical environment. For before Weston could be settled, Fairfield not only had to be settled but had to have sufficient population to make its residents feel crowded enough to be impelled into the back country.

Initially, Fairfield's population was very small. Ludlow might have brought as many as eight or ten families with him when he came from Windsor in 1639, but the town records list the names of only four of the persons who accompanied him; these were Thomas Staples, Thomas Newton, Edward Jessop, and Edmund Strickland. Shortly after the arrival of these first settlers, another group, not much larger in number, came from Watertown, Massachusetts. Still, Fairfield remained a plantation with an extremely small number of residents.[1]

Eventually, the colonial leaders in Hartford recognized the economic folly of supporting such a small settlement; they complained of the "great expense yearly to be laid out to fetch in necessary commodities."[2] To offset these expenses, the Hartford officials adopted a measure designed to encourage the production of staple crops for export. The Connecticut General Court, thus, on February 7, 1641, ordered that one hundred acres of tillable ground and twenty acres of meadowlands be granted to anyone within the plantation who would improve twenty acres the first year, eighty acres the second, and the remaining acres the third. When one considers whatever improvements were made had to be made by the energy that only human beings, aided and abetted by animal power, could provide, the General Court's offer seems less than enticing. But the offer did prove attractive, and soon the promise of land brought persons from other, more crowded, areas of New England to Fairfield. In the summer of 1644, nearly fifteen families from Concord, Massachusetts, led by their minister, John Jones, left that populous town for the open spaces of Fairfield.

Although by 1644 the leaders of Fairfield had bought only a small part of the lands that they would eventually purchase from the Indians, there was land aplenty for the original settlers, as well as for those who were then arriving. Subsequent purchases of land more than kept pace with the influx of new residents. In 1644, what would become Weston remained a vast wilderness, still largely the property of local Indians, still unvisited by the English who inhabited Fairfield.

Originally, Fairfield had been known as Uncoway or Uncoa, the Indian name for the area. But the natural wealth of the region so impressed its residents that they abandoned the Indian name in order to refer to their town as Fairfield, for the "fair" or pleasing fields they found there. From many points of view, the area was rich. The salt marshes provided hay in abundance. Behind the shore was a narrow coastal plain that offered good lands for farming. The town had fine harbors, in particular the one at Black Rock; and several streams provided water power to run the town's mills. By 1654, Fairfield was the fourth largest town in Connecticut and was certainly the leading settlement in the western part of the colony.

Of particular interest in the history of Weston is the way Fairfield dealt with the question of distributing land. The division of Fairfield's northwestern lands would eventually allow population to move to that yet-untrodden wilderness.

Even before the settlement of Connecticut's towns, Englishmen had already developed certain well-defined ideas about how a town should be established. The colonists at Jamestown, in Virginia, as well as those in Ulster, in northern Ireland, had created an example which the founders of Fairfield would follow. The example was one of a nucleated village where the home lots, from which would extend the lands that were to provide pasturage, meadowlands, croplands, and lumber and firewood, stood grouped closely together.[3]

Ludlow had chosen the site of Fairfield carefully. Not only was it close to streams, salt marshes, a good harbor, and rich agricultural land; it was also in a position to be easily defended. The home lots were located around four central squares, and these lots were of more or less uniform size, about two and a half acres each. Also within the center of the town was land reserved for the meetinghouse and for the minister's home. In fact, the meetinghouse stood at the junction of the town's four squares. Streets were created to provide each property owner with access to his property and were not designed to facilitate communication or travel for their own sake.

Beyond the village itself were the vast landholdings of the residents. In the Connecticut colony, the General Court had granted to the towns the "power to dispose of their owne lands undisposed of," once the General Court had granted official recognition to the town's claim to its lands. This meant that Fairfield had the right to make grants to whomever it saw fit. In 1662, the first division of lands beyond the center occurred. The town meeting decided that "a new planting feild" was to be granted "to those inhabetants of the towne that shall desire to have land layd out."[4] Approximately 320 acres were distributed. Each master of a family received half an acre in his own right, a quarter-acre for his wife and for each child, and two acres for every one hundred pounds of assessed real property he held.

This was the first of several land divisions in Fairfield. In 1669, 1671, 1672, 1682, and twice in 1688, similar divisions took place. What eventually developed looked much like the English strip system of land division, where long, rectangular lots were assigned in regular order to various owners. But there was an important difference between the system that grew up in Connecticut and the English open-field system. The size of the average holding in Fairfield was vastly larger than the average holding in an English open field. In England, a reasonably successful man might accumulate as many as fifty acres, these acres consisting of a series of narrow strips, about two rods, or 33 feet, in width, and about a furlong, or 660 feet, in length. In Fairfield, a single lot would be several times larger than an English farmer's holdings. The difference lay not in the arrangement of land but in the amount of land involved.

The residents of Fairfield eagerly participated in these land divisions. One must recall that the first generation of Englishmen to reside in Fairfield were still basically medieval men with medieval values. To be sure, the medieval economic and social system in England had already badly disintegrated. It was a system based upon land; for a person to be powerful economically and socially, he must possess land. But it was nearly impossible to acquire land in England. This was hardly the case in America; and when land became available in Fairfield, men, for a variety of psychological as well as economic motives, demanded to be included in the division. Committed as they were to the sacred tenets of Puritanism, this first generation of Fairfield inhabitants could be surprisingly materialistic when the question of land was at hand.

The economic motives that encouraged interest in these divisions are obvious. The possession of more land meant access to more lumber and firewood; it meant additional acres of pasture or meadow; it meant more land that could be cleared for the plow; it meant land that could be held for speculation. But in addition to being concerned over their own interests, Fairfield farmers also had to be sure that they had enough land to allow their sons to be as prosperous as they were. Primogeniture never flourished in Connecticut. Each of a man's sons expected to own a farm. The practice that developed in Connecticut was one of dividing an estate among all the sons and even holding some land separate for the daughters. This meant that the sons could never inherit as much land as the father, and for them to prosper at all required the father to accumulate vast—at least, by English standards—tracts of land. So Fairfield men participated with genuine zest when land was divided. In 1681, Thomas Staples owned 1,400 acres in Fairfield; Nathan Gold owned even more: 1,500 acres. Fifty-eight persons held more than four hundred acres each.

There were other reasons, as well, for Fairfield residents to favor these land divisions. The distribution of lands in seventeenth-century New England towns, while it failed to eliminate social distinctions, did help to keep the peace by guaranteeing a common concern with agriculture among the residents. The residents were also encouraged in their loyalty to the town, which, after all, was bestowing a great benefit upon them.

The distributions that took place in Fairfield and in other Connecticut towns after 1664 were, at least in part, designed to settle the question of the validity of certain land titles. In 1664, Charles II, who had recently acceded to the throne upon the restoration of the monarchy in England, granted to his brother, the Duke of York, jurisdiction over the lands between the Connecticut and Delaware rivers. Acknowledgement of this grant meant that all undivided lands in Connecticut west of the Connecticut River would become the Duke of York's to do with as he pleased. In the decade that followed this grant, Connecticut leaders took steps to guarantee that these lands would be kept out of the duke's hands. They did this by conveying these undivided lands to individuals. Thus, in Fairfield, there were three land divisions in the ten years that followed the 1664 grant; and, furthermore, the ownership of the undivided lands was placed in the hands of a body of proprietors, who held the lands in common.

All of these various factors prompted the Fairfield town meeting of January 14, 1671, to decree that there "shall be a devission of the greatest part of the Commons of Fairfield to the severall particular Inhabetants for ther propriety to be layd out as the Towne shall conclude hearafter." The town meeting also agreed "that the rule of the devission of the above said Commons to the severall Inhabetants that hath right to divide shall be by persons and the present list of estate," with each person to be valued as follows: "a master of a family thirty pound[,] a wife Ten pounds and a child at Ten pounds: which vallu shall be added to the list of estates: & acording to the Totall sum pertayning to each person they shall receive ther proportions." William Hill accepted the task of preparing a plan for the division of the land. He was to have completed his work within a month's time.[5]

Of all the various land divisions within Fairfield, this one was certainly the most important to the history of Weston. For this division would assign ownership of the lands that make up modern Weston. Although settlement would be slow in coming to northwestern Fairfield, the division of January, 1671, was the first step in the process that would bring population to the area.

On January 26, 1671, the town meeting agreed upon the details of the division. "It is ordered that the west devedent is to begin by norwolke bounds and to run back eight score and soe to run towards the Towne eastward from the said bounds about Two miles and half," the plan began. The dividend land on the east was to begin at the Stratford line and extend west. The town ordered that there should be a common located at the southern end of these lands and that this common should be a half-mile wide. "The Towne hath ordered that ther shall be one mile broad from the above said half mile common to run into the Country to the end of the bounds to remain a common forever." What was created, then, were two commons: the one called the half-mile common, which was a half-mile wide, running roughly

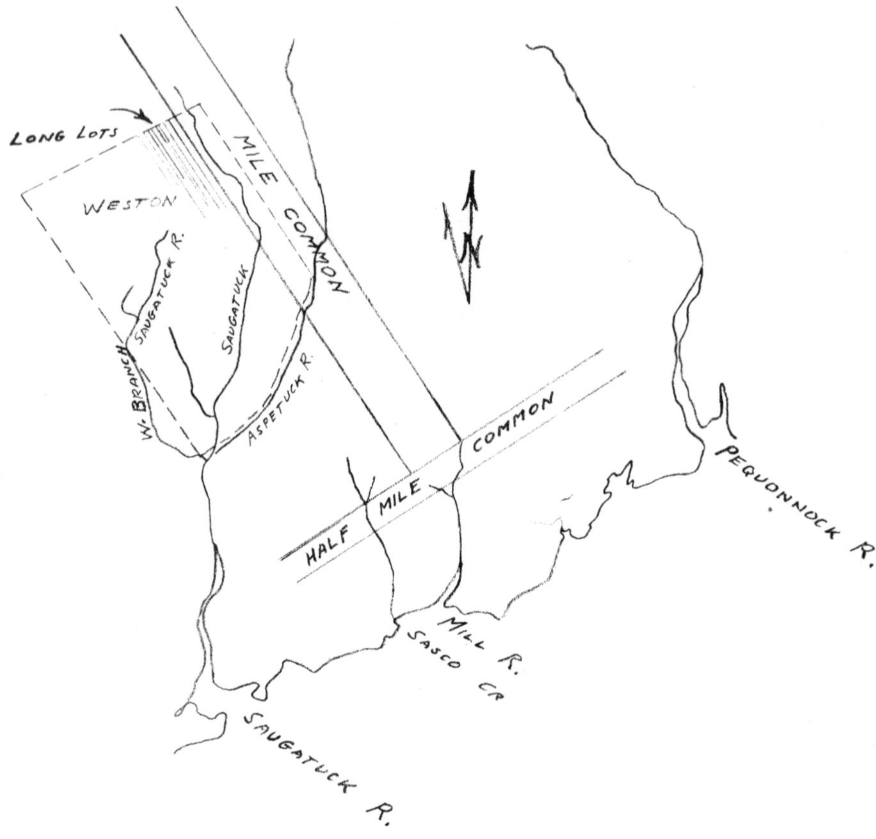

east and west through Fairfield, and the mile common, running north away from the village, which was a mile wide. The two formed an inverted T. On either side of the mile common and north of the half-mile common were the lands that were to be divided. The town meeting agreed that "all the Lands on both sides of the mile common necessary highwayes excepted shall be layd out to the Inhabetants of the Towne that hath right to devid." Each person eligible was to receive his proportionate share, and the location of his share was to be determined by the location of his home within the town. Thus, the meeting directed that the share of "widow wheler [was] to begine next to Stratford bounds and [those of] Simon Crouch [Couch] and Andrews to begin next norwocke bounds and soe the neighborhood to take it up successively inward till all have ther proportions."[6]

Before adjourning, the town appointed John Banks, Seviant Squire, Cornelius Hull, and Josiah Harvey to lay out "to every man his proportion of land." The lands on either side of the mile of common were to begin "next the half mile common and soe to run back to the end of our bounds." Necessary highways were to be included, and the town ordered "that there shall be layd to the parsonage a proportion of common after the rate of Two hundred pound estate" and "to a scoole commonage after the rate of a hundred pound estate."[7]

What the town had created was a system of long lots, each of which began at the half-mile common and extended to the northern boundary of the town. Those long lots that were west of the mile common included more territory than that which would eventually make up Weston. But the land division of 1671 created two special sections in northern Fairfield; they would eventually become Weston and Easton. The existence of Weston was still far in the future, but with the benefit of hindsight, which obviously was unavailable to those who lived in Fairfield in 1671, one can see that a process had begun that would create a community far from the center of life in Fairfield.

The long lots varied in width from roughly fifty feet up to 1,155 feet, and each was named for its first owner, although over the years the names of the lots would change as their ownership changed. But in 1671, the first lot in what would one day be Weston was assigned to Jacob Gray. His property was immediately west of the mile common. Beyond his long lot was the long lot of Jehu Burr, and beyond that the long lot of John Banks, and so forth, until finally the long lot of Simon Couch stood next to the Norwalk line.

Appended to this chapter is a list of the individuals to whom were granted long lots west of the mile common. This is the list as it was recorded on December 30, 1681. Obviously, some significant changes had occurred since the original granting of the lots nearly eleven years earlier. The frequent exchange and sale of the lots, even before the areas had been settled, makes it nearly impossible to establish a precise list of their owners for any given period. A particular lot might be owned by one person in 1671 and by another in 1681 and by yet another in 1691. For example, Simon Couch owned the lot closest to the Norwalk line according to the original division of 1671. But in 1681, John Applegate owned that lot. Originally, the town decreed that there be both school and parsonage lots west of the mile of common. These lots changed hands so frequently that now it would be all but impossible to identify their exact locations.

On January 31, 1672, about a year after the assignment of the long lots, the town resolved to lay out a highway right of way twenty rods (330 feet) wide between the half-mile common and the long lots. This was Hull's Farm Road in Fairfield, now Long Lots Road in present-day Westport. This road, at best only a rock-strewn and rutted path, marked the line between what was for many years the occupied area of Fairfield and the area that remained a vast wilderness. One can imagine the difficulty, given the technology of the late seventeenth century, of establishing the boundaries of these ungainly long lots. Even today the job of surveying a piece of property some nine miles long through unmarked terrain would present formidable problems. So, although the original division was made in 1671, work on the surveying of these lots did not begin until 1675, when the town chose Ezbon Wakeman and Seviant Squire to perform the task, a chore not to be completed for several decades.[8] As late as 1682, the residents of Fairfield had, at best, only a vague idea of the southernmost bounds of the long lots. Until these bounds were established with some precision, permanent settlement could not occur in the area. In other words, although the long lots now existed, at least in the land records of Fairfield, it would be many years before Englishmen took up permanent residence in that part of Fairfield that is now Weston. In the meantime, the men and women of Fairfield, as keen as ever to accumulate real property, bought and sold land that they had never seen at a pace that would amaze their twentieth-century progeny.

Hear followeth a List of the . . . longlots [west of the mile common] granted to the Inhabetants of the Towne [recorded in Fairfield Town Records, Town Meeting Minutes, December 30, 1681]

	Rod	*Q[uarter Rod]*	*Foot*
Jacob Gray	*13*	*3*	*0*
Mr. Jehu Burr	*29*	*0*	*0*
John Banks	*28*	*1*	*0*
Ezbon Wakeman	*11*	*0*	*3*
Tho: Skidmor	*15*	*2*	*0*
Steven Hedges	*10*	*0*	*0*
Cornelius Hull	*28*	*0*	*0*
Mr. John Bur	*30*	*3*	–
obadiah gilbert	*28*	*0*	–
Joshua Jennings	*29*	*0*	*4*
Henery Rowland	*33*	*0*	–
Joshua Knowles	*20*	*3*	*0*
John Cable senr	*15*	*2*	*0*
Richard osborn	*21*	*1*	*0*

Francis Bradly	*22*	*0*	*6*
Tho: Sherwood	*24*	*1*	*0*
Hump Hide	*20*	*1*	*0*
John Hide	*15*	*0*	*0*
Peter Cole	*13*	*3*	*0*
Peter Claphan	*22*	*2*	*2*
John Knowles	*19*	*2*	*3*
John Sturge	*27*	*2*	*2*
John Cable junr	*18*	*0*	—
Danll Lockwood	*17*	*0*	*3*
James Beers	*22*	*2*	*0*
Samll Smith	*16*	*0*	*4*
John Barlowe senr	*13*	*3*	*0*
John Barlowe jr	*13*	*3*	*0*
Eluzer Smith	*10*	*2*	*0*
Robt Rumsie	*16*	*0*	*5*
John Tomkins	*8*	*2*	*0*
Samll ward	*16*	*0*	*0*
Joseph Lockwood	*21*	*2*	*0*
Simon Crouch 1	*20*	*0*	*0*
John Andrews	*11*	*3*	*0*
Danll Frost	*27*	*3*	–
John green	*24*	*0*	*0*
Robt Beachem	*20*	*3*	*1*
John Wheler	*35*	*0*	*0*
Henrick	*7*	*0*	*3*
Rich Lyon	*28*	*2*	*2*
Mr. Wakeman	*23*	*3*	*0*
Georg Squire jr	*5*	*0*	*3*
Parsonage	*23*	*0*	*0*
Scoole	*11*	*2*	*0*
Samll Drake	*9*	*0*	*7*
Danll Finch	*9*	*0*	*2*
Is: Sherwood	*3*	*3*	*2*
Samll godwin	*4*	*0*	*5*
Phebe Barlow	*0*	*15*	*2*
Nath Perry	*0*	*3*	*2*
Mr. Pell	–	–	–
John Bennet	*9*	*0*	*2*
Tho: Lyon	*9*	*0*	*0*
Rich ogden	*26*	*2*	*2*
Jos Patchin senr	*6*	*0*	*2*
John Smith	*9*	*0*	*0*
Tho: Sherwington	*10*	*0*	*7*
John Applegate	*4*	*3*	*0*[9]

NOTES TO CHAPTER 3

1. Elizabeth Hubbell Schenck's *The History of Fairfield,* 2 volumes (New York, 1899) contains a great deal of information about Fairfield's first century, but it offers little in the way of synthesis. This is provided by two modern studies: Bruce C. Daniels, "Large Town Power Structure in Eighteenth Century Connecticut," Ph. D. thesis, University of Connecticut, 1970, and Joan R. Ballen, "Fairfield, Connecticut, 1661-1691," M.A. thesis, University of Bridgeport, 1970. Also useful is Anthony N. B. Garvan, *Architecture and Town Planning in Colonial Connecticut* (New Haven, 1951). Garvan spends several pages on Fairfield. Richard L. Bushman's important work, *From Puritan to Yankee: Character and the Social Order in Connecticut, 1690-1765* (Cambridge, 1967), places many of the events discussed in this chapter in the larger context of social change in the colony generally. Also helpful was Christopher Collier's thoughtful essay on "Saybrook and Lyme: Secular Settlements in a Puritan Commonwealth," in George J. Willauer, Jr., *A Lyme Miscellany* (Middletown, 1977). All of these works have been useful in the preparation of this chapter.

2. *Public Records of the Colony of Connecticut,* I, 58.

3. Ibid., 25.

4. Quoted in Ballen, 107.

5. Fairfield Town Records, Town Meeting Records, I, 51.

6. Ibid., 54.

7. Ibid., 55.

8. Ibid., 100.

9. Ibid., 137, 138.

THE PIONEERING OF WESTON
1681 / 1725

"They valued independence more than the advantages of life in a settled community"

When did the first permanent settlement take place in the area that is today Weston? This is as difficult a question about Weston's history as one could ask. There are several ways to approach the issue. One would be in terms of the dates of some of the oldest houses in Weston. To accept this method, one would have to conclude that permanent settlement began in Weston in the late seventeenth century, for there is a house in Weston which, it is claimed, was built about 1695. Perhaps Englishmen were living on a permanent basis in Weston as early as the 1690s. This point of view seems to receive additional support from the fact that a log building in Easton, unfortunately demolished during the 1930s, was supposedly built about the same time.

One task that historians are particularly badly suited to perform is proving that something did not happen. A great deal of hard evidence is necessary even to cast a shadow of a doubt on some particular legend that has, over the years, developed an enthusiastic following.

Thus, it is all but impossible to prove that people were not living on a permanent basis in the Weston area by the end of the seventeenth century.

But there does exist a tremendous amount of evidence to show that significant settlement in Weston was highly unlikely before the 1730s. In fact, if one compares the evidence marshaled to prove that the old house in Weston and the log cabin in Easton were built in the seventeenth century with the evidence against permanent settlement in Weston until about 1730, he will find it difficult to accept the dates of construction assigned to these two structures. After a careful examination of Fairfield's land records, I am convinced that there was no settlement in Weston until the end of the first quarter of the eighteenth century.

The division that created the original long lots was made in 1671. Even assuming that these lots were quickly surveyed, which they were not, one must recall that powerful forces held men and women in the central village of Fairfield. In the first place, by remaining in town, a person had the advantage of being able to deal collectively with a whole range of predicaments that he would have to face alone if he chose to venture into the wilderness. Many of these situations were basic to his existence. For example, who would grind his corn if he did not have access to millers in the village? Who would repair a broken tool if the blacksmith were a day's travel away? If a tanner were not available, who would mend a broken harness or prepare the hide of a recently slaughtered animal? For those of us who live in a modern age, the trip from Weston to Fairfield is nearly as easily accomplished as thought about. But for a man living at the end of the seventeenth century, the journey from what is now the center of Weston to the center of Fairfield was a more difficult one, although certainly less expensive, than today's journey by automobile from Weston to Washington, D.C., or to Pittsburgh, Pennsylvania. Can a twentieth-century person imagine placing himself in the position of having to make a comparable journey to have an iron tool repaired or to exercise his right to vote? For a seventeenth-century man to move to Weston meant giving up his franchise unless he was willing to travel to Fairfield to participate in town meetings.[1]

The idea of communality, so strong in seventeenth-century villages, demanded that all the townspeople live in a small area so that they could attend public worship and be watched over by the town leaders. This arrangement allowed farmers to live in the village and conveniently walk to their fields, which were nearby. But when a Fairfield farmer thought of putting in crops on his long lot, even on the southernmost part of it, he realized that he would have to walk several miles to his fields. He had great demands on his time. So, after receiving his proportion of the dividend in 1671, even after the lots were laid out a decade later and even after crude roads were established in the southernmost area of the long lots, yet another decade later, the farmer probably did little or nothing with his property north of the half-mile common except hold onto it for future use or sell it to, or swap it with, someone else who would also hold it for subsequent use.

When the farmer got to the point of talking of moving north of the half-mile common in order to take advantage of his property there, his wife would remind him of the consequences. To move a day's travel away meant separation from family and friends. It meant going without education for his children; it meant being cut off from the town's social life; it meant abandoning access to religious services.

All these things the farmer would realize. He also knew that he could not move beyond the half-mile common until he had cleared enough land to provide for himself and his family, and he was unwilling to begin clearing land until he was sure whose land he was clearing. Thus, he would be unwilling to improve his land until he was reasonably certain about the boundaries of his property.

Although the long lots were originally laid out in 1682, the survey was so poorly done that in March, 1706, a committee appointed by the Fairfield town meeting recommended that "the former laying out of the sd long lots should be made null and void. . . ." The town defeated this recommendation but did order that the owners of the long lots try to settle their boundaries among themselves; and that where this was impossible, the owners should submit their contending claims to a committee composed of Peter Burr, John Wakeman, John Meredeth, and John Thompson for mediation.

By 1714, the boundaries of the long lots near Long Lots Road were reasonably clear. But the delineations beyond the fronts of the lots remained very much in question. On December 27, 1714, the town meeting ordered that the boundaries be established all the way to the rear. And while the bounds of the backs of the long lots were generally measured out during the year 1726, as late as 1756 these boundaries remained unclear. On February 16, 1756, the Fairfield town meeting appointed Captain Thomas Hill "to Petition the generall assembly to appoint & enable some meet Persons to fix & Setle some Intermediate *Bounds* between ye *Long Lots* in . . . Fairfield from front to rear in Order to Render ye said Lotts more certain & to *prevent Disputes*. . . ."[2]

The General Assembly responded to this request at its May, 1756, session. It resolved that in order to put an end to the disputes between the owners of the long lots, it was authorizing the Fairfield town meeting "to appoint a committee to measure off the width of each lot the same as they are laid out at the front and rear thereof . . . and erect monuments at the extent of each lot to divide between adjoyning lots." The legislature further resolved that "the bounds fixed and the lines drawn || [parallel] from the front of said lots respectively . . . to the rear of said lots shall forever hereafter be deemed and adjudged to be the true dividing line between each of said lots. . . ."[3]

The town meeting appointed Samuel Sherwood, Joseph Wakeman, Samuel Sturges, and Lyman Hull as a committee to carry out the General Assembly's resolution. On April 28, 1758, they completed their work. Where two or more of the original long lots were consolidated into one, the surveyors "measured the width of them as . . . one Long Lot." In order to achieve the greatest possible accuracy in measuring, the method used "was by a Rod pole, sixteen feet and a half in Length said pole being levelled on all uneven Land by a square and plumb Line. . . ." The results they ascertained, beginning at the mile of common, were as follows:

	Rods	Feet	Inches
Jacob Gray			
Moses Dimon brot into one	26	3	0
John Banks	32	4	2
John Burr	34	3	5
Obadiah Gilbert	24	10	4
Highway	4		
Esbun Wakeman			
Thos Skidmores now called Hills	44	9	0
part of Sarah Wilsons			
Stephen Hedges now called Wilsons	23	5	8
Cornelius Hills	33	15	4
John Burrs	38	8	0
Henry Rowlands	42	15	6
John Cable Senrs	30	5	0
Highway	4		
Richard Osborns	34	13	0
Joshua Knowles	31	11	11
N Perry			
Mr. Herveys now called Staples	31	12	6
Tomkinss	9	14	1½
Bradleys	25	15	4½

Highway	*4*		
Daniel Finches	*10*	*11*	*4*
Thomas Sherwoods	*28*	*10*	*2½*
Peter Coley	*15*	*14*	*9½*
Old Hide	*40*	*1*	*0½*
John Hide one			
John Thompsons	*8*	*1*	*6½*
Peter Clapham	*27*	*5*	*0*
Goodwins	*5*	*3*	*3*
John Knowles	*23*	*12*	*5*
John Sturges	*32*	*6*	*6*
Highway	*4*		
John Cable Jnr	*21*	*5*	*1*
John Applegates	*5*	*10*	*3*
Thomas Lyons	*10*	*10*	*9*
Samuel Drakes	*11*	*1*	*9¼*
James Beers	*27*	*1*	*11¾*
Old Barlows	*16*	*10*	*6*
Saml Smiths	*18*	*15*	*4*
John Barlow Jnr	*15*	*9*	*3*
Eleuza Smith	*14*	*6*	*0*
Robert Rumsey	*19*	*6*	*9*
Daniel Lockwood			
Samuel Ward			
John Smith into one	*51*	*15*	*1*
Highway	*4*		
Richard Ogden			
Danl Frost now called Applegates	*62*	*5*	*6*
Joseph Lockwoods	*24*	*15*	*11½*
Robert Beachum	*24*	*2*	*8¼*
John Green	*27*	*14*	*4¼*[4]

But even this did not end all controversy, for on December 31, 1761, the town once again was forced to appoint a committee "to bound out the Rear of the Long Lotts as they are bounded out at the front. . . ." To point this out, however, is not to contend that settlement had to wait for the 1760s. Certainly, after the original survey of the rear of the long lots in 1726, a family could be reasonably sure that the land it cleared and upon which it built its home was indeed its own land. But until that time, a farmer would have been most foolhardy to take up permanent residence in the area of the long lots.[5]

A clear title was not the only condition demanded for permanent settlement. Before such settlement could be a reality, some system of roads had to tie the long lots to the rest of Fairfield. The object of this

Saltbox house on Davis Hill Road, probably built in the middle 1700s

system was not to provide a means of reaching the towns north of Fairfield. In fact, as late as the end of the colonial period, there were no principal thoroughfares passing through the area that is now Weston. To travel, for example, from Fairfield to Danbury in 1760 or 1770, a traveler would go from Fairfield to Stratford on the Post Road and then up to Newtown and back across to Danbury. So the roads that were needed to encourage settlement were merely small roads that would allow a farmer to travel from the center of Fairfield to his own property in the long lots.

The first upright highways—anything as elaborate as a rutted path qualified to be called a highway—were established by 1692. In that year, those roads were so impassable that the town ordered "Left [Lieutenant] Hull to take the first opportunity to call out the young men to see the highways that were layd out in the long lotts [;] to which hee is to shew to them with the front of thos Long Lotts an to renew ye bounds of thos highways. . . ." Clearly, the so-called highways were so crude that the men were going to have a job even finding them.[6]

Fifteen years later, in January, 1707, the town appointed Peter Burr,

John Wakeman, John Thompson, and James Bennett "to Renew the highways Running up between the Long lotts and to survey the severall Long lotts Lying between the sd highways as Exactly as they may. . . ." But still the matter remained unclear. In 1711, the county surveyor was asked to establish the locations of the upright highways. Not only did the issue remain unsettled, but in 1714 a town committee, again including the familiar names of Cornelius Hull, John Thompson, and John Wakeman, took on the task of determining where the upright highways should be. They reported that the seventh through the twelfth uprights should be located west of the mile of common. These were:

"7th. An highway between Obe'h Gilbert Sen. & Esbond Wakeman's long lot, four rods in breadth be it more or less.

8th. An highway between John Cabel, Sr., & Richard Osborn's long lot, six rods in breadth at the front, & at some distance from the front upward four rods in breadth.

9th. An highway between Francis Bradley & Nathaniel Finche's long lot, four rod in breadth be it more or less.

10th. An highway between John Sturges Sen., & John Cabel jun. long lots, four rods in breadth, be it more or less.

11th. An highway between Eleazer Smith & Robt. Rumsie's long lots, four rod in breadth, be it more or less.

12th. An highway running near the road beyond Machamux which goes to Saugatuck, bounded on the east with the long lot of Simon Couch, & on the west with Norwalk line, the south east side hath at the front a great oak tree betwen the said Couch, & said highway with an heap of stones."[7]

But an exasperated town meeting decided in 1738 that the issue was still confused and formed a committee "to clear the highways that run between the Long Lotts. . . ." It seems safe to assume that until about the end of the first quarter of the eighteenth century, the upright highways existed only in the southernmost part of the area north of the half-mile common and in the minds of Fairfield's town fathers. Remembering that the long lots began at Long Lots Road, well south of the present boundary of Weston, it seems unimaginable that permanent settlement could have existed in Weston before 1725. The tasks of hauling in the contents of a house and of maintaining even the barest communication with Fairfield could hardly have been accomplished before this date.[8]

A look at a modern map of Weston provides a clue to the location of the upright highways. The westernmost north-south—actually north-northwest by south-southeast—road ran along the Fairfield-Norwalk boundary. What remains of it today is called Cavalry Road or Wampum Hill Road. The second upright highway, taking these roads from the Norwalk line to the mile of common, was a highway that ran on the west side of Applegate's—at other times Ogden's and Frost's—long lot and was referred to as Applegate's Highway. It is the present Weston Road and Georgetown Road. The third upright highway ran between the Cable, also Wakeman, and Sturgis long lots. It is now North Avenue, Kettle Creek Road, and Old Hyde Road. Between the Finch and Bradley long lots was the fourth upright highway, now called White Birch Road and Good Hill Road. The fifth upright was between the Osborn and Cable long lots and is now Fanton Hill Road. The sixth, nearest the mile of common, was between Wakeman's and Gilbert's long lots and was called Gilbert's Highway. It is now Eleven O'Clock Road and Davis Hill Road.

In addition to the upright highways, running north and south, a system of cross highways, running east and west, was necessary for people to be able to reach conveniently all sections of their long lots. In December, 1734, the town voted that Samuel Sherwood and John Andrews "open the Twenty rod highways on the West side of the Mile Comon. . . ." Little progress was made on the project, so in February, 1746, a new committee was formed by the town and ordered to lay out the highways. At the same time, the town voted to reduce the width of the highways from twenty rods to six rods.[9]

Ultimately, Samuel Sherwood, Daniel Bradley, and Thomas Hill established the cross highways in the area west of the mile of common, but they did not complete their work until 1758. The first cross highway was located in what is today Westport, and is now called Cross Highway. The second was what is presently Coleytown Road and Catamount Road, although the Catamount section was subsequently exchanged for land that ran along the Aspetuck and followed today's Route 136. The third began at the home of David Godfrey, which was located at what was then the Fairfield-Norwalk town line, now the Weston-Wilton line. It followed what is presently Broad Street to Good Hill to Cartbridge Road to Lyons Plains Road. An extra cross highway was put in south of the intersection of Cartbridge and Lyons Plains Road. This is now the Old Easton Turnpike. The fourth cross highway was located four and a half miles from the front of the long lots and corresponded to what is today Norfield Road and Steep Hill Road. The present Lords Highway was the fifth, and Godfrey Road the sixth. The seventh and final cross highway was located

Once a tavern, this house on Gifford's Hill dates from the eighteenth century.

in the Redding parish, then a part of Fairfield but soon to become a separate town, in 1767.

Certainly, permanent settlement in the Weston area did not have to await the completion of the cross highways in 1758. But it is certain also that settlement had not existed long in this region before demands for a cross-highway system would have been heard. Because this problem first received the town's attention in 1734, it is likely that settlement began shortly before this date. Thus, evidence gleaned from the development of the upright highways tends to confirm that settlement first took place in Weston about 1725.

This conclusion is further substantiated by the Fairfield land records. A careful search of these records failed to uncover a single reference to a dwelling house in the area that is now Weston until the 1740s. Recognizing that a person would be unlikely to build a home only to sell it in a few years, one could still expect, however, a record of the transfer of such property within a decade or two. Thus, the land records also seem to confirm the judgment that permanent settlement waited until about 1725.

Probably those Englishmen who first lived in Weston did so on a part-time basis. As land became scarce in that part of Fairfield close to the village—the area, as has been seen, where most persons preferred to live—farmers would be forced to travel farther and farther from home to obtain lands for crops or livestock. Eventually, these farmers would be spending so much time walking that they would lose a good part of each day. They might also be making this walk to cut firewood, or logs to be hewn into beams or sawed into lumber. Because Weston was blessed with large stands of chestnut trees, which were highly valued by colonial carpenters, and because a sawmill was established in 1704 on the Aspetuck near what is now Redding Road, probably the Weston region was initially of interest to loggers.

But whether herders or farmers or lumbermen, the first Englishmen to spend any large period of time in the Weston area did so for a few weeks at a stretch, perhaps for a few months. They lived in crude shelters that could be constructed easily and that offered few of the comforts of home. As rough as these shelters were, they were not log cabins; for the concept of a dwelling, even a hut, constructed of logs was unknown in early eighteenth-century New England.[10]

Eventually, some of those who dwelt temporarily in Weston decided to make the traumatic move, decided to leave friends and family and meetinghouse and schools and whatever conveniences they had known, to become "outlivers." Those who moved out tended to be less well-to-do than those who remained behind. If one owned sufficient land in town to provide for himself and his family, he would have little reason to leave. The land near the town's center was also more valuable than that off in the wilderness. Those who moved to Weston were also different from most Fairfield people in another respect: They valued lumber or cattle or land or possibly independence more than they did the advantages of life in a settled community. They moved because they did not want to walk for an hour or two or three each day to the sites of their work. But the typical Fairfield man or woman of 1725 or 1735 found other means of dealing with this inconvenience. Those who left were the exceptions.

But eventually, some were forced to leave. Fairfield became crowded. The population grew. Greater and greater demands were placed on a constant supply of land. Younger sons found themselves heirs to land away from the town's center. Poorer men were unable to afford the prices of land in town. These sorts of individuals were crowded out and found new homes in areas like that which would become Weston.

By 1725, then, there was a permanent settlement in Weston. The population of the area undoubtedly grew slowly at first. Again, judg-

The Weston Road about 1910, looking up Gifford's Hill

ing from the land records, more persons moved into Weston between 1750 and 1756, when it became a parish, than from the beginnings of settlement until 1750. Between 1756 and 1776, the population increased approximately three times. In 1756, the population of Weston—that is: the Norfield Parish, as it was then known—was approximately 350 persons. By 1770, that number had increased to about 875, and by 1776, to almost 1,000. Until the completion of the Merritt Parkway in 1940, Weston would never again experience such a tremendous increase in population.

The population of the future Weston was not evenly divided throughout the area. In what is now southwestern Weston was an area known as the Oblong or Albany. Here, about 1750, lived, among others, David Godfrey, Nathan Gray, and John Lockwood. Close by, in what is today Westport and Wilton, were other families, giving this area a sufficient population to have a school by 1744. About this same time, in the Fanton Hill and Lyons Plains section of Weston lived several families, including those of Ebenezer Thorp, Peter Thorp, Thomas Treadwell, John Lyon, Joseph Banks, and John Fanton. Around what is today the center of Weston were the homes of Nathan Morehouse, Nathan Gray, and Benjamin Dean. One of the busiest areas in Weston in the mid-eighteenth century was the area in the extreme northeast, at what is today the northern end of the Newtown Turnpike. In this area lived Peter Bulkley, Shubal Gorham, and John Rowland. This area was close to Redding, a section of Fairfield that developed much earlier than Norfield did. Redding became a separate parish twenty years before Norfield did and a separate town twenty years before Weston did.

It was many decades after the land division of 1671 before people moved into the future Weston. But once the process started, its momentum grew until the area's population was nearly as great as it could bear. Once the population had arrived, the people of the area began to think of themselves as separate from Fairfield. Ties to the old community began breaking down; a new sense of community was developing.

NOTES TO CHAPTER 4

1. My reading of Richard L. Bushman's *From Puritan to Yankee: Character and Social Order in Connecticut, 1690-1795* (Cambridge, 1967) and Kenneth A. Lockridge's, *A New England Town, The First Hundred Years: Dedham, Massachusetts, 1636-1736* (New York, 1970) was of great help in writing this chapter.

2. Fairfield Town Records, Town Meeting Minutes, II, 378, 397; III, 496.

3. *Public Records of the Colony of Connecticut*, X, 512.

4. Fairfield Town Records, Land Records, XIV, 554-557.

5. Fairfield Town Records, Town Meeting Minutes, III, 509.

6. Ibid, II, 239.

7. Ibid., 377, 388; Elizabeth Hubbell Schenck, *The History of Fairfield*, 2 volumes (New York, 1889), II, 37-38.

8. Fairfield Town Records, Town Meeting Minutes, III, 469.

9. Ibid., 465, 480.

10. Harold R. Shurtleff's *The Log Cabin Myth: A Study of the Early Dwellings of the English Colonists in North America* (Cambridge, 1939) proves that eighteenth-century New Englanders did not use log cabins as dwellings. J. Frederick Kelly unsuccessfully challenged Shurtleff's thesis in an article in *Oldtime New England: Bulletin of the Society for the Preservation of New England Antiquities* XXXI (October, 1940), 28-41. In fact, what Kelly was attempting to do was to justify certain errors that Shurtleff had discovered in his previous work, *Early Domestic Architecture of Connecticut* (New Haven, 1927). See Shurtleff, pp. 206-207.

NORFIELD BECOMES A PARISH 1725 / 1783

"To walk together in Brotherly love & Christian Communion"

Permanent settlement in the Weston area began about 1725. Twenty-five or thirty years would pass before the region had developed a strong sense both of being separate and different from Fairfield and of being a community in its own right. The sense of being different from Fairfield came earlier and more easily to the outlivers than did a sense of their own community, but eventually both ideas profoundly influenced the area's development.

Some of the factors that encouraged individuals to move to the back country also prompted them to think of themselves as different from the neighbors they left behind. A sense of being different arose when younger sons were forced out of town onto the marginal lands and saw the relative advantages which their older brothers enjoyed by merely being in town. Likewise, when poor newcomers to town also found themselves shunted out to these same lands, they were aware of the benefits of membership in an old family that held land in the village. In both cases—younger sons or poor newcomers—the relative poverty of the outlying areas as compared to the parent town was apparent.

The present Norfield Congregational Church, dedicated in 1831

Homogeneity had once existed within the old village; now that homogeneity was a thing of the past, the outlivers were not the equals of those in town, and—even more important—the outlivers realized this.

It took only a short time for tensions to develop between those who did move out of town and those who stayed behind. Controversies could arise over hundreds of small concerns. Would the town be willing to spend money from its treasury to build roads in the hinterland? It would not, if the people in the central part of town had their way, and they usually did, because they outnumbered the outlivers. Would the town be willing to establish new schools in these areas? Again, the interests of the outlivers and of the townspeople ran counter.

Out of these differences, a sense of "us against them" developed among the outlivers. This was easily encouraged, because within the outlying area the population was amazingly homogeneous. The means by which one man sustained himself and his family were the same means used by his neighbors. To be sure, some of the outlivers were wealthier than others, but the distance between the wealthiest and the poorest was hardly significant, and social distance was nonexistent. The economic and social distances that separated outlivers from townspeople were more real and, therefore, more significant.

The greatest deterrent to this sense of "us against them" was the continued dependence of the outlivers on the town. Initially, at least, the outlivers were constantly dependent upon the services the town could provide. The craftsmen and artisans were in town. So were the merchants and the schools. But gradually the outlivers became more and more self-sufficient. The process of becoming self-sufficient was largely accidental and certainly not self-conscious. It happened like this: A farmer might discover that he had a knack for working with leather and so would abandon his plow temporarily to make or mend harnesses or boots for his neighbors; eventually, so many neighbors would call upon him for help that he would forsake his plow and become a tanner. Another man might discover that his talent was in working with iron. He could have begun by building or repairing iron items for himself, but if he was a reasonable craftsman—he did not have to be expert, for he had little competition—his neighbors would bring their work to him. Soon the outlivers would have in their midst not only a tanner but also a blacksmith, men whose roles in the nascent community were absolutely essential.

In addition to the benefits provided by craftsmen, the outlivers also needed the services that could be offered only by millers. As long as they had to rely upon the mills in Fairfield, the outlivers could not even pretend to be self-sufficient. So mills were built in what is now Weston, where water power was abundant. A sawmill had existed on the Aspetuck as early as 1704. James Davis's sawmill was located where the fourth cross highway entered the mile of common. Possibly as early as 1767, Nathaniel Squier began operating a mill on Godfrey Pond. This was primarily a sawmill but was able to perform other tasks as well. Squier subsequently sold the mill to Jonathan and Silliman Godfrey, who vastly expanded its operation. From an early date, David Coley ran a mill at what is now the bridge on River Road. This mill also performed a variety of tasks for local residents.

As outlivers began to provide more and more of their own needs, they came to think of themselves as a distinct community. This feeling developed slowly, but after Englishmen had lived together in this section of hinterland for twenty-five or thirty years, they possessed a strong sense of their own community, a sense expressed at different times and in different ways. In 1744, the residents of the Oblong insisted that they be given the right to establish their own school. This was hardly a radical request and was easily accepted by those who lived in the settled part of Fairfield. But it was the beginning of greater and greater demands for autonomy. Within a dozen years, the outlivers would request the privilege of forming their own ecclesiastical society.[1]

An ecclesiastical society in mid-eighteenth-century Connecticut corresponded roughly to an English parish. Its origins were ecclesiastical, but by this time it had also become a political body. In its role as a political body, it was referred to as a parish and performed numerous functions. It built and maintained the meetinghouse, hired and paid the minister. It had the power to levy a "society rate"—a tax which it used to pay the minister and meet its other financial obligations. It had charge of the schools in its district; these were financed by student fees and by a special school rate. In order to accomplish all these duties, the society elected a slate of officers. Of these, the most important were the committeemen; they were the executive and administrative agents of the society. The society also elected a clerk, a treasurer, and a rate collector.

In addition to the creation of a parish, the establishment of a society also meant the installation of a church. The parish and the church, however, were not the same. The church dealt with matters of theology, the covenant, church membership, and church discipline. The church meetings were limited to church members—those who adhered to the covenant—and so were much smaller than parish meetings. To participate in parish meetings, a person had to be either a freeman—that is: eligible to vote in elections for the General Assembly—or a full communicant of the church. The General Assembly had authority over ecclesiastical societies and was the only agency empowered to authorize the formation of new societies. In 1650 and 1658, the legislature had granted itself this exclusive power. By a 1728 law, the Assembly enabled the societies to carry out their various functions.

The outlivers saw many opportunities for themselves in the formation of new societies. Generally, the leaders of the town and of the existing society were men who lived in the central village. These were men who had easy access to parish and town meetings. The outlivers, on the other hand, had trouble getting to these meetings and so played a much less important role in them. But when a new society was formed in an outlying area, the outlivers would be the ones to take up the new positions and, therefore, to begin to have more control over their own affairs. They could then become leaders, themselves.

The men who eventually requested the creation of a new ecclesiastical society in the Weston area were more concerned with exercising additional control over their own lives and with projecting themselves into positions of leadership than they were with religious matters. For these men, unlike Roger Ludlow and the other founders of Fairfield, were not Puritans; they were Yankees. For example, most of them would become members of the church that they formed, but they, unlike their ancestors from the previous century, no longer regarded the church as an agency of social control. By the 1750s, the church in Connecticut was so racked by theological disputes that it failed to speak with one voice and had lost the authority it had once enjoyed. The church no longer set the moral or intellectual tone of the colony.

The decline of church influence meant that the men who lived in the Weston area in the 1750s were guided by other examples. Whereas the active pursuit of riches had been at least partly condemned during the age of Ludlow, it was an accepted way of life by the 1750s. The men who would soon call for the new society were men who were very much aware of the main chance. After all, many had given up the benefits of living in a settled community to seek their fortunes as outlivers.

Cupidity was only one of many impulses that men of the 1750s could

The interior of the Norfield church

acknowledge but which men of the previous century had been compelled to hide. They could acknowledge that they were more concerned with their own independence and liberty than they were with the benefits of social order. The Puritan generation had valued order above all social virtues. The generation of 1750 was less willing to sacrifice its own liberties for the sake of order and more likely to interpret pronouncements supporting law and authority as oppressive. The men who would found the new ecclesiastical society in Weston had traveled a great distance from the seventeenth century. They had physically forsaken the village established by Ludlow; but even more, they had abandoned many of his ideas.[2]

The initial step in the move for a new society came in 1755. In that year, inhabitants of northwestern Fairfield petitioned the General Assembly for the privilege to hold back one-fourth of their parish rates in order to use this money to have their own minister during the three stormiest months of winter. The petitioners claimed that they were so far from the meetinghouse that travel back and forth in the winter was nearly impossible. The men who made this petition were members of the Green's Farms parish, a society which had itself broken from the original society in Fairfield. That part of Fairfield that eventually became Weston was, in fact, frequently referred to as the northern part of Green's Farms. The 1755 petition was granted, and for three months the Weston area had its own minister.

But this was just the beginning of the area's petitions. Being less interested in religion than in politics, local leaders planned, in 1756, to request the authority to become a separate society. Generally, the Assembly required that a settlement have fifty or sixty families and estates that were valued at £4,000 before the area could qualify to become a parish. The settlement in the northern part of Green's Farms had slightly fewer than fifty families, and its list of real property totaled only £3,500, but the residents prepared their petition nevertheless.

The petition that was finally sent to the General Assembly was drafted by persons from the northern part of the Green's Farms Society, the northwestern part of the Greenfield Society—also in Fairfield—and a small part of the Wilton Society, which was then in Norwalk. In fact, the principal name on the petition was that of Cornelius Dikeman, who lived in Wilton. The petition stated that the residents of this area lived a great distance from their places of worship and that they had the ability to support a minister. The petition, dated October, 1756, was referred to a committee of the General Assembly for review. Jonathan Maltbee, of Stamford, and John Read and Samuel Olmsted, of Fairfield, considered the appeal and reported back to the legislature the following May. Typically, the Green's Farms Society opposed the creation of the new society. Its creation would mean a loss of taxes, thus raising the proportionate share of those who remained in the old society. In this case, a new society would mean the loss of approximately one-third of the assessed list of the Green's Farms Society. The old society's opposition failed to influence Maltbee, Read, or Olmsted, and they recommended the creation of the new society. The General Assembly agreed with the committee's findings and in May, 1757, created the Norfield Society. Finally, that part of Fairfield that would eventually become Weston had a name of its own.

The boundaries of the Norfield Society were different from the boundaries of modern Weston. The northern and western limits of the society were essentially the same as those of today. The southern boundary was so located that the Aspetuck River was included within the society, and the eastern boundary was different in that the society extended only as far east as today's Eleven O'Clock Road and Davis Hill Road. Thus, the society continued considerably farther south than modern Weston does but stopped short of the present town's eastern boundary.

These boundaries were soon changed, however. In October, 1757, the eastern line was moved further east to where Old Stage Coach Road is now found. This was the western boundary of the mile of common. Likewise, in May, 1760, the southern boundary was slightly altered to allow Asabel Raymond, Jr., of Norwalk to associate with the Norfield Society. John Cable, James Davis, and Daniel Morehouse also joined the new society after the boundary adjustment of October, 1757.

The first meeting of the Norfield parish assembled on June 23, 1757. David Coley, Nathan Morris, and David Godfrey summoned the meeting. The initial order of business was the election of a moderator. Nathan Squier was selected. The meeting then elected David Andrews as clerk and David Coley, David Adams, and John Lyon as committeemen. The meeting instructed the committeemen to "call the west parish of farefield [Green's Farms] and Greenfield to account for oure Rite [share] in the overplus mony and parsanage mony and scool mony, and our Rite in the meating house and othere things that they shall think proper." Whether Norfield was able to collect its share from the other parishes remains a mystery. If it did, the clerk never bothered to make note of this in the parish records. The final order of business at the first meeting was to summon Samuel Sherwood "to preach with us upon probacion."[3]

At the next meeting of the parish, the question of Sherwood's settling in Norfield was again discussed. The parish decided to offer him "fifty pound lawful money, for the first three years, from this dait, July the fourth Day, 1757. At the end of three years to give him Sixty pound a Yeare annually. . . ." David Coley, John Lyon, and David Bulkley agreed to meet with Sherwood and invite him to come to Norfield.[4]

The three men convinced Sherwood to take charge of the new church, and his ordination was scheduled for August 16, 1757. Representatives, both ministers and laymen, were present from area churches to participate in the ceremony conducted under the auspices of the Council of the Western District of Fairfield County. The ceremony opened when the Norfield committeemen appeared and produced a copy of the act of the General Assembly creating the Norfield Society. They also displayed "a Copy of the Votes of the People chusing Mr. Samuel Sherwood to settle among them in the work of the Gospel Ministry. . . ." Sherwood then came forward and announced

Old pewter Communion cup of the Norfield church

his acceptance of the society's offer and presented himself for examination. The Council questioned him "as to his Experimintal Acquaintance with Religion, his views in undertaking the Work of the Ministry, his Principals & his thoughts, and approbation of the Saybrook Platform* and Confession of Faith. . . ." The Council was "all well Satisfied with him, and unanimously and cheerfully agreed to proceed in his Ordination." At this point, the ordination process was adjourned until seven the next morning.[5]

In the morning, visiting clergymen offered prayers, the charge, and a sermon. Then local residents who were members of existing churches presented themselves for membership in the Norfield church. They, "having been admitted to Communion with Churches professing the Doctrine and practising the Discipline agreed upon by the General Consociation of the Churches of Connecticut at their Meeting in Saybrook 1746 and being inhabitants of the Parish of Norfield," agreed "to become a particular Church, as the Constitution aforsd. and covenant with each other to walk together in Brotherly

*The Saybrook Platform established a system of government for the churches of Connecticut.

love & Christian Communion as becomes brethren. . . ." Those who signed this covenant were Samuel Sherwood, Samuel Lyon, Thomas Whitlock, Thomas Pike, David Bulkley, Nathan Gray, John Rowland, David Coley, David Godfrey, Shubal Gorham, Michael Dunning, and John Meaker. The church was then proclaimed to be one of the Consociation churches, and the ordination was concluded.[6]

During the next month, several other persons became church members, bringing the membership to sixty-two. Of these sixty-two, forty-three had belonged to the Green's Farms Society, fifteen at Greenfield, two at Wilton; the affiliations of two others were not disclosed. The former members of the Greenfield church lived in the Lyons Plains area and included Samuel Lyon, James Lyon, John Lyon, Peter Thorp, James Davis, Joseph Davis, John Meaker, Thomas Pike, and John Cable. Those from Green's Farms lived in the western and northern parts of Norfield.

Samuel Sherwood was the most important member of the new church. The second son of Samuel Sherwood, of Green's Farms, he was born on February 10, 1730. His mother, Jane Burr, was the sister of the Reverend Aaron Burr, the president of the College of New Jersey (later Princeton), who was the father of the more famous Aaron Burr. After graduating from Yale in 1749, Sherwood moved to New Jersey to become a tutor at his uncle's college. While he was there, he studied theology with Burr, and on July 23, 1751, was licensed to preach by the Western Association of Fairfield County. But he shortly left Connecticut to spend another year in New Jersey. He did eventually return to Connecticut to assume the pastoral duties at Stratfield parish, now Bridgeport, and later at Kensington, part of what is presently Berlin. From Kensington, Sherwood went to Norfield, where he remained the rest of his life. He died on May 25, 1783, leaving a substantial estate that included two slaves.

From the few sermons of Sherwood that have survived to the twentieth century, it is possible to develop a general picture of Norfield's first minister's theology. Sherwood believed that the single greatest duty that God required of man was "to repent and be converted and sincerly believe in his Son Jesus Christ." Where this was not done, he contended, nothing of good could ever be accomplished. Even if a man is "externally regular and civil in Life" but has not been "born again," he cannot hope to escape God's "Wrath and Vengeance." Unless a man was converted, unless he discovered a new heart and a new life, he "must then be cast into Hell . . . and be eternally confined to that awful Place of Torments where there is everlasting weeping and wailing and gnashing of Teeth."[7]

This is the message that Sherwood presented over and over again. Jesus, he preached, was "able to heal the Souls of men of that dreadful Desease of Sin," and sin is the most dangerous of all diseases for it renders men "vile and abominable in the Sight of the blessed and glorious God" and must, therefore, expose the sinner to God's "Displeasure and Wrath." But through Jesus it is possible to be cleansed of sin and so allowed to glorify God by being pure of heart.[8]

The advice that Sherwood offered was full of warnings. Life is a period of probation, he contended, a time when a man must prove his worthiness to God. In fact, life "is the only Season in which you can do good for yourself or others. It is the only Season in which you can prepare for your eternal State." Death, on the other hand, "fixes your eternal State. If you are unprepared when it meets you, you must remain so forever." His sermons were admonitions about the sinfulness of man, admonitions about the wrath of God, admonitions about "an Eternity of Misery in Hell." The single hope was Jesus Christ; his love was the only sunshine in the otherwise gloomy picture painted by Sherwood for his congregation. From 1757 until 1783, he warned the unholy of their fate.[9]

The arrival of Sherwood in Norfield meant that the new society needed a meetinghouse. On October 30, 1757, the parish voted to build "a meating house for Divine worship" and appealed to the County Court* in Fairfield "to set a Stak and fix a Spot for us to erect a meating house." Because the location of the meetinghouse would determine the location of the town's center and because it would also significantly affect the values of property in the area, the question of locating the meetinghouse was too delicate to be left up to the parish members. Thus, the parish took the question to the County Court and hoped to find objective justice there.[10]

Apparently, the County Court selected a location either later that autumn or during the following spring. In May, 1758, additional plans for the meetinghouse were considered by the parish meeting. At the meeting of May 10, the voters debated "whether or no wee wold Build a meating house forty feate long and thirty feate wide and nineteen feate posts." The meeting approved this plan and then decided to begin work as soon as possible "and Raise it and Cover it, thro Dawn the floore and put in the glass, By next December A.D. 1758." The

*Connecticut's judicial system was organized by counties at this time, the Fairfield County Court sitting in Fairfield.

building committee was then ordered to "persead and Lay under pinin . . . in the new place perposed."[11]

In September, after considerable work should have been completed, the parish voted to raise the projected building "upon generosity." The failure of the parish to decide how to finance the construction until September seems to indicate that work had not proceeded according to the schedule of the previous May. Apparently, the site selected by the County Court was unsatisfactory to large numbers of Norfield residents. So, on September 27, 1758, representatives of the County Court chose a new location for the building. The meeting then directed the building committee to transport the partly completed frame of the meetinghouse from the old to the new location. Either the two sites were close to each other or else little work had been accomplished. At any rate, the first meetinghouse was finally to be built on land that had belonged to John Gilbert, Jr. The site was located near the present intersection of Norfield Road and Old Hyde Road.

By December, 1758, the building committee, which consisted of David Coley, David Bulkley, and John Cable, had completed the frame. Financed by a tax of threepence per pound of assessed property, the meetinghouse, the meeting decided, was to be shingled "all over." The meeting also voted to hire David Coley, Jr., for one month to lay the floors and case the "winders" of the structure.[12]

Exactly when work on the meetinghouse stopped would be difficult to determine. In August, 1760, the meeting voted to build a pulpit and place seats on the lower floor. The voters, at the same time, appointed Daniel Andrews, Humphrey Ogden, and John Lyon "a committee to mark out fifteen pues in the meating house on the Loer flore to the Inhabitants of the Society of Norfield, acording to theire highest Lists [assessments] in the Year 1760. . . ." David Coley, David Adams, and Ebenezer Squire had the task of constructing the remainder of the seats on the lower floor and of finishing the pulpit.[13]

This work was not finished quickly. In February of 1761, the parish meeting decided that each person who wanted a pew should pay the cost of having it built and also should "Pay his full perporsion of Cost acording to his List towards building the pulput and seates in the meating house." After this entry in the parish minutes, several years passed before the problem of the meetinghouse was again discussed. But in 1774, the parish again took up the question. From these discussions, it is clear that the building was never completed. In February, 1774, the meeting appointed Ebenezer Squire, Daniel Andrews, and

Daniel Duncan to receive subscriptions of money "& of all others that may be subscribed in woork or meterels that is wanting to repair sd house. . . ." The building continued to be used, but it must have been a crude affair, at best.[14]

On November, 1778, the Norfield Society voted to "put a rof on the meating house & git bords & thro Down on the Galary flores & make one paire of galary Chamber Staires . . ." during the following year. Apparently, the gallery remained unfinished and could be reached only with the assistance of a ladder. What the exact condition of the building was as late as 1783 is something of a mystery, for in August of that year, the meeting agreed to the following enigmatic resolution: "Voted that we will repaire the meating house as it now stans on the Sils." This brief entry was clear only to those who attended that parish meeting. But what is obvious is that Norfield's first meetinghouse was hardly an architectural delight. Perhaps this lack of concern over a temporal structure was in keeping with the theology of the Reverend Sherwood, who told his flock that their thoughts should be with the life hereafter, or perhaps it indicated a general indifference to church affairs.[15]

The parish had other concerns besides building and maintaining a meetinghouse. It had taxes to collect. The first tax levied by the new society was a tax of four pence on the pound. Jeremiah Sturgis was the collector, and he received twenty shillings for his task. The society was also charged with responsibility for the schools. David Coley, Humphrey Ogden, and David Adams collected the school tax and divided the moneys collected among the three school districts. These first districts were located at Lyons Plains, at the center of Norfield, and at the Oblong (Kettle Creek). John Cable was the school committeeman for the Lyons Plains (actually called Lyons Woods) district, Humphrey Ogden for the central district (called the Cross Highway), and Nathan Morris for the Oblong. Related to the task of operating the schools was the job of attempting to recover part of the money that the Norfield inhabitants had previously paid to the Green's Farms Society for schools. The Norfield parish appointed Daniel Andrews as an agent to press this matter. Typically, the parish clerk neglected to record whether or not he was successful.

During the early years of the parish, the schools were in session for six months of the year. This is not to say that each of the schools operated for half the year; rather, each of the three schools was in session for two months, allowing the parish to claim that it provided a total of six months of education. The responsibility of paying the

The Emmanuel Episcopal Church, completed in 1846

school expenses for each year was shared by the parish and the parents of the students. As the parish minister stated, "What the School Mony Dont pay shall be paid by the Scholers, each School shall have theire money according to theire List"—that is: according to the percentage of taxes paid by a given district of the parish into the school fund.[16]

Just as Norfield's population generally was growing rapidly during the 1750s and 1760s, so also was its school population. The three schools that had existed in 1757 had become five by 1769. There is no way to determine if the two new schools were as large as the three original ones, but given the tightfisted attitude of the parish leaders, they were unlikely to expand the school system unless there was no way to avoid it. Clearly, the Norfield parish was a growing concern.

But if the parish was a success, there is reason to believe that the Norfield church had, by the beginning of the American Revolution, already begun to languish. Perhaps this was to be expected, given the nature of Norfield's population. After all, the earliest Norfield settlers had been willing to leave meetinghouses far behind when they departed for the wilderness. Also, the growing excitement over the differences between Great Britain and her American colonies had diverted attention from religious issues during the 1760s and 1770s. These factors, combined with the general malaise the established church was suffering in Connecticut during these same decades, meant that the new church was founded at a most unpropitious time. The failure of Norfield parish even to finish its first meetinghouse is some indication of its priorities.

By the autumn of 1774, the church's position had eroded so badly that a special church meeting was assembled to deal with the problem. The meeting, after a lengthy discussion, reached a set of six conclusions. First, the meeting decided that all baptized persons are "under the Watch & Care of the Church and Subject to its Discipline." In the second place, the special assembly resolved that all church members should be urged to attend communion services. Next, the meeting urged that all children from twelve to fourteen years old be required "to attend Catechatical Lectures till they take upon them bond of the Covenant." The fourth resolution called for the establishment of a Committee of Enquiry, Inspection, and Information. The committee was composed of David Coley, Daniel Andrews, Shubal Gorham, Nehemiah Beers, David Godfrey, Eleazer Godfrey, and Ephraim Lyon. Its function, according to the fifth resolution, was "to give a full information of the true State of our Ecclesiastical Society with regard to the religious & moral Conduct of its Members, particularly as to their attending public Worship, Family Religion & Gospel ordinances with a view to assist and bring forward in gentle & Gospel Method, all delinquents to the practice of their Duty." The final resolution simply called for this committee to meet with the Reverend Sherwood to decide upon how it should function. Unfortunately for the church, during the final nine years of Sherwood's tenure, there occurred no great rebirth of religious fervor in Norfield. In fact, the political issues of these years continued to divert the inhabitants' attention.[17]

The Reverend Sherwood probably was more responsible for igniting Norfield to the cause of the American Revolution than anyone else in the parish. Certainly there was no more zealous patriot in Norfield. He, in fact, was more than just a zealot. He wrote several pieces supporting the patriot cause that were both well argued and widely read. As might be expected, these pieces, subsequently published, were originally sermons. One of his most important was a sermon delivered in Norfield on August 31, 1774, and later printed in New Haven. This sermon was written in response to the Intolerable Acts, a series of laws passed by the British Parliament and designed to punish Massachusetts in general and Boston in particular for allowing the Boston Tea Party to occur. Sherwood began his dissertation by reminding his readers that "there is but one general distinction that is of essential importance in the cause now depending, and that is to be made by drawing the dividing line between the true friends to the rights of humanity,—our dear country, and constitutional liberties and privileges, civil and religious: And the base, traiterous and perfidious enemies thereto." The issue was clearly joined in Sherwood's mind. He warned his readers that they were "threatened with being deprived of all our civil privileges, and brought under a most cruel, arbitrary and tyrannical kind of government." The only way to avoid such a disastrous plight was for all "to unite our hearts and hands with all lovers of the rights of humanity, in upholding and defending this most valuable and important interest." There was no question about where Sherwood stood on the political questions of his time.[18]

The Norfield minister's most famous sermon in behalf of the revolutionary cause was entitled "The Church's Flight into the Wilderness." The sermon, delivered January 17, 1776, was dedicated to John Hancock and the other members of the Continental Congress and to the "patriotic Heroes, who are spirited by Heaven to exert their superior abilities . . . for the defense of our distressed country, bleeding under the cruel and murderous hand of unexampled tyranny and oppression. . . ." In this sermon, Sherwood sought to prove that Great

Britain was a conscious agent of the devil's plan to destroy the "glory and prosperity of Christ's church." But this scheme is bound to fail, he assured his audience, for "it will soon be said and acknowledged, that the kingdoms of this world, are become the kingdoms of our Lord, and of his Christ." Six months before the Declaration of Independence, Sherwood was calling for a separation from the mother country.[19]

Once independence was declared and it became clear that the issues between the colonies and England were too real to be talked out of existence, Sherwood gave his full support to the war. He argued "that a just defensive War is not forbidden but may be fully justified from the Scriptures. . . ." Now is the time, he warned, "to exert ourselves for our common Safety and Defense before the Destruction actually occurs." In Samuel Sherwood, Norfield had its greatest patriot.[20]

In general, the Norfield parish agreed with its minister about the virtues of the American cause. Likewise, the town of Fairfield, of which Norfield was obviously still a part, was a staunch Whig—that is: patriot—town throughout the Revolution. In September, 1774, it established a committee to aid the people of Boston, who were then suffering under the effects of the Intolerable Acts. Serving on this committee were Ephraim Lyon, John S. Andrews, Hezekiah Bradley, Daniel Andrews, and Humphrey Ogden, all of Norfield. The people of Fairfield contributed 634 bushels of rye and 116 bushels of wheat to the relief of Boston. In December of the same year, the town meeting voted to support the economic boycott of British goods established by the Continental Congress and agreed that "if any Person or Persons shall directly or indirectly with intent to diswade disunite or otherwise prevent us from strictly complying with and conforming to said Agreement & association Publish Vend or Sell or otherwise dispose of any Books Pamphlets or publications in this Town directly tending thereto," such persons were to expect quick and harsh treatment. Norfield in particular and Fairfield in general entered the American Revolution thoroughly committed to the patriot cause. Neither the parish nor the town would be troubled with any significant dissent.[21]

Many Norfield residents served in the war. Since its establishment as a parish, Norfield had had its own company of militia. The existence of the militia company meant that the men of the parish had some passing acquaintance, at least, with military training. For many years, Daniel Andrews, the same man who was so active in the Norfield church, was the commander of the local company. He, like other militia officers, was elected by the men in his charge. Until 1768, he and his successor, David Coley, held the rank only of lieutenant. Because the population of the area was small, the number of men in the company was correspondingly limited, and so the highest rank allowed the Norfield men was that of lieutenant. By 1768, the company had become sufficiently large to warrant the designation of a captain's company. In that year, David Coley became the company's first captain. Coley served for only one year in that rank, resigning in 1769 because of his age. His replacement was his son, Ebenezer, formerly company sergeant and at the time of his election twenty-eight years old.

In June, 1775, Ebenezer Coley submitted a pay list for his company. Included were the names of the fifty-six men who had reported for training the previous autumn. These men were:

Aaron Boing
Albert Lockwood
Brush Marvin
Christopher Godfrey
Daniel Dunkin
Daniel Godfrey
David Morehouse
David Osborn
Daniel Andrews, Jnr.
David Bulkley
Daniel Morehouse, Jnr.
David Beers Jnr.
David Morehouse, Jnr.
Ebenezer Squire, Jnr.
Ebenezer Lockwood
Elijah Gray
Edmund Ogden
Ebenezer Guyer
Elias Godfrey
Eli . . . Brown
Ebenezer Bixby
Eliphalet Gray
Fanton Beers
Giddeon Lockwood
Gillad Gray
Hezekiah Osborn
Jonathan Squier
Joseph Dickson
John Silliman Andrews
Isaac Osborn
Jonathan Beers
Isaac Godfry
John Gray
John Olmstead
Jabez Sherwood
Isaac Sturgis
Jonathan Godfry
Jonathan Coley, Jnr.
James Sturgis
Joseph Gray
John Lord
Isaac Beers
Jabez Elwood
Joel Gilbert
Justes Gray
Joseph Green, Jnr.
Jeremiah Sturgis, Jnr.
Jonathan Cole
Joseph Gray, Jnr.
Josiah Green
Jeremiah Johnson
Joseph Whitlock
Elias Godfrey
Lockwood Gray
Moses Godfrey
Moses Burr[22]

When news of the outbreak of fighting at Lexington and Concord reached Norfield, the men of the parish were quick to respond. Among those who immediately answered the alarm were Nathan Thorp, Daniel Morris, Jr., Ebenezer Squire, Joseph Green, and Shubal Gorham. Although these men served only a few days, the residents of Norfield were equally quick to respond to subsequent demands for troops. During the summer of 1776, after the British had abandoned Boston, General George Washington called for men to help defend New York City from an expected British attack. Norfield men who replied to this call included Elias Bennett, David Burr, Pinckney Beers, Fanton Beers, Isaac Godfrey, Jonathan Godfrey, David Morehouse, Jr., Edmund Ogden, Nathan and Thaddeus Thorp, Jonathan and Nathaniel Perry, Stephen Hurlbutt, David Whitlock, and Joseph Green.

It was while they were en route to New York that some of the Norfield men first learned of Congress's decision for independence. These men had boarded ship in Fairfield and were on Long Island Sound when they encountered a vessel from New York. The commander of the transport hailed the ship and inquired about the situation in New York. The reply came through a speaking trumpet: Independence had been declared. Isaac Godfrey, who was on the transport, later admitted that he and many of his fellow soldiers had no real concept of what this news meant, either for themselves or for the new nation. From New York City, some of the Norfield men went on to Long Island. British forces had been gathering on Staten Island since the second week in July, and Washington decided that he must prevent the British from using Brooklyn Heights to bombard lower Manhattan. Eventually, the British attacked the American defenders on Long Island and forced Washington to order a retreat to New York City. Thaddeus Thorp of Norfield later recalled the evacuation of the wounded from Brooklyn Heights; that they were able to escape at all was a credit to Washington.

From Long Island, the British proceeded to New York City itself and, in the early autumn of 1776, occupied the city. Again included among the defenders were Norfield men. Although involved in various stages of the fighting, Isaac Godfrey, the man who had initially failed to comprehend the meaning of the Declaration of Independence, managed to escape harm. Nathaniel Perry did not fare so well. He fell into British hands and was sentenced to the prison ship *Jersey*. He never fully recovered from the privations suffered aboard that ship.

Hardly a battle was fought in the northern United States that did not involve Norfield men. Jonathan Godfrey and his nephew, Isaac, both fought in the Battle of White Plains. Jonathan was more fortunate than Isaac, for the younger man's good fortune ran out during this battle. He was one of the 2,818 American captives taken by the troops of Sir William Howe. This battle occurred in October, 1776. In December of the same year, Fanton Beers and Edmund Ogden crossed the Delaware River with General Washington and participated in the successful assault on Trenton, New Jersey. A year later, Beers would spend a grim winter with Washington at Valley Forge.

In the spring of 1777, the war struck close to Norfield. In April, General Howe ordered William Tryon, formerly governor of New York, to proceed to Danbury, there to destroy a cache of American stores and provisions. The expedition sailed from New York on the twenty-third and landed at what is now Westport's Compo Beach the following day. From the coast, Tryon and his men marched to Redding Ridge, Bethel, and eventually to Danbury. The line of march avoided Norfield; the road to Redding was a better road. On April 26 and 27, the raiders completed their mission in Danbury and began their return to Long Island Sound. At Ridgefield, the Americans challenged Tryon and his party. A pitched battle ensued. The militia, eager to fight under the command of Benedict Arnold of New Haven, performed well but failed to block the British withdrawal. Because the British troops were so close to Norfield, many men from that parish answered the alarm. Isaac Godfrey, who had been paroled after his capture at Fort Washington, fought at Ridgefield and helped to harass the British as they retreated to Norwalk. His uncle, Daniel Godfrey, was there, as well; in 1777, he was commander of the Norfield militia. Daniel Rowland was wounded at Ridgefield. Jonathan Cole, Jonathan Perry, Elias Bennett, and Joshua Adams were also among those who resisted Tryon.

Joseph Ogden, the brother of Edmund, and a miller in Norfield, was an enthusiastic patriot. He certainly would have been among the rebels at Ridgefield had he not enlisted in the Continental Army in January, 1777. Ogden was present at the American defeat at Germantown in October, 1777, and at the standoff at Monmouth in June, 1778, when General Charles Lee nearly brought disaster onto the American army by attempting to cut off the British rear guard, an attempt that resulted in his losing control of his men totally and having to retreat in disorder.

Of all the battles in which Norfield men participated, none was

The interior of the Emmanuel church

more important than the fighting that took place around Saratoga, New York, in October, 1777. Seventeen Norfield men, under the command of Captain Daniel Godfrey, participated in these actions. How such a large number of men from the parish came to be part of the American force at that time is a complicated story. It began in July, 1777, when a band of Indians fighting with the British seized two women hostages at Fort Edward in New York. The more important of these hostages was Jane McCrea, the daughter of a Presbyterian minister from New Jersey. She had gone to Fort Edward in hopes of seeing her fiancé, a Tory officer assigned to duty with General John Burgoyne. Her Indian captors were unimpressed by stories of her Tory connections and decided to take her to Fort Anne, also in New York and then controlled by the British. On the way, the Indians began to argue about who was to guard her. Eventually, one of the Indians shot her, scalped her, and took all her clothing. When Burgoyne heard of the incident, he ordered the arrest of the murderer but later pardoned him for fear of losing support among the local Indians. The murderer bore the suitably fierce name of Wyandot Panther.

This incident was nothing more than a minor atrocity in the midst of many greater atrocities. But the event became immensely important.

Jane McCrea was soon a martyr to the rebel cause. Her story appeared in newspapers throughout the northern United States. It was told in countless taverns and around innumerable dinner tables. Especially in New England, the story excited patriotic imaginations. When, in the fall of 1777, General Horatio Gates called upon the men of New York and New England to oppose Burgoyne's army, the response was unlike anything that American officers had seen before. By October 4, Gates had 7,000 men; by the seventh, he had 11,000. Among them were the Norfield men.

The details of the battle of Saratoga are too complex to be retold here. It is enough to say that it was a colossal American victory. Burgoyne surrendered to the Americans, and with him over 300 other officers, almost 400 noncommissioned officers, 197 musicians, and 4,836 of the rank and file. In addition, the Americans seized twenty-seven artillery pieces and 5,000 stand of small arms. One can imagine the humiliation of the British regulars as they passed in review before their captors. One British officer described the appearance of the American troops like the ones that Daniel Godfrey had brought from Norfield: "Not one of them was properly uniformed, but each man had on the clothes in which he goes to the field, to church or to the tavern. But they stood like soldiers, erect, with a military bearing which was subject to little criticism. All their guns were provided with bayonets, and the riflemen had rifles. The people stood so still that we were greatly amazed. Not one fellow made a motion as if to speak to his neighbor; furthermore, nature had formed all the fellows who stood in rank and file, so slender, so handsome, so sinewy, that it was a pleasure to look at them and we were all surprised at the sight of such a finely built people. And their size! . . . The officers . . . wore very few uniforms and those they did wear were of their own invention. All colors of cloth . . . brown coats with sea-green facings, white linings and silver sword-knots; also gray coats with straw facings and yellow buttons were frequently seen. . . ."[23]

Whatever their appearance, these men, although they did not realize it, had turned the tide of the war. They would, however, better understand the importance of their victory when France responded to it by forming an alliance with the infant United States.

In the summer of 1779, war again came close to the fields and forests of Norfield. In July, William Tryon came back to Connecticut. This time, he came not to destroy military supplies but rather to destroy the morale of the Connecticut people. He and his commander, Sir Henry Clinton, believed that a series of hit-and-run raids would convince

Connecticut's people of the folly of further resistance. To accomplish his mission, Tryon struck first at New Haven. The attack came as a surprise, and the British were easily able to gain control of the town. But by the following day, July 6, a large force of militia had gathered to prevent any further penetration of the area. Among the militiamen who answered the alarm were Captain Daniel Godfrey and the men of his company.

From New Haven, Tryon traveled by sea to Fairfield. The town guard, which included Daniel Thorp of Norfield, first sighted the enemy ships as they approached the town about four o'clock on the morning of July 7. Isaac Jarvis, commander of the fort at Black Rock, ordered the alarm gun to be fired. Word of the raid spread quickly to all parts of Fairfield, and when the British finally struck, about three that afternoon, a considerable force of defenders had gathered. Daniel Godfrey and his company were again present. Nathan Lyon was working in Norfield when he heard of the attack. He rushed to Fairfield and joined the company of Captain Benajah Bennet, a Redding company. Both Bennet's and Godfrey's men remained on duty throughout the night of July 7-8 and "harrass'd [the British] very much at their embarkation, till afternoon when they all got on board. . . ." The militia was so energetic in its pursuit of Tryon's men that Sir George Collier, the commander of the British naval units supporting Tryon, had to dispatch gunboats to McKenzey Point in Fairfield to drive the militiamen back from the beach.[24]

Not only did Norfield men aid in the defense of this town, but Norfield itself provided a refuge for people fleeing Fairfield. Priscilla Burr, wife of Thaddeus, was an example. Shortly after hearing of the British raid on New Haven, she sent word to a friend in Norfield asking him to bring his team to town to help her remove some valuables from her home. She was afraid, she explained, that the British would come next to Fairfield. By the time the friend, his team, and wagon reached Mrs. Burr's home, the Tryon force had arrived. After loading the wagon with all it would carry, she headed off to Norfield to the home of Parson Sherwood. When she arrived, the Sherwood home was full of refugees from Fairfield and Green's Farms.

Tryon's departure left a toll of eighty-three houses, fifty-four barns, forty-seven shops and stores, two schools, two churches, the jail, and the courthouse all destroyed by fire. At the Fairfield town meeting of July 20, 1779, the town voted "to put about subscriptions to raise a sum of money, as a reward for any person or persons that shall captivate or take prisoner General William Tryon, who commanded the British troops when they burnt this town. . . ."[25]

After the raid at Fairfield, the British fleet made its way to Huntington Bay, Long Island, there to receive fresh supplies, to make repairs on ships and equipment, and to fumigate the transports. But by July 10, the raiders were back at work. They struck next at Norwalk. Again, Norfield provided a refuge for town residents as well as defenders for the property they left behind. Daniel Godfrey and his men, nearly exhausted from the ordeal of the past days and nights at both New Haven and Fairfield, answered the alarm. Marching from Norfield to New Haven and then to Fairfield and holding off the British, these men had had little rest during the past week. Nathan Lyon had not even returned to Norfield after participating in the defense of Fairfield before he received word that the British had landed at Norwalk. His commanding officer, Captain Bennet, ordered him to ride to Greenfield Hill to collect ammunition. This he brought back to Norwalk; the ammunition was used in the counterassault on the British. On July 11, Tryon, having burned Norwalk, withdrew, much to the relief of its exhausted defenders.

By 1779, the war was all but over in the North. But Norfield men remained in the rebel army right until the end of the fighting. Joseph Elwood, for example, was not discharged until October 28, 1783, at the very end of the war. He had been serving under Captain William Munson in the Fourth Connecticut Regiment. Elwood had been at Yorktown on October 19, 1781, when Lord Charles Cornwallis, with 7,247 of his men, surrendered to General Washington. Elwood was among the American troops who, "though not all in uniform, nor their dress so neat, yet exhibited an erect, soldierly air and every countenance beamed satisfaction." And well satisfied Elwood must have been.[26]

Generally, the Norfield men in the Revolution served in Elwood's unit, the Fourth Connecticut Regiment. Norfield's Daniel Godfrey was commander of the Fourteenth Company of that regiment. Most Norfield men, of course, served in this company, but they were also well represented in the Sixth and Seventh Companies of the regiment.

But Norfield's service was not limited to the Fourth Regiment. Thomas Banks, who for many years would operate a tavern on Lyons Plains Road, served with Colonel Elisha Sheldon's Light Dragoons, one of the most famous and glamorous cavalry units in the Revolution. On the other hand, Trowbridge Crossman and David Smith never did anything more exciting than stand watch in the fort at Black Rock Harbor in Fairfield. David Squire lost both hands and an eye while on duty at the same post. Some Norfield men cast their lot with the fledgling American navy. Edmund Ogden served on board various vessels, in particular the *Bonhomme Richard,* under the command of John Paul Jones. This was the ship that Jones was commanding at the time of his famous battle with the British warship *Serapis.* Jones ultimately captured the *Serapis.*

If any single individual stood out for his military exploits during the War for American Independence, it was Daniel Godfrey. Born on March 30, 1739, Godfrey was from a staunchly patriotic family. His father, David, was too old to fight in the war, but his brother, Jonathan, as has been noted, participated in various engagements. No less a soldier was Isaac Godfrey, Daniel's nephew. Captain Godfrey fought in the war from beginning to end. He was chosen captain of the Fourteenth Company in 1776, and in that year, he and his men were on guard duty along the coast at Fairfield and Green's Farms. At that time, he had thirty-seven men under his command. In 1777, Godfrey fought at Ridgefield and was present at Burgoyne's surrender at Saratoga and the following year was serving in the Continental Army. He and his men helped defend New Haven, Fairfield, and Norwalk from Tryon's raiders. Later in the year, he was on guard duty at Stratford and Green's Farms. In 1780, Washington issued a call for additional men; Godfrey responded and took his men into service in the Connecticut line. Although he was never the hero of any battle and never attained a rank higher than that of captain, Godfrey represented the sort of patriot who was willing to serve a cause in which he believed deeply whenever and wherever he was needed.

It would be a mistake, however, to conclude that all of Norfield's men were as eager as Godfrey to serve the ideal of American independence. The case of Jonathan Coley is an example of a less than enthusiastic patriot. He was called into service in 1778. Before answering the call, Coley and several other local draftees decided to have "a frolick at the house of John S. Andrews in Weston [Norfield], and late in the evening Capt. [Daniel] Godfrey and a fill of men, one of which was Joseph Meeker, surrounded the house for the purpose of taking the men who had been drafted, 7 or 8." As soon as the revelers realized what was happening, they began to flee. "Girls and all," Coley later stated, "fled through the doors and windows and scattered in all directions." All escaped except Coley, who was captured and taken to the home of Humphrey Ogden. But about dawn the next morning, when all of his captors had fallen asleep, Coley ran from the house in the direction of what he thought was freedom. But Joseph Meeker

The 1978 Emmanuel church fair

came after him "with a pistol in hand." Coley was so frightened he fled into the woods and escaped. Ultimately, he avoided service by hiring a substitute.[27]

Even among those who served, not all did so to the credit of Norfield. During the summer of 1776, when General Washington was preparing the defenses of New York City, he wrote to Governor Jonathan Trumbull of Connecticut, requesting that Connecticut militia be sent to join the defense. Trumbull ordered several regiments to proceed to New York. Among these was the Fourth Regiment, then commanded by Lieutenant Colonel Ichabod Lewis. Lewis ordered the company commanders in his regiment to bring their men to Fairfield on August 13 to embark for the voyage down the Sound. Lewis later reported to Governor Trumbull that "Capt. [Ebenezer] Cooley of Norfield did not attend. Liut. [Jonathan] Squire of Capt. Cooleys Company attended. Informed me that Capt. Cooley had never Read to his Company any orders that I had sent him, and utterly refused to take up arms against the Kings forces." Lewis then ordered Squire to call out the company and to join the regiment at Fairfield without delay.

For his disobedience, Coley was haled before the governor. What occurred during that interview has been lost to history, but on

November 18, 1776, General Samuel Huntington wrote to Lieutenant Colonel Abraham Gold, who had replaced Lewis as commander of the Fourth, and directed him to order the election of a new commanding officer for the Norfield company. According to Gold, Coley and Ensign Michael Lockwood, also of Norfield, had been "guilty of numbers of notorious crimes" against the United States "and in particular manner last summer when Orders came from the Capt. General of this State for the western Militia of this state to March for New York to the assistance of Genl. Washington. . . ." Coley and Lockwood, Gold stated, declared that they "would not pay any further regard to the Orders" and that if they took up arms they "should be immediately damned; and ever since [have] continued to act conformable to the same principles, and a few days ago did declare that if . . . [they] did take up Arms it should be on the side of the King."[28]

The Norfield company did hold a new election and selected Daniel Godfrey to replace Coley. The company chose John Olmstead to become ensign in place of Lockwood. Whether Coley and Lockwood were truly loyalists is unclear; their disobedience may have been prompted by some specific grievance. In any case, neither man suffered further for the stand he took in 1776. This would lead one to believe that if they were loyal to George III, they remained quiet about it and took a neutral stand during the war.

Other individuals in Norfield were clearly loyalists. In December, 1776, Thaddeus Burr, sheriff of Fairfield County, complained that Samuel Lord and David Morehouse, Jr., both from the parish, had, on November 28, attempted "to join the Enemies of this State and of the united States and with a View to join such Enemies did go from their Respective dwellings [and] did Travel toward the Sea Coast in order to Cross the Sound to Long Island in the State of New York where said Enemies then were and now are. . . ." Burr also charged that Lord and Morehouse used "their Influence to persuade and Induce one Isaac Sturges of Norfield Parish in said Fairfield and sundry other Persons to the Complainant unknown to join said Enemy. . . ." All of this, asserted Burr, was "against the Peace of this State destructive of the Safety thereof and is against the Form Force and Effect of one Statute of Law of this State entitled an Act for the Punishment of High Treason and other Atrocious Crimes against the State."[29]

Justice of the Peace Jonathan Sturges heard Burr's complaint and ordered Lord, Morehouse, and Levi Morehouse, an accomplice from Ridgefield, to appear before him on December 3, 1776. At the conclusion of this appearance, Sturges decided that "they each of them are guilty and have thereupon Considered that they each of them give Bond (with Surety) of £500 for his appearance before the Superior Court . . . to answer said Complaint. . . ." Because they could not provide the bond, the men "were by a proper Warrant ordered to Gaol there to be held untill Lawfully discharged."[30]

Ironically, two days after this hearing, the men whom Lord and the Morehouses had encouraged to go to Long Island with them made it to the enemy on their own. These men were Isaac Sturges—mentioned in the unit—Thaddeus Squire, David Osborn, Lockwood Gray, Gilead Gray, Daniel Morehouse, Thaddeus Sturgis, Samuel Lockwood, and four slaves. All were from the Norfield parish.

But Lord and Daniel Morehouse paid for their loyalism. In February, 1777, the Superior Court found the two guilty of "Atrocious Crimes" against the state and sentenced them to serve a year in the jail at Norwich and to pay the costs of the prosecution. The men never served their entire sentences, because, at the beginning of 1778, a group of neighbors, including such important local figures as Benjamin Dean and Increase Bradley, petitioned for their release, promising to "have a careful watch over them." The petitioners also stated that many of those who fled to Long Island subsequently returned, disillusioned with the enemy. The case was thus closed. Loyalism was subsequently not an important issue in the parish.[31]

The existence of a few loyalists in Norfield encouraged zealous patriots to keep a watch for anything that might be regarded as suspicious behavior. When danger was close at hand, these individuals were especially active. For example, following Tryon's raid on Danbury in April, 1777, several Norfield residents were accused of aiding the enemy during the attack. David Adams, Jr., Squier Adams, Gideon and Albert Lockwood, and David Coley, Jr., were all charged with "being inimical and unfriendly to the Liberties and Priviledges of this and the rest of the United States of America." Their accusers claimed that each of these men "did at Norwalk . . . on the twenty eighth Day of April A.D. 1777 unlawfully wickedly and Traiterously join himself to the Army of the King of Great Britain then in Norwalk aforesaid at open War with and acting in an Hostile manner against said States. . . ." Furthermore, their accusers asserted that each did "unlawfully and Traiterously aid and assist the said Army in their Hostile Operations against said States."[32]

Apparently, these men were less than enthusiastic patriots, but also it is apparent that their only crime was to wander over to the Wilton parish to watch the British troops return from Danbury. While they

St. Francis of Assisi Roman Catholic Church, completed in 1966

were waiting to satisfy their curiosity, they encountered Jabez Lockwood, the loyalist brother of Gideon and Albert. Jabez was one of Tryon's party. Evidently, the Norfield men spoke briefly with him, and during this short conversation he warned them to return to their homes. This they did, but not before they had been seen by some of their vehemently patriotic neighbors. Undoubtedly irritated by the refusal of the Lockwoods and the others to aid in the defense of their homes, these neighbors assumed that the Norfield men were playing the same traitorous role that Jabez was.

These men were briefly imprisoned, but because of the weakness of the evidence against them, they were shortly released. David Coley, Jr., was a miller, and Parson Sherwood, Daniel Andrews, Benjamin Dean, Ephraim Lyon, Daniel Duncan, David Morehouse, and Humphrey Ogden, all of Norfield, attested to the essential role he played in Norfield's economic life and urged his release. They assured the court that he was not an enemy of his country. Gideon Lockwood later enlisted in the Continental Army, and his brother, Albert, served the Connecticut militia as a teamster. The two Adamses took an oath of fidelity to the state of Connecticut and also pledged to work as teamsters for the militia. Possibly these five men were lukewarm in their support of the Revolution, but more likely they were victims of the doubt and fear that existed in Connecticut after each of Tryon's raids.

One other important result of the American Revolution for Norfield was the coming of Freemasonry to the area. During the winter of 1778-1779, General Israel Putnam and his men were encamped at Redding. Among the officers in his brigade were several who had been active in the American Union Lodge of Masons; it had been organized among the Connecticut Line during the siege of Boston three years before. These men brought the ideas of Freemasonry to Fairfield County. Although it would be eighteen years later before William Heron, Nathan Wheeler, and Benjamin Hall would finally establish the Ark Lodge in Weston, the steps leading to that development began in the War for Independence.

Norfield's role in the American Revolution was hardly momentous. But the parish certainly did its part. For every Samuel Lord or Jabez Lockwood in Norfield, there were literally a dozen Daniel Godfreys or Thaddeus Thorps, men ready to answer the calls of General Washington or Governor Trumbull for soldiers. At the same time, Samuel Sherwood was composing convincing sermons for American independence. In the process, Sherwood, as well as the war itself, was focusing Norfield's attention more and more closely on political questions and diverting the parish from theological and church concerns. This change in emphasis would mean that the parish of Norfield would soon become totally subservient to the town of Weston.

NOTES TO CHAPTER 5

1. Again, this chapter has profited by my reading of Richard L. Bushman's *From Puritan to Yankee: Character and Social Order in Connecticut, 1690-1765* (Cambridge, 1967) and Kenneth A. Lockridge's *A New England Town, The First Hundred Years: Dedham, Massachusetts, 1636-1736* (New York, 1970).

2. Bushman described the transformation of Puritans into Yankees as well as anyone has.

3. Weston-Norfield Congregational Church Records, Connecticut State Library, II, 31.

4. Ibid.

5. Ibid., I, 1.

6. Ibid., 1-2.

7. The only significant body of Sherwood sermons is located in the Samuel Sherwood Papers in the Beinecke Rare Book and Manuscript Library, Yale University. These quotations are from a sermon dated August, 1763.

8. Ibid., January, 1771, and July, 1777.

9. Ibid., July, 1777.

10. Weston-Norfield Congregational Church Records, II, 29.

11. Ibid., 28.

12. Ibid., 10.

13. Ibid., 26.

14. Ibid., 4, 23.

15. Ibid., 35, 42.

16. Ibid., 10.

17. Ibid., 5-6.

18. Samuel Sherwood, *A Sermon, Containing Scriptural Instructions to Civil Rulers . . . Delivered on the Public Fast, August 31, 1774* (New Haven, 1774).

19. Samuel Sherwood, *The Church's Flight into the Wilderness . . . Delivered on a Public Occasion, January 17, 1776* (New York, 1776).

20. Sherwood Papers, October, 1776.

21. Fairfield Town Records, Town Meeting Minutes, III, 546-547.

22. Connecticut Archives, Revolutionary War, Series I, II, 48-49, Connecticut State Library.

23. R. W. Pettengill, ed., *Letters from America, 1776-1779* (Boston, 1924), 110.

24. Quoted in Thomas J. Farnham, "The Day the Enemy Was in Town: The British Raids on Connecticut, July, 1779," *Journal of the New Haven Colony Historical Society* XXIV (Summer, 1976), 48.

25. Ibid., 51.

26. James Thacher, *Military Journal of the American Revolution* (Hartford, 1862), 346.

27. Donald L. Jacobus, *History and Genealogy of the Families of Old Fairfield,* 3 volumes (New York, 1912), III, 208. Jacobus is the source of most of my information about the service records of individual soldiers.

28. Connecticut Archives, Revolutionary War, Series II, XII, 2240, 2243, Connecticut State Library; Ichabod Lewis to Jonathan Trumbull, August 15, 1776, Jonathan Trumbull Papers, V, 148, Connecticut State Library.

29. Connecticut Archives, Revolutionary War, Series I, XIII, 214-216, Connecticut State Library.

30. *Connecticut* v. *Lord,* Superior Court Records, Fairfield County, Confiscated Estates and Loyalist Cases, 1770-1789, Connecticut State Library.

31. Ibid.

32. *Connecticut* v. *Coley,* ibid., Connecticut Archives, Revolutionary War, Series I, XIII, 258-260.

THE PARISH BECOMES A TOWN
1783 / 1787

"The Privileges of freemen to elect rulers, enact law, and lay taxes"

Although the American Revolution had begun a process that would eventually weaken the Norfield church and virtually eradicate the Norfield parish, the people of Norfield in 1783 were still oblivious of this. The war was now over, and supposedly life would return to normal. The fact that they had their own parish meant that Norfield people had much more control over their own affairs than they had had when they were merely a geographic section of Fairfield. They now elected their own constables, tithingmen, listers, surveyors of highways, as well as parish officers. They no longer felt so completely under the thumb of men who lived miles away and who were little interested in the problems of the outlivers.

The war had barely ended when the people of Norfield decided that they had to do something about the wretched condition of their meetinghouse, which remained unfinished and was an embarrassment to the parish. Furthermore, its location was unsatisfactory to many Norfield residents. On November 4, 1784, the parish meeting voted to "Chus a Comtt. from other Sociaties to look into the Situation of Norfield Sosiaty respecting the Situation of the Inhabitants, and the plase where the meating house now stands & if the sd. house does not stand in the right Plase to Comidate the half of the Inhabitants of sd. Sosiaty that sd. Court should set a Stake for sd. Purpus, where they thought the meeting house ought to Stand Considering the Situation of the ground and the Situation of the Inhabitants of Said Society." Why the site of the meetinghouse was so intolerable is unclear. Perhaps it was just inconveniently located. Or perhaps its location hindered in one way or another the development of the parish.[1]

The parish meeting then went on to decide that if the committee believed the meetinghouse ought to be moved, the committee should proceed to select a site. The parish would then recommend the site to the County Court, which would make the final decision. This question must have been fiercely debated, an extremely rare occurrence in the parish meeting, for the vote on the question was recorded: "It is to be noted that 30 is in the Vote & 11 against it." The minutes of the parish meetings almost never indicated the outcome of a vote, probably because most questions were decided by consensus. The decision to list the vote clearly indicated that no consensus could be had; the parish had to resort to the unhappy device of allowing those with more votes to inflict a decision upon a reluctant minority—not a welcome situation.[2]

Since the committee recommended that the meetinghouse be relocated, the parish meeting voted a month later to "Pull Down the old Meating house, and so much as will Dew to erect a new house." The meeting of March 21, 1785, imposed a tax of threepence per pound of assessed real property to pay for the new building. John Gray, Thomas Banks, Ebenezer Coley, Daniel Godfrey, Benjamin Dean, Ebenezer Bixby, Eliphalet Coley, Nathan Adams, Samuel Rowland, and Zebulon Fanton formed the committee charged with its construction.[3]

The location of the second meetinghouse was very close to the site of the present Norfield church, but the sites were not identical. The second meetinghouse eventually stood slightly northeast of the existing structure. It was built on land donated by Samuel Rowland to the inhabitants of the parish "so long as the said Inhabitants shall maintain a House of Publick Worship thereon. . . ." Rowland made his gift on February 2, 1785. Actually, on October 16, 1784, Thaddeus Burr of Fairfield had given the parish a piece of land "for a place of Parrade to do Military Duty on and build a Meeting House and School House thereon, as the People Shall think proper. . . ." The residents of Norfield used Burr's land to conduct militia drills and used Rowland's gift for the meetinghouse. In either March or April, 1785, work began on the new building.[4]

At the end of May, the parish auctioned off the fifteen most desirable pews to the highest bidders. David Coley, John S. Andrews, Jeremiah Rowland, Samuel Rowland, Ebenezer Bixby, Thomas Whitlock, Thomas Banks, Ebenezer Coley, Daniel Godfrey, Eliphalet Coley, John Gray, Zebulon Fanton, Christopher Godfrey, and Daniel Duncan (who bought two pews) paid between six pounds and nine pounds thirteen shillings for the honor of reserving these pews for themselves and their families. In August, the building was plastered and put into use.

While the parish was acquiring a new meetinghouse, it also obtained a new pastor. The Reverend Sherwood had died in May, 1783, and during the following November, the parish invited John Noyes, Yale 1779, to preach at Norfield on a temporary basis. The young man apparently made a strong impression, for the following October the parish voters invited Noyes to settle among them permanently. The minister informed the parish leaders that he was still unprepared to assume sole responsibility for a church. Therefore, the discussions between Noyes and the leaders did not reach the point of negotiating the terms of his settlement. A year later, however, Norfield did make a formal offer to Noyes. The inhabitants of the parish invited him to become their minister. His salary would be seventy-five pounds and forty loads of wood a year. Furthermore, the parish offered him a settlement of one hundred pounds to be paid over four years to cover the costs of his establishing himself in Norfield.

Noyes rejected this offer, still preferring to avoid a permanent post. He informed the inhabitants that he intended to spend a year in Rhode Island before settling down. He had agreed to preach for a year at the Little Compton church.

Apparently, Noyes was a talented minister, because at the same time that Norfield was inviting him to settle there, at least two other societies were vying for his services. The Great Hill Society in Derby had offered him eight pounds and fifty loads of wood a year, plus a settlement of one hundred and fifty pounds to be paid in four years. Noyes flatly rejected this offer; Derby held no attractions for him. The Little Compton Society also wanted Noyes. It offered a settlement of one hundred and eighty pounds to be paid in three years, plus "the yearly Income or Improvement of all the Ministry Lands belonging to sd. Church & Society in Little Compton & further to have the Interest yearly of the Donation Money belonging to sd. Church & Society and that sd. Society will Cut & cart for Mr. Noyes & familie to the Door a Sufficiency of fine Wood. . . ." In addition to all this, the Society promised to build a house for Noyes. He refused this offer, deciding to spend only the winter of 1785-1786 at Little Compton.[5]

The following spring, Norfield renewed its offer to Noyes, and he accepted it. On May 30, 1786, the Norfield church ordained its second minister. Sherwood had led the church for twenty-six years. Noyes, in one capacity or another, would serve the church for almost twice that long.

John Noyes was the second son of John Noyes; the grandson of Joseph Noyes, pastor at the Center Church at New Haven, and the great-grandson of James Noyes, the minister at Stonington and one of the original trustees of Yale. His mother was Mary Fish, daughter of another Stonington minister. When her husband died at thirty-two, she married again, this time to Gold S. Silliman; thus Noyes was the half-brother of Benjamin Silliman, one of the great scientists of the first half of the nineteenth century.

After graduating from Yale, John Noyes studied theology, and received his license to preach from the Western Association of Fairfield County in 1783. His first sermon was delivered at Norfield during his temporary stay there. One reason for his decision to settle in Norfield was the fact that he had fallen in love with a local girl, Eunice Sherwood, daughter of the first minister. In March, 1786, the two were married; the couple eventually produced seven sons and two daughters. Two of the sons became prominent physicians: Samuel Sherwood Noyes of New Canaan and Burr W. Noyes of New York City. Another son, William, would become the operator of a general store in Weston.

Like his predecessor and father-in-law, Noyes was an ardent patriot. Although he never served in the military, he had been at New Haven when the town was attacked by Tryon; the experience cemented his patriot inclinations. At the conclusion of the American Revolution, Noyes delivered a Thanksgiving sermon at Norfield. He argued that just as God had driven the heathen from the land of Canaan and made it safe for the Israelites, so had He also driven the British out of America. "The remarkable interposition of Providence in our favor" was, he contended, the determining factor in the outcome of the Revolution.[6]

Although the Norfield church was less important in 1786 than it had been in 1757, and although its influence would continue to decline, John Noyes remained an extremely important figure in the life of the parish. In an age and a region where entertainments were few and far between, Noyes's sermons were among the most exciting events in a generally dull routine. Many people who were not necessarily enthusiastic about religion attended his services for the social life available at church. In the process, they heard the message that the minister delivered.

Most of Noyes's sermons, hundreds of which have been preserved by the New Canaan Historical Society, contained a great deal of common sense. He had advice for his flock on how to enjoy life genuinely. "If you would enjoy life moderate your desires & affection for earthly things," he suggested. "Look not for high advancement. If you do, you will be restless till you attain it, disappointed if you fall short of it, and if attained, it will not satisfy you." While he urged that his congregation be diligent in their business, he also suggested that they be content with their lot in the world.[7]

He hoped his flock would find serenity in life. "Amidst the fluctuating scenes of life, possess your mind unruffled. Be like the heavy laden ship which plows the billows, and not like the skiff which is tossed by every wave. Enjoy what you have with moderation & thankfulness, and trust God. . . ." Serenity, he believed, would come only with reliance upon God. "Make him your portion thro' Christ, and less of this world will satisfy you. Be persuaded that his way is perfect; acquiese in his will & rejoice that he reigns." Like his father-in-law, Noyes believed that one must glorify God and that the best way to do so was by accepting His will, whatever it might be. "We cannot glorify God so much in any other way as by doing and suffering his whole will with that faithfulness, patience and constancy which characterized the apostles and which is our duty under all circumstances of life."[8]

Also like Pastor Sherwood, Noyes constantly warned his people of their fleeting existence upon this earth. "Bear on your mind that nothing here is trust worthy: that worldly enjoyments are evorescent [evanescent], that soon all earthly scenes will be closed, and all worldly distinctions be done away." While in this life, all must "be kindly affectioned towards all your friends & connexions, & treat every one with due courtesy remembering who it is that maketh one to differ from another." He urged everyone to "do all the good you can. Live devoted to God; watch & pray, keep near the throne of grace; walk by faith; go on your way rejoicing, and be ready to depart at any moment. . . ." He reminded his followers "that your great concern should be to prepare to meet your God, and that you will be saved or lost according as you improve gospel grace." Noyes's messages were

Osborn cemetery on Old Farm Road in the Georgetown section of Weston

essentially similar to those of Sherwood; a strong continuity was thereby maintained in the Norfield church.[9]

The greatest difference between Noyes and Sherwood was the emphasis which Noyes placed upon the impermanence of man's earthly existence. Even as a young man, Noyes was obsessed with the idea of death. "Remember that you are born to die; and that the great business of life is to prepare for death," he wrote to his thirteen-year-old son, Benjamin. Another son, Samuel, was nineteen when his father warned him "what a bubble is human life! How transitory all earthly bliss!" When, two years earlier, Samuel's sister Eunice died of diphtheria, his father suggested that he "be mindful of your own frail state & consider who it is that continues you in life while one of the tender branches of the family is cut off by death." This morbid fascination with death became even more pronounced after Noyes's son Benjamin committed suicide at the age of eighteen. No one died in the Norfield church without the death's prompting a sermon or letter from Noyes describing the uncertainty of life.[10]

Noyes's obsession did not lessen the esteem in which his congregation held him. From his arrival, the church members seemed bent upon making his life as comfortable as possible. As soon as Noyes arrived in Norfield, the parish inhabitants offered to help him build a home. Some contributed labor, ordinary farmers and craftsmen doing the heavy work while the well-to-do acted as overseers or contributed the services of sons or servants. Fifty-three individuals gave a total of sixty-three days' labor. Daniel Andrews, a deacon in the church, worked for four days on the construction of the house. In addition to labor, the Norfield people also donated building materials. Seely Squire gave 200 feet of timber, 200 feet of boards, and 200 feet of siding. Samuel Rowland donated 500 feet of boards, while Moses Burr, Ebenezer Bixby, and John Silliman Andrews each contributed 300 feet. Daniel Duncan gave 500 feet of siding, and Benjamin Dean offered 200 feet of boards and 200 of siding. Others donated smaller amounts.

The Norfield inhabitants contributed only a part of the cost of building Noyes's house. The remainder came from his own pocket. The following is a partial list of the expenses that he recorded and the names of those to whom he made payments:

TEAM WORK

		£ : s : d
Capt. Dean	*1 day carting stones*	*0 : 6 : 0*
John Lockwood	*Carting kiln lumber*	*0 : 6 : 0*
Lemuel Wood	*2 days sledding stone*	*0 : 14 : 6*
Lemuel Wood	*Carting 5 load of shells*	*1 : 15 : 6*
Mother Sherwood's	*team carting sand, clay & window frames*	*0 : 9 : 0*
Mother Sherwood's	*team the value of half a day levelling the bank & drawing Piazza Posts*	*0 : 3 : 0*
Capt. Dean's	*team carting clay*	*0 : 7 : 0*
	Carting 3 load brick from shore	*0 : 17 : 6*

COMMON LABOUR

About 12 days	*work's value given in fall in digging cellar*	*1 : 16 : 0*
Thomas Wood	*1 day tending plasterers*	*0 : 3 : 0*

MATERIALS

Better than 1200 foot pine boards	*3 : 18 : 0*
300 feet oak boards of Mr. Bulkley	*0 : 15 : 0*
2,000 brick @ 20/m	*2 : 0 : 0*

40,000 short shingles @ 10/	20 : 0 : 0
8,000 shingle cut nails @ 2/6	1 : 0 : 0
200 Wt. of nail rods	2 : 17 : 9
100 feet 7 by 9 glass & expenses	3 : 16 : 6
6 pr. cupboard hinges @ 19d, 2 do. @ 8d	0 : 5 : 2
6 lb. white lead & 5 Qts. fish oil	0 : 5 : 3
1 brass nob door latch, 3/5 doz. scres @/6	0 : 5 : 6
6 bushels of hair of Peter Sturges	0 : 6 : 0
TRADESMEN'S WORK	
Mason's work stoning cellar	3 : 12 : 6
Carpenter 2 days in cutting timber	0 : 8 : 0
George Abrahams at hewing & framing	0 : 9 : 4½
Mr. Coles 8½ days his work at plastering	2 : 11 : 8[11]

Even if his parishioners had failed to give him a home, as the people of Little Compton had promised to do, they were ready to help in other ways. On one occasion, Noyes wrote to his son Samuel saying that "yesterday my people carted wood for me, & their coming on early prevented my writing further till this morning. They bro't me 40 loads of good wood, bro't in materials for a chicken pot pie & a number of women came in & performed the service of cooking & waiting. Liquors were also brought in, and the people seem'd all to be pleased." Obviously, strong ties connected Noyes to his church members, especially the zealous ones.[12]

But the problem was that church membership was becoming less and less important to the people of Norfield. There were fewer people committed to the church in the way a Seeley Squier or a Samuel Rowland was. Noyes had been minister of the church only a short time when the church meeting established a committee to meet with those who were missing public worship and those who were guilty of "anything scandalous." The committee attempted "to convince them of their sin & of their duty." Those who regularly failed to appear at worship services and who violated other tenets of church discipline were evidently numerous enough to warrant the appointment of such a committee.[13]

There were other indications of declining support for the church. Although Noyes was well liked by the faithful, the faithful became so few that Noyes's salary failed to keep pace with the expenses of his growing family. He was forced to borrow money and then found that he was unable to repay what he had borrowed. He wrote to Daniel Duncan, from whom he had obtained money, to explain his plight. "I have not a dollar in money in the world," he wrote, "nor have I recd. half of one from the Parish since my giving the note. As for grain, it is with difficulty I can get eno' to eat from one week to another. . . ."[14]

The enthusiasm that Norfield had once reserved for its church and parish was now being committed to its growing political interests. The creation of the Norfield Society had vastly increased the inhabitants' control of their destinies. But the increase in their autonomy had occurred way back in 1757, and since then the American Revolution, with all of its emphasis on freedom and liberty, had vastly whetted the appetite of Norfield for even more independence. By the late 1780s, there was much talk in the parish about becoming a town separate from Fairfield. The problem was that Norfield lacked sufficient population to be incorporated in its own right. To offset this problem, representatives of the parish began talking informally with persons from North Fairfield, another of Fairfield's parishes, about joining forces and applying jointly for incorporation. North Fairfield, which was to become Easton, was directly east of Norfield and had come into being in 1762.

On March 15, 1786, these informal negotiations reached fruition when the Norfield inhabitants voted "that they were willing that Norfield should be set off with Northfairfield to be a town." The inhabitants elected Daniel Duncan, Benjamin Dean, Samuel Rowland, Squier Adams, and David Coley, Jr., to be a committee to work with a similar committee from North Fairfield to press the issue of incorporation.[15]

All seemed to be going well when the plan for union with North Fairfield ran into a snag. What this snag was is impossible to determine from the distance of two hundred years, but on February 13, 1787, the Norfield parish meeting decided "to try the minds of the Inhabitants to see if they will be willing to be Set off with the Parish of Northfairfield to be a town by themselves." The question—strangely enough, in light of the vote of the previous March—was not only defeated but defeated unanimously. The issue was far from settled, however. On March 26, the question was once again considered, and this time Norfield voted to join with North Fairfield in requesting incorporation. On April 12, the Norfield meeting selected Samuel Wakeman of North Fairfield to be "an Agent to go to the Assembly [in Hartford] to try to get to be a town. . . ."[16]

Later that same month, the two parishes submitted a petition requesting to be a separate town. The petition noted that the two societies were, together, about eight miles wide and six miles deep.

The two societies, it continued, contained 355 families and 2,400 persons, of whom 1,020 were twenty-one years old or older. The total amount of assessed real property in the parishes was £140.9.2. The petition also noted that most of the inhabitants of the two societies lived in the northern sections of the parishes and few in the south. On the average, the petitioners lived ten miles from the Fairfield town house, and some lived as far away as fifteen. They protested that the town house, where all town business was conducted, was "too much inconvenience, trouble & cost when they attended as freemen." Frequently, they claimed, they were unable to attend the public meetings "or use the Privileges of freemen to elect rulers, to enact law, lay taxes, and transact the business of this state." The result of this unfortunate situation, the societies' inhabitants contended in the language of the Revolution, was taxation without representation. Therefore, they asked to be made a separate town. Before closing their petition, the two societies requested to be granted their share of all school and tax money then in the Fairfield treasury. They also agreed to accept their share of any debts that the parent town might have.[17]

The General Assembly acted quickly on the petition. Without offering any explanation, the legislature rejected the request. Possibly, Fairfield's opposition killed the petition. For the time being, the question was closed.

But Norfield and North Fairfield refused to allow it to be closed for long. In September, 1787, a second petition went to the Assembly. This application traveled first to the lower house, which agreed to grant incorporation. The upper house then confirmed this decision. The matter seemed to be settled, but the General Assembly decided to review the case again and appointed a committee to interview representatives from Fairfield, which, of course, still hoped to avoid losing parts of its lands, population, and especially town money. After these interviews, the committee recommended that the Assembly reject the petition. The legislature accepted this advice, and for the second time Norfield and North Fairfield lost their case.

Apparently, at this point a meeting took place between the leaders of Norfield and North Fairfield, on the one hand, and those of Fairfield, on the other. The result of the meeting was a compromise: Fairfield would withdraw its opposition to the creation of the new town in return for the two parishes' abandoning their claims to school, parsonage, or other public money in the Fairfield treasury. On October 25, 1787, the idea was presented to the Fairfield town meeting, and the meeting agreed that Norfield and North Fairfield should be a

Headstone in the Norfield (Coley) cemetery is typical of those dating back to the late eighteenth century.

separate town, yet the meeting considered it "unreasonable that the Memorialists [petitioners] should be allowed any part of the ... Public Monies in the Town because sd. monies were created by a vote of the Town many years ago and before the existence of the Memorialists as Parishes. . . ." The final obstacle to incorporation was removed.[18]

At the close of its October, 1787, session, the General Assembly voted to create the town of Weston. The Assembly granted to Weston all the rights and privileges of other towns except that, because of its small population, it was allowed only one representative in the General Assembly. The new town was to accept its share of responsibility for the poor and for its share of the debts of both Fairfield and Stratford.* It was also granted its portion of the state moneys and public securities in the Fairfield treasury, its right to these moneys never having been contested by the parent community. From Stratford, however, it received its part of the school and public moneys in addition to the state moneys and public stock. Thus, the compromise with Fairfield was honored.

The birth of the new town was not without additional complications, however. A problem arose because some residents of Weston owed back taxes to Fairfield and Stratford. The General Assembly ordered the selectmen of Fairfield, Stratford, and Weston to meet before June, 1789, and establish a list of those whose taxes were in arrears. This list, with the amount owed by each person, was then to go to the state treasurer, who would indicate to the Weston selectmen the amount to collect in behalf of the older towns.

More complicated was the issue of the boundary between Weston and Fairfield. The parent community wanted the boundary adjusted slightly to the north of the old parish boundary. Dudley Baldwin presented the Fairfield petition. The Assembly then requested Samuel Wakeman and Nathan Wheeler—both of Weston, although specifically of the North Fairfield parish—to appear and explain why the adjustment should not be made. The new town decided to oppose Fairfield's petition and appointed Abel Hall, Daniel Bennett, Nathan Seeley, and David Coley, Jr., to collect evidence to support Weston's counterclaim. David Coley, Sr., took the responsibility of presenting the town's case to the legislature. The Weston meeting authorized him to use his "own method in opposing the Town of Fairfield provided it bring no cost on the Town. . . ." Weston lost its case, but the adjustment of the boundary meant no significant loss of territory. For the time

*A small section of North Fairfield had been part of Stratford.

being, at least, the differences between Weston and Fairfield were settled.[19]

The joining of Norfield and North Fairfield was clearly a marriage of convenience. It was a union of two separate communities, separate both physically and emotionally. Norfield and North Fairfield pretended to be one in order to become a town; each was too small to apply in its own right. But the separate identities of the two communities persisted despite the creation of the town.

In several respects, the Norfield parish and the new town played complementary roles. One important function that the parish performed was nominating officers for town government. Beginning in November, 1787, the parish regularly presented to the town meeting a slate of nominees. In that month, the parish nominated David Coley, Jr., as selectman, and on December 17, the town meeting selected Coley to be one of three selectmen. The other two, John Sherwood and Samuel Wakeman, were from North Fairfield. Norfield presented the names of Benjamin Dean and Squier Adams to be constables. The town selected only Dean, Nathan Wheeler of North Fairfield being chosen to fill the other place.

The Norfield parish nominated persons for minor as well as major town offices. In November, 1787, the parish nominated eleven men to be surveyors of the highways. These were Jesse Morehouse, Samuel Rowland, Daniel Duncan, Adbel Hilton, Joshua Adams, Jeremiah Rowland, David Smith, Nehemiah Cable, Daniel Banks, Silliman Godfrey, and Nehemiah Beers. Jeremiah Rowland and Daniel Banks were suggested as listers, Daniel Andrews and Squier Adams as fence viewers, and Ebenezer Bixby and David Smith as tithingmen. Names were also presented for the offices of sealer of leather, grandjuryman, hayward, gauger, packer, and sealer of weights and measures.

Exactly how long this nominating scheme lasted is unclear. On November 22, 1796, the parish clerk noted that henceforth he would not bother to record "nominations made in this meeting for town offices." Probably the system died before the nineteenth century. In any case, it shows how the parish and town functioned together, and it also indicates the lack of cohesion within the town. Where the two principle regions of the town functioned like political parties, clearly the town had yet to become a unified whole.[20]

The society also worked with the town in operating the schools within its bounds. From the founding of the town down until 1795, Norfield Society and North Fairfield Society technically had charge of the schools but actually ran them in co-operation with the town. The school districts were the creations of both the parishes and the town. In 1792, the town meeting appointed a committee of nineteen to form the districts. Apparently, the committee established districts, but in 1794 the town meeting voted that Norfield should be redistricted. The new districts were devised by the parish. There were six districts. As described in the parish minutes, these were: "Southern Destrict No. 1 Senter near Capt. John Gray's Called Southern Destrict [;] Southwestern Destrict No. 2 Senter near Left. James Gray's, called Kettle Creek District [;] Eastern Destrict No. 3 Senter near Mr. Joseph Banks called Lyon Destrict [;] North East Destrict, No. 4 Senter near Mr. David Bulkley's called Den District [;] North West Destrict No. 5 Senter near Mr. John S. Andrews, called Upper Parish Destrict [;] Middle Destrict No. 6 Senter on Cross highway near the meeting house, called Bushy Ridge District." These districts were used only for a year, because in 1796 the town, which now had much greater control over the schools through the establishment of school societies, decided to draw its own districts.[21]

The parish and the town worked together in other areas as well. One of these concerned the Staples Free School. Samuel Staples was a thrifty and hard-working farmer from North Fairfield. On April 25, 1781, Staples, then seventy-three, became convinced that he was about to die. He, therefore, summoned Rev. Robert Ross of Stratfield, Rev. Samuel Sherwood of Norfield, and Rev. James Johnson of North Fairfield to explain how he wanted to disperse his estate. Staples was a bachelor who had no close relatives. He told the three clergymen that he wanted to establish a free school in North Fairfield which would be available to the children of that and of neighboring parishes in Fairfield. (Weston, of course, had yet to be founded in 1781.) The clergymen called upon Andrew Rowland, a Fairfield attorney, to draft the documents necessary to create the free school. But in drafting the documents, Rowland indicated that the school was to be built in Fairfield. When Staples objected to this error, Rowland assured the old man that the error was unimportant because Ross, Sherwood, and Johnson knew Staples's intent. Staples then signed the legal papers, asserting again his demand that the school be built in North Fairfield.

Staples's health was better than he had believed, and he lived to regret ever signing the papers. In August, 1781, the trustees of the school met and voted that the school should be in the Greenfield parish. Staples was outraged, but the trustees defended their action, arguing that what they had done was in the best interest of the town of Fairfield. In 1782, the trustees moved the school to the center of

Fairfield, and in 1783, to Stratfield.

Norfield residents wanted the school located in their parish and began a political campaign in 1786 to accomplish this. But once the town of Weston was established, Norfield reluctantly joined in supporting North Fairfield's claim to the school. In April, 1792, North Fairfield petitioned the General Assembly to locate the school permanently in that parish. Only after much debate was the petition granted and construction of the school begun. Ultimately, Norfield parish's halfhearted support of the North Fairfield claim helped bring the Staples Free School to the North Fairfield parish of Weston, and the existence of this free academy benefited Norfield as well as North Fairfield children.

Town-parish co-operation was evident in another matter dealing with the estate of Samuel Staples. In addition to the money that he provided for the free academy, which served older children, Staples also provided an income to pay the district school tuitions of younger children from poor families living in Norfield and North Fairfield. This trust—which consisted of Staples's farm and other real estate—was administered by three guardians chosen by the parishes and accountable to them. The trust was known as the Guardian Fund. The Norfield parish worked closely with that of North Fairfield in overseeing the administration of these moneys. When the probate court ordered the sale of some Staples land, the Norfield parish reacted by forming a committee "to act with the Comtt of Northfairfield ... to look into the Settlement of Mr. Saml. Staples Decead. Estate to proceed & take out an appeal to the Superior Cort, from the Judgments of the Cort of Probate wherein he orders the Sale of the land of the Estate ... & in every other Judgment of sd. Cort of Probate that they shall think fit to Appeal. ..." Thus, again, the parish demonstrated that it was an important adjunct to the town.[22]

Shortly after the creation of Weston, the Norfield parish took upon itself the task of establishing a lending library. Individuals from the parish, "being desirous to improve our minds in useful knowledge & wishing to promote the good of society," contributed money for the books. Pastor Noyes received the money and was charged with "purchasing such books as he shall judge best calculated for entertainment & instruction." The town provided no library; again the parish demonstrated how it could supplement the town's efforts to improve life in Weston.[23]

But this usefulness became less and less significant as the town matured. Within a dozen or so years, the parishes had abandoned the

Wing at right of house on Steep Hill Road was built in 1774. The main section was added about 1840.

practice of nominating candidates for town office. In 1795, the General Assembly revoked the ecclesiastical societies' control over the schools and placed this control in the hands of school societies, which were extensions of the town. Likewise, the school societies assumed responsibility for the Staples Guardian Fund, while the Staples Free School was by this time functioning on its own, without either assistance or interference from the Norfield parish. Even the library failed to be a great success; interest in it waned and it did not fulfill the hopes of its founders.

The declining influence of the parish should not be surprising. Before the creation of the town, the parish had been the center of political activity for the people of Norfield. It, along with the North Fairfield parish, had really been the parent of the town. But once the town came into being, the importance of the parish inevitably diminished. The town meeting was now the scene of important political action; town, not parish, offices were now the powerful positions. The parish had created the town, but now the town usurped the parish's prestige.

The Norfield church had been declining in influence even when the parish was thriving. The distraction of the American Revolution was the most devastating of a series of blows to the institution's importance. Noyes did what he could to maintain the church, but in March, 1806, his health failed and, as a consequence, he lost his voice. He rested for a year, hoping to recover both his health and his voice, and when he did not, he asked to be released. On May 26, 1807, the parish voted to dismiss him.

Unfortunately, Noyes was not replaced by a resident minister. A variety of itinerant clergymen preached in Norfield. In the fall of 1808, Noyes, still a resident of Weston, resumed occasional preaching duties. The parish paid him five dollars per sabbath until 1823, when he assumed more regular duties at the church and accepted an annual salary of $250.00. In 1812, the Norfield parish had offered Noyes $216.00 a year to preach. To his son he wrote: "I tho't the sum inadequate and besides, I judged that if I should engage for a year steadily that the genl. impression would be that I had (virtually at least) resettled with my old charge. . . ." The irregular direction that the church received created great problems. In August, 1816, the congregation established a committee "to inquire into any cases of public scandal in the Church & endeavor to bring the offender to a sense of his sin. . . ." Clearly, the church had fallen on hard times.[24]

Its role as moral arbiter of the community, which had never been especially important, dwindled even further. For example, in August, 1828, Jeremiah Rowland, of the church, accused David B. Godfrey, also a member, of the sin of intemperance. A church meeting convened to deal with the problem. There, Hannah Lockwood testified that on June 14, she had seen Godfrey pass her house "evidently in a state of intoxication as appeared by his reeling on his horse." Sarah Brumel declared that Godfrey "fell from his horse & that she & her daughter helped him on his horse again & that his fall was evidently the effect of intoxication & that he intimated as much by saying: 'You know my failing. I am not fit to any business to-night.' " The church voted that the charge was supported and informed Godfrey that he had been found guilty of the sin of intemperance. "This admonition is not given you out of any illwill to your person . . . but in love to your soul & in obedience to Christ Jesus who has made it our duty to watch over one another," the church told him. "We do it that you may be recovered from the error of your way & be reconciled to God, & to his Church, that you may not be cut off from the Communion of the Church here nor be excluded from the Church triumphant above."

Godfrey was unimpressed and showed his disdain by ignoring a summons to appear before the church meeting. The church's influence had all but disappeared if it could not even intimidate the town drunk.[25]

The decline of the Norfield church did not necessarily mean a general decline in religion. A partial cause of the church's problems was the rise of other denominations in the area. Although the Norfield church remained the only church in the parish, local residents were finding their way to services at other churches in other areas. Episcopal services were available in Wilton to those Norfield persons who lived in the western part of the parish. In fact, these services, conducted by Richard Caner and Joseph Lamson, had been held on an irregular basis since before the establishment of the Norfield Society. In 1762, Episcopal worshipers began meeting in North Fairfield at Gilbert Town. For twenty-five years, they were sustained only by occasional visits from British missionary priests and by the extraordinary work of their own lay persons. Finally, in 1787 (the year of Weston's incorporation), they were formally organized as the Episcopal Society of Weston. The present parish of Emmanuel Church on Lyons Plains Road is the successor to that first congregation. The Reverend Philo Shelton served as rector of the Episcopal Society of Weston from its founding until 1825. Mr. Shelton was the first priest ordained in the Episcopal church in North America, being ordained in 1785 by Samuel Seabury, the first American bishop. The location of this church in North Fairfield was convenient for persons of this persuasion residing in eastern Norfield. Since 1795, a Methodist church had served the people of Fairfield and surrounding areas, and in 1813, easier access to Methodism for Norfield persons was provided by the construction of a Methodist church in North Fairfield. None of these churches was as convenient as the Norfield church; but if a person were willing to endure the inconvenience, he certainly did not have to accept Norfield as his only option. In Norfield, as in the rest of Connecticut, growing denominationalism meant that the Congregational church, which would continue to enjoy privileges in Connecticut until 1818, had lost its monopoly of those eager to affiliate with an organized group. Between those who had forsaken interest in formal religion and those who now found it elsewhere, the Norfield church had lost much support.

The years ahead for the church would be no brighter. In 1835, Noyes retired, to be succeeded by a whole series of ministers, each of whom served for a few years and then left. For example, George Hall, in

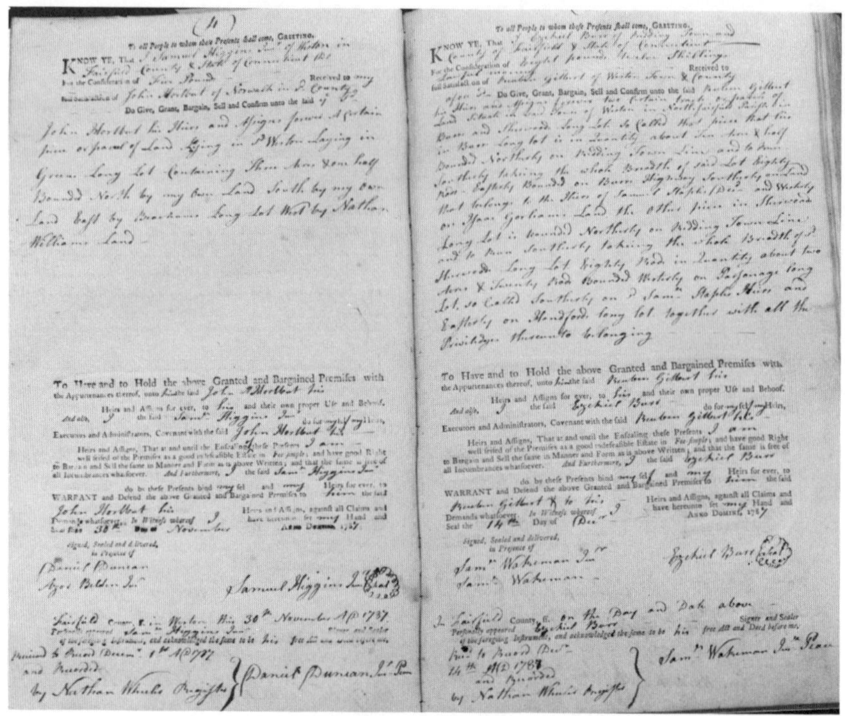

One of the first land transactions in Weston, recorded in 1787

October, 1840, asked to be relieved of his pastoral duties because of "the inadequacy of his support and the divided State of the Ch and congregation." When the church hesitated in answering his request, Hall merely abandoned his post.[26]

Strangely enough, it was during this period of acute decline that the Norfield parish decided to build a new meetinghouse. On March 9, 1826, the parish meeting adopted the concept of the new structure and on September 14, 1829, decided to locate it "on the parade ground in Norfield." This was the land that Thaddeus Burr had given the parish forty-five years earlier. Levi Coley, Eliphalet Coley, Justus Platt, Samuel Rowland, Silliman Godfrey, John Gray, and Ward Nichols oversaw the building's construction. Unfortunately, two men were nearly killed before it was done. Peter Smith and William Hurlbutt were working on the steeple when the gin pole gave way and the steeple partially collapsed. How they avoided serious injury was a mystery to them both. In 1831, the building was dedicated and came into regular use. The structure is today a classic example of New England church architecture. Perhaps when the people of Norfield decided to build it, they did so with the hope that the future would hold more promise for the Norfield Society than recent years had. For by the time the meetinghouse was built, the parish's important functions had been lost to the town, and the church, which had long known hard times, was in more serious straits than ever. The church would one day recover; the parish remained an institution with no function. The town of Weston, despite its being formed from two distinct communities, was now the object of Norfield's attention; the ecclesiastical society had given way to the town as the focal point of community life.

NOTES TO CHAPTER 6

1. Weston-Norfield Congregational Church Records, II, 48, Connecticut State Library. (Hereinafter cited as WNCCR).
2. Ibid.
3. Ibid., 50.
4. Fairfield Town Records, Land Records, XXII, 432, 451.
5. Minutes of the United Church and Society in Little Compton, January 4, 1786, in the Noyes Collection, New Canaan Historical Society.
6. John Noyes, Sermon of December 11, 1783, ibid.
7. John Noyes, The Way to Enjoy Life, ibid.
8. John Noyes, *A Sermon Written for the Occasion of the Sixtieth Anniversary of His Ministry* (New York, 1846).
9. Noyes, The Way to Enjoy Life.
10. Noyes, *A Sermon*; John Noyes to Benjamin Noyes, June 19, 1809; John Noyes to Samuel Noyes, February 13, 1804, and February 25, 1806, in Noyes Collection.
11. An Account of the Assistance Granted Me by My People, 1786, ibid.
12. John Noyes to Samuel Noyes, February 25, 1806, ibid.
13. WNCCR, III, 15.
14. John Noyes to Daniel Duncan, November 13, 1798, Noyes Collection.
15. WNCCR, II, 63.
16. Ibid., 66-67.
17. Connecticut Archives, Towns and Lands, X, 124 a-d, Connecticut State Library.
18. Fairfield Town Records, Town Meeting Minutes, III, 593.
19. Weston Town Records, Town Meeting Minutes, I, 7, Weston Town Hall.
20. WNCCR, II, 93.
21. Ibid., 85.
22. Ibid., 76.
23. Notes on the library are in Box 50 of the Noyes Collection.
24. John Noyes to Benjamin Noyes, April 17, 1812, ibid.; WNCCR, III, 19.
25. WNCCR, III, 21.
26. Ibid., 26.

TOWN GOVERNMENT
1787 / 1807

*"Without any fee or reward . . .
only the sincere thanks
of the town"*

When the General Assembly created the town of Weston, it ordered that the citizens of the town gather on November 14, 1787, at 2:00 P.M. in the North Fairfield meetinghouse. Samuel Wakeman of that parish agreed to summon the meeting and to be its moderator. This gathering, which took place according to the legislature's directive, was Weston's first town meeting.

The principal business of the meeting was the election—by voice vote—of town officers. The town chose Nathan Wheeler to be its first clerk. He was the first official selected and immediately set to work keeping the minutes of the meeting. The town elected seven selectmen; they were Abel Hall, John Sherwood, David Coley, Jr., Nathan Wheeler, Samuel Wakeman, Benjamin Dean, and William Prince. Wakeman also was chosen town treasurer. The first constables were Josiah G. Leavitt and Benjamin Dean. The meeting also voted for surveyors of highways and key keepers. Before adjourning, the town voters agreed "that the warnings for Town Meetings shall be put up one on a Birch tree near Henry Summers, one on the Post in the Society of Northfairfield and one on the post in the Society of Norfield."[1]

The officers chosen in the first meeting served for only slightly more than a month, because elections for town posts were held again in December. The reason for this repetition was to bring Weston into conformity with other Connecticut towns, which normally elected officials in late December. Nathan Wheeler again became town clerk, a post he would hold for more than two decades. The number of selectmen was reduced from seven to three; they were John Sherwood, David Coley, Jr., and Samuel Wakeman, who was also the meeting's moderator and was again chosen town treasurer. Nathan Wheeler and Benjamin Dean were the constables. The meeting then chose twenty-eight surveyors of highways, five fence viewers, four listers, one collector, two leathersealers, two grandjurymen, five tithingmen, two haywards, two gaugers, two packers, one sealer of weights, one sealer of measures, and five key keepers. (The duties of these functionaries will be described later in this chapter.) Having elected all these individuals, the meeting then began to worry about paying them. It came up with an eminently practical solution and one that was typical of early Weston. "Whereas it often happens that large sums arise against Towns for the services of the several Town officers appointed by sd. Towns which to prevent," began Weston's second town resolution, "we the inhabitants of the Town of Weston in town meeting assembled do vote and agree that we will for the year ensuing transact and perform all town business which by law or reason is or ought to be required of us . . . without any fee or reward. . . ." Furthermore, the town decided that "whoever shall be chosen to any town office in this town . . . are hereby notified that he is to expect or receive no other reward for his services, only the sincere thanks of the town and if any person so chosen is not willing to serve as above described they must make their objections to this meeting and shall be excused." Apparently, no officer objected. The meeting then adjourned until December 27.[2]

The December 27 meeting was the first held in Norfield. The business of this gathering was to select additional town officers, including three more selectmen. Nathan Wheeler, Samuel Rowland, and William Prince were added to the three already in office. The town also selected a committee to buy, sell, and exchange highways within the town. This influential committee had the power to determine the specific locations of highways. Several prominent local men served on this committee, including Abel Hall, Samuel Wakeman, William

Prince, David Coley, Jr., Daniel Duncan, and Samuel Rowland. Their willingness to work on this body indicated its importance. When the meeting adjourned, all town posts had been filled, and the town government was now ready to function.

To understand how the new town operated, it is first necessary to understand the franchise in eighteenth-century Connecticut. There were two kinds of voters in Connecticut, freemen and town voters. In 1729, the General Assembly assigned the towns the task of deciding who was eligible for freemanship. A town inhabitant would appear before the selectmen for examination. He—women were ineligible—would qualify if he possessed a freehold producing an annual income of forty shillings. He might also qualify if he possessed a personal estate worth forty pounds. In addition, the applicant had to be twenty-one years old, willing to swear the "Freeman's Oath," and known to be a person of quiet, peaceable behavior and civil conversation. If he met these criteria, the selectmen would certify in writing the applicant's admission. In fact, the Weston selectmen were most liberal in interpreting the law, and most applicants eventually qualified. A substantial number of Weston males, however, were too apathetic to apply. This resulted in a significant section of the adult, male population's excluding itself from freemanship.

The freemen met twice a year—once during the first week of April and once during the first week of September. During both these sessions, they voted for representatives to the General Assembly. At the September meeting, each freeman also voted for up to twenty men as nominees for governor, deputy governor, and assistants. The town constables then collected the votes and sent them to the Secretary of the State, who, at the October session of the General Assembly, would announce the names of the twenty individuals receiving the most votes. At their April meeting, the freemen voted for one of these nominees as governor, one as deputy governor, and twelve as assistants. The final results became public at the legislature's May session. In Weston, as in other Connecticut towns, great care was taken to maintain the separateness of the town and freemen's meetings.

The qualifications to become a town-meeting voter were equally elaborate. All freemen were eligible to vote in their town's meeting. In addition, all lawful male inhabitants of Weston who were twenty-one years old and who possessed a freehold estate valued at fifty shillings or more or a personal estate valued at forty pounds could participate. Town meeting voters also had to be "known to be of honest conversation and shall be accepted by the major part of the town; or by authority of the selectmen of the town." The law was specific. "No person not meeting the above shall be allowed to vote, intermeddle, act, or deal in any town meetings, in the choice of officers, granting of rates, or any other town affairs." Yet despite this harsh-sounding law, in Weston, and probably throughout Connecticut, virtually all adult males could participate in the town meetings. To have excluded a substantial number of persons from these meetings would have been to create a disgruntled minority in town. This would have been the height of folly, since one function of the town meeting was to foster a sense of community by finding a common position on local issues. Furthermore, when new people arrived in town, they found that they were welcome at the meeting. Instead of insisting that they demonstrate their good character, the selectmen were willing to assume it until proven wrong.[3]

During Weston's early history, the town meeting normally met only twice a year. The principal business of the meeting was the election of officers, the setting of taxes, and the appointment of committees. Otherwise, the meeting seemed to do little more than confirm the policies formulated by the selectmen. Few decisions were made in the meeting, but it could prove to be a useful forum to resolve differences and find a consensus. The meeting was directed by a moderator chosen only for a single meeting. Generally a man of great prestige, the moderator rarely had trouble maintaining order.

The most important officers of eighteenth-century Weston were the selectmen. Between town meetings, they exercised both legislative and administrative powers for the town. Although it seldom happened, the town meeting might later reverse a decision of the selectmen; but the real power in the town lay in their hands. They administered a complex welfare program by looking after the poor and maimed, idiots and insane persons; they had the authority to make grants to widows and to forgive the town rate for unfortunates. During the previous century, selectmen in towns like Fairfield had performed most of the tasks necessary to the town's operation themselves. By the time Weston elected its first selectmen, these officers had assumed a more supervisory role, leaving the performance of specific duties to lesser officers.

Next in importance to the selectmen were the town clerk and the town treasurer. During the early years of Weston, these posts were held by the same man, Nathan Wheeler. The town elected Wheeler over and over again because he was a man of unsullied reputation and great prominence. The oath that Wheeler swore upon becoming town clerk contains a reasonable description of his duties: "Swear by the dreadfull name of the ever-living God that you will keep an entry of all grants, deeds of sale or mortgages of lands, and all marriages, births, deaths, and other writings brought to you and deliver copies when required of you." As town treasurer, Wheeler had charge of all the town's financial affairs.[4]

The town constables had once enjoyed considerable power, but by the end of the eighteenth century, much of it had disappeared. They remained the chief law enforcement officers of the town. At one time they had also had the responsibility for maintaining standards of social conduct, but this function was lost as the towns generally abandoned the overseeing of mores. The constables were assisted in their duties by the tithingmen and grandjurymen. Both watched out for violations of the law. If a man were cruel to his animals, he might find his cruelty reported to the constable by a tithingman or grandjuryman. The grandjurymen also formed the pool from which the County Court selected juries.

Listers and collectors performed tasks associated with taxation. The lister assessed the personal and real property of each town inhabitant. This list then became the basis, not only for the town tax, but for the state tax as well. A taxpayer could appeal his assessment to the selectmen; but if they agreed with the lister's judgment, the appeal process ended. In fact, the taxpayer had a considerable role in determining his own tax. He was required by law to estimate the value of his property and submit his estimate to the lister, who could either accept or reject it. If the lister accepted it, the taxpayer's estimate became the basis of his tax; if the lister rejected it and found it to be underestimated, the taxpayer had to multiply the difference between his estimate and the lister's assessment by four and add this amount to his tax. The collectors were the men who actually collected the tax. Generally, different persons collected town and state taxes.

Surveyors of the highways oversaw the work done on the roads. They had the power to command town residents to work as many as four days a year on the town roads. The surveyors were men known for their fairness and for their ability to demand respect. Many of the town's most prominent men served year after year in this capacity. The fence viewers could also demand work of any Weston male, in this case work on the town-maintained fences. The fence viewers were additionally charged with responsibility for locating inadequate fences around the fields of individual farmers. If the farmers refused to repair their fences, the fence viewer would mend them and charge the farmers double the cost of the repairs. To the modern world, the positions of surveyor of the highways and fence viewer seem as remote as feudalism. But in an age that expected the local population to maintain its roads, that had never heard of the idea of the division of labor, and that knew the disastrous consequences of allowing unfenced animals to trample or devour crops, these two positions were completely relevant.

Two other town officials worked closely with fence viewers; these were key keepers and haywards. Key keepers watched for animals that had escaped through dilapidated fences overlooked by the fence viewers; they then placed these animals in pounds which they maintained. Delinquent owners could collect their animals but only after paying a fine to the town and a fee to the key keeper. Haywards cared for the stock that was kept on common lands. Because there was little common land in Weston, the haywards were relatively unimportant.

The last of the town officials in early Weston were the leathersealers, packers of beef, gaugers, and sealers of weights and measures. The first three were all involved in inspecting products exported from town. Leathersealers and packers of beef placed their marks on leather or meat to indicate that it was produced in Weston and was of reasonable quality. The gaugers did the same for items produced by local craftsmen—in particular, blacksmiths. The sealers of weights and measures guaranteed that weights and measures used in Weston corresponded to the standards set by the state.

These, then, were the town officials who served Weston. (School officials, it will be remembered, were initially officers of the parish and then of the school societies.) The needs of this small, agricultural community were reflected in the posts that the new town created. These positions existed because they were needed. The persons who occupied them did so realizing that the community depended upon them to fulfill some essential function. They also realized that in this small community, their failure to perform their duties well would be as obvious as their doing their jobs conscientiously. This was a strong incentive to do well by the town.

Mention should be made of two other public officials. According to the town's charter, Weston could elect one representative to the General Assembly. In 1800, after Weston's population had grown considerably, the Assembly authorized it to send two, as most towns did. The men selected were among the most respected in town. Equally esteemed were the justices of the peace. Chosen by the legislature, they heard minor cases in what were called justice courts. They also

Water turbine used to drive sawmill at Godfrey Pond in the mid-1800s. Original mill was constructed in 1783.

had the authority to issue warrants against persons whom the fence viewers had found to neglect their fences and against malingerers who refused to do their share on the roads. Furthermore, the justices witnessed the recording of all land transactions by the town clerk. Justices seldom simultaneously held town offices, but they frequently represented the town in the General Assembly while they served as justices.

Fortunately for the men who guided the fate of the young town, the range of town concerns was much more limited at the end of the eighteenth century and the beginning of the nineteenth than it is now. Many items, such as zoning, that are today a concern of the town would never have been regarded as public business in 1787 or 1807. Zoning was no problem, because property values were unaffected by the juxtaposition of residential and either industrial or commercial property in a community of subsistence farmers. In fact, it would have been nearly impossible to distinguish between commercial and industrial property, on the one hand, and residential, on the other, because most persons—whether blacksmiths, farmers, or merchants—worked and lived in the same place. Additionally, many of the problems that draw our attention now were not even recognized as problems during those earlier times. In a community of small farmers, there was no reason for the town to ponder the recreational needs of its inhabitants; too much work had to be done to allow leisure to be a problem. Even when problems might have been recognized, town leaders ignored them because the town had only enough tax dollars for absolute necessities.

Probably no concern occupied more of early Weston's time than roads. Connecticut roads were notoriously bad, and within Connecticut few towns had a worse reputation for poorly maintained roads than Weston. The town roads were at best wide swaths cut through forests and fields. They were rough and uneven, crossed by small streams, and littered with stumps and boulders. Drivers had to be alert to avoid ruts, holes, stones, and fallen trees. On infrequently traveled roads, second-growth trees quickly rose to obscure the former pathways. In fact, Weston periodically appointed committees to examine the surreptitious cutting of firewood on publicly owned roads.

Because of the rivers that flowed through Weston, the town had to keep up several bridges along with its roads. These bridges, like the roads, were built and maintained by local residents as part of their regular highway duty. The early bridges were simple structures, usually consisting of hewn logs placed in such a way as to allow a team of horses or a yoke of oxen to pass gingerly over them. Weston residents were consistently unable to build bridges that could endure the high waters of spring or the ice of winter. Unlike the bridges of England, many of which date back to the seventeenth century, not a single colonial bridge is left in Connecticut, much less in Weston.

In addition to being the object of the highway surveyors' attention, roads were the special concern of the town-appointed committee to buy, sell, and exchange highways. This committee either sold or traded little-used roads for land upon which to build new thoroughfares. It also had the power to remove encroachments from the highways not in use.* These encroachments usually consisted of fences that farmers might extend across one of the town roads. Both the committee to buy, sell, and exchange and the surveyors were responsible to the selectmen.

---

*Some of the "highways" were not in any sense thoroughfares, or even trails. They were simply straight lines plotted arbitrarily on maps, with no reference to actual terrain.

Each surveyor had charge of a highway district. In December, 1799, the town divided the Norfield Society into eleven districts. These were the Southern District, located in the southeastern section of the parish; Kettle Creek District; Goodhill District; Eastern District, near the North Fairfield line; Lyons District; Western District, along the Wilton line; Middle District, located near the Norfield meetinghouse; Norwest District, in what is now Georgetown; Burr's District, along the Redding line; Den District; and Southeast District, bounded on the south by Fairfield and on the east by North Fairfield. These districts remained in use until 1807, when the eleven were reduced to seven. It is hard to imagine how more awkwardly constructed districts could have been drawn than those of 1807. The southern district is a good example. It was "Bounded Southerly on Fairfield Line, Easterly on Sturges Highway to run on the west side of said highway as far North as the foot of the great Hill above Samuel Coley's taking all the Inhabitants on the west side of said highway then running Easterly at the same distance North of the said Cross-highway as far as Gilberts highway so called, then following Gilberts highway Northerly to the Cross Road to the Road near Northfairfield Line then on the west side of said Road to the East Side of the Publick Highway leading from Redding to Saugatuck, then on the East Side of said highway including all the Inhabitants living on both sides said highway to Redding line, then running Westerly on Redding line to the East side of the Branch so called, then running Southerly on the Eastside of the Branch so called to Wilton line, then Bounded Westerly on the Line of the Towns of Wilton & Norwalk. . . ." Why such complicated districts were constructed is unknown; it certainly could not have been to simplify the work of the surveyors.[5]

Occasionally, the town would decide that all able-bodied men in one or the other of the two parishes should work on a particular road. On December 27, 1791, the town voted that all Norfield men should work for one day during 1792 on Sturges Highway (now Fanton Hill Road). But usually the surveyors decided what work needed to be done within their districts. They failed, however, to keep the roads in sufficiently good condition to avoid complaints to the County Court. In 1792, the town meeting found it necessary to appoint an agent to oppose a complaint made in the court about the Weston road that connected Redding with Saugatuck. This sort of complaint against Weston was to be heard regularly in the years ahead.

One reason for the poor condition of the roads was the town's refusal to use tax money to finance highway repairs. What was done to the roads was accomplished by the labor of local residents and with the materials at hand. In December, 1800, the town meeting considered the idea of using tax moneys to pay for repairs, but voted it down. This decision had barely been made when, on February 21, 1801, a town meeting was called "to appoint an Agent to appear before the County Court now Setting & oppose the Complaint made against the Town for not Repairing the Road leading from the Turnpike Road in Redding through the Town of Weston to Saugatuck Shores." Benjamin Hall was the agent chosen, but he failed to convince the court that Weston had not been negligent. Therefore, the town, in April, 1801, appointed Samuel B. Sherwood, son of the first pastor, as agent "on behalf of the Town, to represent to the County Court the situation of the Road in Norfield Condemned by the Court and request the Same to be altered." At the same time, the town finally came around to voting a tax of one cent on each dollar of assessed property for repairing the roads.[6]

Unfortunately, Sherwood lost the appeal; furthermore, the one-cent tax proved inadequate to pay for any real improvement in the roads. Thus, in November, 1801, the tax was increased to three cents on the dollar. The town voted to use this tax in the following way: "One Cent on the Dollar of sd. Tax to . . . pay the Execution now against the Town in favor of Andrew L. Hill, Esq." and the remaining two cents to be used to finance repairs. Hill was the justice of the peace who had granted the execution against the town.[7]

This was not the end of Weston's problems with its roads. In December, 1802, a similar three-cent tax was levied. Apparently, the Norfield roads were even worse than those in North Fairfield, because the town appointed David Coley and Squier Adams to oversee the expenditure of two-thirds of this money in Norfield. Any money left at the end of the year was to be used to pay Andrew Hill, to whom Weston still owed money.

The highway tax first levied in 1801 was payable either in money or in labor. In 1803, the selectmen submitted to the town meeting a detailed report on how the tax should be collected and used. They suggested first of all that tax money or labor from a particular district be used in that district. The price of a day's labor, they contended, should "be from 30th of April to the 15th of June for a Man, he to keep himself and furnish his Tools to work with, Sixtyseven Cents, and for a Man and a yoke of Oxen, Cart & Chains or Plow One Dollar thirtyfour Cents. . . ." Between September 1 and October 15, the town was willing to allow only fifty cents for a man and one dollar for a man and a yoke. Obviously, a man's time was more valuable in the spring, when crops had to be planted, than in the fall. Also obvious was the necessity to repair the roads after the damage of winter and early spring. The selectmen recommended that the surveyors in each district collect the tax in that district and expend the money collected. "If any Person shall not work when Called on by the Surveyors, he first giving legal notice of the Time and place of Working . . . he Shall pay three fourths of his Tax by the 15th day of June next in money and the other fourth by the 15th day of October next." Finally, the selectmen urged "that the Surveyors be directed to purchase the Timber for Bridges in their respective Districts in the best manner they are able and with the least expense. . . ." The surveyors were to give an account of their expenses to the selectmen. This report was adopted by the town meeting, and it now seemed that some order had been imposed on a previously chaotic system of road maintenance.[8]

But Hill's execution against the town was still only partially paid. David Coley had agreed to lend the town the money to pay part of it, and the town now had to reimburse him for both principal and interest. Thus, the selectmen had to borrow again. Then, in December, 1803, the selectmen had to dip into the highway fund to repay the loan. Eventually, the town fathers straightened out their finances, paid Hill, and paid off the town's debt. The execution, which amounted to less than $200, had created the greatest financial crisis that Weston faced during its first two decades.

Roads continued to be an issue. In 1805, the town agreed "that the price of Labour on the highways be One Dollar for a man and two Dollars for a man & Team in the Spring and Sixtyseven Cents for man and One Dollar thirtyfour Cents for a man and Team in the fall. . . ." The meeting also decided that all residents must accomplish two-thirds of their work in the spring, when the roads needed the most attention. This system of maintaining the roads lasted until about 1850. There were occasional modifications. In 1806, for example, the town appropriated six dollars for each highway district to purchase "an Ox Shovel or Drag." But basically, in a community of small farmers who had little notion of the division of labor, the system of residents' maintaining the roads was a perfectly satisfactory one. The roads were never good, but they were generally adequate to meet the needs of local residents.[9]

At the end of the eighteenth century, an economic innovation appeared that promised to eliminate some of the burden of keeping up the roads. This was the privately owned turnpike. Weston welcomed the idea of private companies' building toll roads. The first of these roads to be located in the Weston area was the Fairfield, Weston, and Redding Turnpike Company. It was incorporated in May, 1797; although it avoided Norfield, it did pass through part of North Fairfield. In the years ahead, six more turnpike companies would function in the town of Weston, but not until well into the nineteenth century. For the time being, at least, Weston's roads remained a source of regular inconvenience to travelers and of periodic embarrassment to local pride.

In addition to the highway tax, the residents of Weston paid a town tax. The first tax, that of 1787, was one of "five pence on the Pound on all the Polls and Rateable estates of the town. . . ." The tax rate at first varied greatly; in 1788, the rate was cut in half, and in 1790, it was once again reduced. But during the rest of the 1790s, it remained fairly constant. By no means was the tax burden of Weston residents great. In 1797, for example, when the rate was eight mills on the dollar—dollars having finally replaced pounds as the unit for measuring value—the median tax paid by a resident was ninety cents, the equivalent of one day's labor. The low tax rate was in keeping with the idea that the functions of the town were limited and that the residents would rather donate their time, which was plentiful during certain seasons, than their money, which was usually scarce.[10]

Being an agricultural community, Weston regularly had to deal with questions involving livestock. In March of 1788, for example, the town voted to admit swine to its common pastures so long as they had rings in their noses. This remained standard practice in Weston until 1810, when the town decided that its earlier ordinance was too general to satisfy the complexities of the situation. Thus it ruled "that all Swine be lawful Commoners untill ten Weeks old without a Ring, and lawfull Commoners after ten weeks old with a Ring in their Noses." Male sheep were a bigger problem, especially during their mating seasons. So in 1788, the Weston meeting decreed "that all owners of Rams in this Town shall restrain their Rams and not suffer them to run at large in this Town from the first day of Septmb. untill the first day of Novemb. in each year and if any owner of any Ram in this town shall suffer his Ram to run at large in the Town during sd. term of time he shall forfeit and pay the sum of Ten Shillings lawful money into the Town Treasury." To a twentieth-century resident, such a regulation would be irrelevant, but to a farmer of early Weston, one concerned with the bloodlines of his stock, the possibility that his ewe might become inseminated by some wandering, but determined, ram was a serious matter.[11]

Because Weston was in reality two communities, it lacked a center. Unlike most of its neighbors, it was without either a green or a town building. In 1775, the town of Fairfield had established a parade—that is, an area for militia exercises—in North Fairfield, and this continued to be used for the same purpose after the establishment of Weston. In 1811, the town voted to sell this land and to establish a new parade, but it, too, was located in North Fairfield. The Norfield militia used land given the parish by Thaddeus Burr until 1805 and then moved its militia exercises to a field near the Coley (Norfield) Cemetery, owned by the Coley family. Thus each parish maintained its separate identity through separate militias and separate training grounds.

The first town meeting was held in the North Fairfield meetinghouse. Although occasionally meetings gathered in Norfield, most continued to be held in North Fairfield, either at the meetinghouse or, after 1816, at the Episcopal church. In December, 1791, Weston considered the idea of building a town hall. It appointed a committee of twelve persons, six from Norfield and six from North Fairfield, to decide if and where a town center should be established. The committee planned to report to the next town meeting. In the meantime, the voters agreed that "the town meeting shall be held in the same manner as they have hitherto been held untill the Town House shall be erected in the place where the committee shall fix for the center without any expense to the Town by way of Tax, but the Town House to be built wholly by subscription." No action on the committee's report was ever taken, and Weston remained without either a center or a town hall, symbolizing the fact that Weston was truly two communities.[12]

One of the town's most important tasks was the care of paupers. The selectmen had the job of placing the poor with town families and providing for their upkeep. Samuel Thorp, for example, kept Aranias Brush in his home and billed the town for the cost of boarding and clothing him. In many cases, the town was surprisingly generous in its treatment of paupers. In 1788, it voted to "allow Old Mr. Booth now Supported by the town one Quart of Rum pr. month." But the cost of keeping these persons, although their number was small, was a great burden to the town.[13]

In an attempt to reduce this expense, the town decided, in 1803, to appoint a committee to confer with representatives from Fairfield, Norwalk, and Wilton about establishing a joint poorhouse. The com-

Old tollhouse on Newtown Turnpike, which linked Norwalk and Newtown

mittee presented its report at the December, 1804, town meeting. The report suggested that the towns, in order to reduce the drain of caring for the poor, should build a poorhouse at a cost of about $1,000, including furniture. Each town was to finance the cost in proportion to the size of its tax list. A tax of seven mills on the dollar was believed to be sufficient to pay for the project. Each town was to contribute to the support of the poor according to the number of persons it sent and according to the length of each pauper's stay. The facility would be operated by a committee of two representatives from each town and was to be located near the intersection of the boundaries of the four towns. The report anticipated that Weston would save about one-third of what it had been spending for the poor. The town meeting adopted the report, as did the meetings of the other three towns.

In April, 1805, the four towns purchased land in Weston from Gershom Burr, a Fairfield resident. They paid $275 for this property and also leased additional acreage from the Norfield Society. Work began immediately, and by the end of the year the poorhouse was a reality. It stood on the site of modern Weston's library. Weston allowed its selectmen to oversee the poorhouse; only rarely did the town meeting interfere with its operation. In 1807, the General Assembly granted Weston, Wilton, Fairfield, and Norwalk permission to convert their poorhouse into a workhouse and to "ordain such By Laws, as they may judge necessary relative to the Persons to be committed to such Work-House. . . ." The state, however, reserved the right to appeal this permission if conditions were found to be "unreasonable and unjust." Although the residents of the workhouse were now required to work for their keep, the institution was apparently reasonably well managed, for it continued to function until 1831. In that year, the towns involved decided it was too expensive to operate and sold the facility to Eliphalet Coley for $500. Weston resumed its former practice of letting out its paupers to town residents.[14]

Technically, the operation of the schools was not the duty of the town. Yet the town maintained something of a veto power over the work of the school societies; and as the years passed, the role of the town became larger and larger. As early as 1792, the town decided that new school districts were needed, and in 1795 the town meeting rejected the school districts established by the school societies. Clearly, its role in school management was real, despite the technicalities of the law.

These were by no means the only areas of concern to the town; they were merely the most important. In fact, many areas of life sooner or later caught the town meeting's attention. Roads, taxes, livestock, paupers, schools, and the question of a town center were perennial issues. But the town meeting also found time to do such things as vote "that we will admit of innoculation for the small pox in the Town under proper regulation" and insist that David Lambert of Wilton accept responsibility for the welfare of his slave, Pegg.[15]

Finally, mention ought to be made of the atmosphere that pervaded the early town meetings. Many twentieth-century people believe that eighteenth- and early nineteenth-century meetings were the scenes of vigorous public debate, of independent farmers standing up and speaking their minds. Such a generalization really applies much more to twentieth-century gatherings than to those of earlier times. The sort of outspoken democracy that the modern age attributes to the early 1800s really came only after a degree of diversity had arrived in Weston. During the town's early years, its population was amazingly homogeneous. It was a population of impecunious, yeoman farmers whose ancestors were uniformly English and who were themselves at least nominal Protestants. In the years before Weston's people had differing religious beliefs or contending economic interests, before

Original fireplace, crane, and warming oven in the Wakeman Bradley house on Valley Forge Road, probably built before 1800

division of labor, before immigration and cultural diversity, the town meetings reflected the unspoken consensus that existed on almost all issues. The Weston farmers of that age were more interested in harmonizing their interests than in asserting their individual rights.

Such an attitude fitted nicely with Weston's desire to shape its policies to coincide with the course of action desired by the whole community. Town leaders went to great lengths to formulate actions that were as universally satisfactory as possible. They were as careful to provide adequate warning of all town meetings as they were reluctant to place any arbitrary limits on the town franchise. Within the meetings, no mention was made of the tally when the town voted on some issue or for some candidate. Also, when committees were created, great care was taken to represent differing opinions on them so that small differences could be resolved in consensus. The committee to locate the town's center included a variety of points of view. On those rare occasions when a common course could not be found, issues were regularly shunted off onto the County Court. For example, the question of the site of the Norfield meetinghouse was put to the County Court. The object was the maintenance of peace and harmony, of a sense of community within the town.[16]

During the first two decades of the town's life, there did, however, remain a serious challenge to the idea of community; this was the fact that Norfield and North Fairfield remained in practice two separate entities. This challenge was to remain real; it refused to be cajoled out of existence. North Fairfield was more populous than Norfield and was the site of the town meetings, as well. The official parade was there. So, too, was the building that for all practical purposes was the town hall; this was the home of Nathan Wheeler, for twenty-eight years Weston's town clerk. All of these things created jealousies in the minds of Norfield men and women. In 1787 or 1797 or 1807, these jealousies remained very much under control. Ultimately, the tensions between Norfield and North Fairfield would become too intense to be so easily contained. But that was in the future, and for the time being, the two parishes walked, not as one, but at least side by side.

NOTES TO CHAPTER 7

1. Weston Town Records, Town Meeting Minutes, I, 5, Weston Town Hall. (Hereinafter cited as WTR, TMM.)

2. Ibid.

3. Quoted in Charles S. Grant, *Democracy in the Frontier Town of Kent* (New York, 1972), p. 131. Grant's work and two works by Bruce C. Daniels are especially useful in describing the operation of eighteenth-century Connecticut towns. Daniels' works are "Large Town Power Structure in Eighteenth Century Connecticut," (Ph.D. diss., University of Connecticut, 1970), and "Connecticut's Villages Become Mature Towns: The Complexity of Local Institutions, 1676 to 1776," *William and Mary Quarterly,* XXXIV (January, 1977), 83-103. I have relied heavily on these three works.

4. Quoted in Daniels, "Large Town Power Structure," pp. 49-50.

5. WTR, TMM, I, 69.

6. Ibid., 41, 42.

7. Ibid., 44.

8. Ibid., 50, 51.

9. Ibid., 61.

10. Ibid., 6.

11. Ibid., 7, 9, 81.

12. Ibid., 17.

13. Ibid., 8, 26, 27.

14. Connecticut Archives, Civil Officers, Series II, XXIV, 158, Connecticut State Library.

15. WTR, TMM, I, 18.

16. Michael Zuckerman's fine analysis of Massachusetts town meetings, *Peaceable Kingdoms: New England Towns in the Eighteenth Century* (New York, 1970), describes the consensus-seeking function of these meetings; Kenneth A. Lockridge's *A New England Town, The First Hundred Years: Dedham, Massachusetts, 1636-1736* (New York, 1970), demonstrates how democracy requires diversity.

WESTON'S EARLY LEADERS 1787 / 1807

"Let this hypothetical public servant's name be 'Sherwood Fanton' "

Weston's success depended as much upon the men who guided its fortunes as upon the rules around which it was organized. Thus, Weston's early leaders are of special interest. Unfortunately, these men had neither the leisure nor the inclination for keeping diaries or writing long, descriptive letters. With few exceptions, Weston's early leaders were as anonymous as was Weston's population generally. But while little is known of these men individually, much information exists about them generally. By creating a hypothetical person—let his name be "Sherwood Fanton"—and attributing to him all these general characteristics, one can obtain a feeling for the kind of men who served the new town between 1787 and 1807.[1] Fanton's hypothetical career represents the total of the careers of all of Weston's early leaders; he is the sum of thirty-seven men who were the leaders of early Weston. Many of his real neighbors—nearly three hundred of them, in fact—held public office during Weston's first twenty years, but only thirty-seven occupied the

The Pickney Dimon house on Kellogg Hill Road, built about 1802

prestigious positions of selectman, moderator, or representative to the General Assembly. Fanton and his fellow leaders constituted a small and highly select group.

Fanton made his living as a farmer, as did not only most of the men of Weston but also most of the town leaders. Some men had second occupations as well. Samuel B. Sherwood was an attorney; David Coley, Jr., operated a mill; Nathan Wheeler was involved in a variety of financial enterprises. Fanton was assuredly of English descent and was a member of the Congregational church, either in Norfield or in North Fairfield. By the time he was elected to a major office, he was forty-seven years old, his family was largely grown, and his social and economic position well established in the community. All his fellow leaders were married, and only one, Samuel B. Sherwood, had held major office before he was thirty. Sherwood became a selectman at twenty-five. Fanton had enjoyed little formal schooling; his education included barely more than what was offered at the district schools. A year at the Staples Academy was as close as he came to any instruction beyond the three Rs. He had only one colleague among the town leaders who had attended college. That was, again, Samuel B. Sherwood, the son of Norfield's first minister and brother-in-law of the second minister. Born in November, 1767, Sherwood attended Yale after preparing for college with his father. He was at best a mediocre student at Yale and failed to gain admission to Harvard when he attempted to transfer to that school at the end of his junior year. Yale officials refused him readmission until he agreed to spend a year studying with the Reverend Timothy Dwight, then minister at Greenfield Hill. Sherwood finally graduated from Yale in 1786 at the ripe old age of nineteen, almost a year older than his average classmate.

Fanton had been a zealous supporter of the American Revolution and had served for a brief time in the Continental Army. Again, some of his colleagues differed from him in this respect. Both David Coley, Jr., and Squier Adams had been only lukewarm patriots, and local officials had charged them with actions inimical to the interests of the United States. Fanton's life was generally free of indiscretions or of incidents that he would rather forget. He was in all respects a solid, upstanding citizen and family man. Benjamin Dean, who served three terms as a Weston selectman, had at age nineteen found himself in the predicament of having impregnated his teenage sweetheart. This situation was resolved by a hastily planned wedding. But Fanton himself was not only above accusation but was even above suspicion.

Only after they had seen him prove himself in a variety of lesser positions did the people of Weston agree that Fanton should serve in a major office. Although he was too young to have held office in the parent community of Fairfield, many of his slightly older associates had. The senior David Coley, for example, had served on Fairfield's highway committee; Daniel Duncan had been a key keeper in the parent town; and Samuel Rowland had helped to collect the town tax. Even more impressive were the roles that Benjamin Dean, Nathaniel Seeley, David Silliman, Samuel Wakeman, and Nathan Wheeler played in the political life of Fairfield; these men had each held major town offices.

Other of Fanton's colleagues, like himself, had demonstrated their administrative skills in other ways. Joshua Adams had helped guide the fortunes of the Norfield parish. Jabez Wheeler had been a deacon in the North Fairfield church. Thus, both parish and church provided training for future leaders; Fanton was active in both. One might also receive training in the Weston town government. Before he became a selectman, Fanton had served for several years as a surveyor of highways, a fence viewer, a grandjuryman, and a member of several ad hoc committees. He was a member of the militia; and although he never attained a captaincy, several other leaders had. Abel Hall, of North Fairfield, served as a militia captain. So, also, did John Sherwood and Jabez Wheeler, both of that same parish.

Compared to his neighbors, Fanton was financially successful. His property was valued at about $1,200, as compared to a median valuation in town generally of only about $130. To be sure, he never attained the success some other leaders did. Samuel Wakeman's property was valued at nearly $4,200 and John Sherwood's at about $3,800. But certainly Fanton enjoyed genuine success. His estate of $1,200 overshadowed not only that of the typical town resident but also that of the typical minor officeholder. The median value of the fence viewers' property, for instance, was only about $730. Obviously, prosperity, as well as a successful period of apprenticeship, was necessary before Fanton could become a leader.

Although no effort was made to establish the hypothetical location of Fanton's residence, he probably lived, not in Norfield but in North Fairfield. This is true because most of Weston's selectmen, town meeting moderators, and representatives to the General Assembly between 1787 to 1807 came from that parish.

Fanton served four terms as a selectman and three terms as a representative. He had two colleagues, John Sherwood and Samuel Wakeman, who were selectmen for thirteen years, and another, Samuel B. Sherwood, who served eleven terms as a representative. But only three men served more than ten years as selectmen and only five served five terms as representatives. On the other hand, Fanton saw thirteen of a total of thirty-four selectmen serve only single terms and nine of a total of eighteen representatives likewise win election once. Thus, he must never have felt especially secure in his role as a major officeholder. Regular rotation of officers indicated that early Weston was hardly a pocket borough controlled by a handful of oligarchs.

But while this was generally true, Fanton knew that there were certain men who possessed a magical power to win election. David Coley, Jr., for example, won election as selectman nine times in the twenty years between 1787 and 1807. John Sherwood was even more successful. During those same years, he was selectman thirteen times and moderated twenty town meetings. Additionally, he served five terms in the General Assembly. Samuel Wakeman was moderator eleven times, selectman thirteen times, and representative five times. No early leader held so many offices as did Nathan Wheeler. He was, in twenty years, town clerk nineteen years, selectman eleven years,

The former home of artist Wood Cowan on Godfrey Road West, built in the latter part of the eighteenth century

town treasurer five years, and served five terms in the General Assembly.

As Fanton must have realized, men like Wheeler, Wakeman, Sherwood, and Coley served year after year, not because their neighbors were cowed by them, but because these men were able to serve and were competent to serve. That there was generally considerable turnover among major officeholders indicates that early Weston's political life was a dynamic one and that to be a perennial officeholder was a genuine tribute to a man's abilities. Favoritism and nepotism played an insignificant role in Weston's early history. The leaders had few favors to dispense, and where they could confer advantages, as in the case of the establishment of roads or bridges, they were careful to act judiciously. Nepotism was also minimal. David Coley's son, David, was, like his father, a selectman, as was Nathan Wheeler's nephew, Stephen. But in a small community like Weston, these occasional instances were bound to occur. They were neither regular nor normal.

How, then, in the final analysis, did Fanton and his fellow leaders

Joseph Buckley's iron works and forge on the Saugatuck River at Valley Forge, as it appeared in the late nineteenth century

stack up? They were men who became leaders only after demonstrating, through a long apprenticeship, their ability to do so, either in Fairfield, or in one of the parishes or churches, in Weston town government, in the militia, or, most likely, in several of these institutions. They were, by Weston's standards, wealthy men, but wealth was less a criterion for officeholding than the device that permitted certain individuals to serve. Their wealth was ultimately the town's profit, for it gave them the leisure to enter politics. Once in office, these men were offered little security because turnover was rapid, and once in office, Fanton and his colleagues demonstrated themselves to be fair men who sought the best for their community. Fanton was clearly a man with some political ambition, but his object was not the creation of a self-perpetuating oligarchy. Rather, he was a man with a genuine sense of community who exercised restraint in office and who earned the respect of his contemporaries and the admiration of his progeny.

NOTES TO CHAPTER 8

1. The statements about the political life of Weston's early leaders are based upon examinations of the Weston Town Records, Town Meeting Minutes, I. Biographical information came from Donald L. Jacobus, *History and Genealogy of the Families of Old Fairfield*, 3 volumes (New York, 1912). The leaders' financial status is disclosed in one of the few extant Weston tax lists, that of 1797. It is to be found in the Fairfield Historical Society. Ways of approaching the subject were suggested by Charles S. Grant's *Democracy in the Frontier Town of Kent* (New York, 1972) and Kenneth A. Lockridge's *A New England Town, The First Hundred Years: Dedham, Massachusetts, 1636-1736* (New York, 1970).

EARNING A LIVELIHOOD 1787 / 1830

"1 one horse Sleigh $8 . . . 9 Sheep $9 . . . 6 winsor Chairs $1.25 . . . the Dwelling House $150"

Early Weston was as much an economic unit as it was a political entity. Today, Weston's economic life is intimately involved with those of its neighboring towns and that of the nation as a whole, but the community during the eighteenth and early nineteenth centuries was a largely self-sufficient economic microcosm; it supplied virtually all its own needs.

The contrast between the economies of early and modern Weston would be astonishing to a person who had dwelt there in that former time. If the Reverend Noyes could look back from the perspective of the late twentieth century, he would find the differences overwhelming. Perhaps the somber-faced clergyman would be ideally suited to illuminate the town's early economic life for the reader of the twentieth century; certainly most of what is known of that life comes from the letters and papers left by Norfield's second minister and his family.

Noyes would surely be amazed by the fact that today all aspects of economic life are not only subject to change but are *expected* to change. Occupations that existed ten years ago are obsolete now; professions that are flourishing today may be dying a decade hence. During Noyes's life, the town's economy was stable to the point of being static. In 1820, it was essentially unchanged from what it had been when Noyes's father-in-law had become the first pastor seventy years before, or, for that matter, from what Fairfield's economic life had been when Noyes's great-grandfather had been overseeing the founding of Yale College. Today's economic uncertainty was unknown to Noyes and his neighbors. Political and social changes were realities to them, but economic change was part of a world of which they knew nothing.

Noyes would also be impressed that modern people work in large groups, frequently with strangers, and away from their places of residence. In his time, economic activities took place in much more familiar surroundings. When Noyes or his contemporaries went to work, they had to go no farther than their barns or shops. Men and women worked in small groups and with people they knew intimately. Fathers and sons harvested rye and repaired fences and butchered cattle together; mothers and daughters labored side by side in front of the fireplace, preparing meals and preserving meat and making candles. Economic life went forward in the presence of familiar faces and familiar objects. Even a hired man—Noyes was never able to employ one regularly—became a virtual member of the family. The idea of an impersonal office staff or work force was as alien to Noyes as the concept of work as a family affair is to most Americans of 1978.

The Reverend Noyes lived in the village that had, by 1787, grown up around the Norfield meetinghouse. Some of his fellow townspeople lived in the village with him, others in the village of North Fairfield, and still others in the countryside of Weston. For the most part, the village dwellers, like Noyes, made their living in the same way that men residing in the countryside did; all were farmers. The village dwellers, however, frequently combined two occupations; they were farmers and lawyers or ministers or merchants or artisans. John Noyes is a perfect example. He was the minister at the Norfield church, but he was also a farmer. Stephen Perry, one of Noyes's parishioners, operated a mill; the mill could not support him and his family, so he additionally farmed. Even Samuel Burr Sherwood—Noyes's brother-in-law, one of the few college graduates in town, and the closest thing Weston had to a successful attorney—was also a farmer. An examination of the estate inventories left by the residents of early Weston shows that, while virtually every able-bodied man in town was a farmer, some men engaged in other occupations, as well. But the age of specialization was still part of the future.

Within the town, Noyes knew a variety of part-time businessmen. Thomas Banks kept a tavern. Thomas Davis and Gabriel Baldwin were physicians. Burr Gilbert was a merchant. Ebenezer Coley operated a mill. Aaron Buckley was a blacksmith, and Walter Smith and Squire Gilbert were cobblers. Thomas Elsey and James Johnson developed local reputations for their skill as carpenters. All of these men had two occupations; they were farmers who also pursued some other business.

The country storekeepers—in this case, Burr Gilbert and his partner, Isaac Bennett— found that their activities at the store did not prevent their operating farms. Business was usually dull, because Weston's population was too impecunious to purchase many manufactured goods. The store, located in Osborn Town,* stocked a variety of agricultural items, including livestock, as well as spirits, both wine and rum, and manufactured items such as knives and mirrors. Although the store existed well after the establishment of the United States, the owners kept their books in pounds, shillings, and pence. In 1800, a pound was equal to $3.33 and a shilling to 16 cents. They sold a looking glass for 6s. 6d. Two oxen brought £15 and four sheep £1 10s. The price of a gallon of rum varied with the quality of the product, but 3s. 6d. (54 cents) was a typical price. Strangely enough, the price of molasses was usually almost precisely the same as that of rum. Paper was expensive, selling for a penny a sheet, but salt was more reasonable, nine shillings a bushel. A silver-hilt sword, of which Gilbert and Bennett sold only one, brought £4 16s. in an age when a man's saddle cost only three pounds.[2]

Frequently, Gilbert and Bennett accepted services of one kind or another in lieu of payment. Local farmers would lend draft animals to the proprietors as a method of paying debts. More often, payment took the form either of carting goods for the store owners or of cutting ship lumber (oak planking), which Gilbert and Bennett then sold. In fact, the production of ship lumber became a principal interest of the firm. Lumber, along with feathers and flax, was virtually the medium of exchange in the store. But people who had no access to any of the three commodities might pay their debts by repairing a barn door or

*Osborn Town was the early name for Georgetown.

building a stone wall. Joseph Lyon repaid a debt of 5s. 6d. by working for two days building walls for Bennett. He must have worked slightly less than two full days, because the going rate for a day's labor was three shillings (48 cents). A man with a team, of course, earned more. Ebenezer Bradley paid a six-shilling debt in a single day by hauling manure for Gilbert and Bennett with a sled and a yoke of oxen.

Because John Noyes's Weston was much more self-sufficient than it is today, considerable manufacturing took place in the town. Most of what was produced, such as soap, candles, and cloth, was manufactured in the homes of Weston residents. The Noyeses produced all of these items. Other manufactured products were created in the shops of local craftsmen—joiners, blacksmiths, and cobblers. In fact, in 1819 there were nineteen grain mills, an iron foundry, four distilleries, four tanneries, three carding machines, and three fulling mills scattered throughout the two parishes of Weston. Almost nothing that was produced in Weston was produced for a market beyond the town's borders. Neither were the manufactured goods produced by people who depended upon the income they derived from that activity.

Along its rivers, visitors to early Weston would find dams and mills with their water wheels operating slow-moving vertical saws, the grinding wheels of gristmills, the hammers of forges and fulling mills, and the bellows of forges. To the gristmills, like the one operated by Ebenezer Coley, local farmers brought corn and rye to be ground into flour. Job Perry's sawmill was always busy, as was that of David Godfrey. Ebenezer Coley also operated a fulling mill, a simple machine for shrinking and dressing cloth which had been spun and woven in the farmhouses. He even had a carding machine, which prepared the wool for spinning.

By the early nineteenth century, there was a small iron industry in the Valley Forge section of Weston. That industry had had its origin about 1760, when Oliver Sanford established a forge in Sanfordtown, an area in Redding. He eventually married Rachel Coley, the daughter of the older David Coley, and brought his shop to Weston in 1805, when a freshet destroyed his operation in Redding. Valley Forge was then called Princetown, after William Prince, a large property owner in the area. Sanford established his forge in an old grist- and sawmill and, using primitive methods, began the production of iron.

This operation required a supply of iron, a supply of wood for charcoal used as fuel, and the water power necessary to operate both hammers and bellows. Much of the iron came from Salisbury or Kent. What Weston had that made the industry possible was an abundance of wood for charcoal and an abundance of water power. In the years ahead, other aspiring iron manufacturers would follow the lead of Sanford and come to Weston to establish forges.

One should be careful to avoid imagining the existence of a modern industrial establishment in Valley Forge. Sanford was, in addition to being a manufacturer of iron, the proprietor of a farm. The operation of the forge depended, not on any regular schedule, but upon the demands of the farm and the whims of nature. During haying season, Sanford made little iron. The forge was likely to close down completely during the dry season of August and September. The ice and heavy rains of spring might also force the closing of the forge. John Noyes's daughter, Mary, wrote in 1807 that "we had a heavy rain on Saturday. The bridges & milldams have been swept off by means of the overflowing of the water & ice. Members have sustained a considerable damage." Sanford had to stop operation.[3]

Most of the iron that Sanford produced ended up in the hands of local blacksmiths. During the War of 1812, he sold iron to the United States government, but the expense of transporting the iron to New Haven, a six-day round trip, seriously cut into his profits. Except in unusual times, the demand for his product was insufficient to allow him to make a living at his trade. So he had to resort to farming. The same was true to an even greater degree of other craftsmen. The distinction between their farming and their work as millers or cobblers or distillers or blacksmiths was so blurred as to be unreal. This lack of specialization is obvious to anyone examining the financial records of Aaron and Nehemiah B. Buckley, Weston blacksmiths. The products and services that they sold were by no means necessarily related to the skills of a blacksmith. In their daybook, they recorded that they charged Thomas Davies $.42 for "Sharpening & setting Horse shoes round" and Ward Buckley $.75 for "setting oxe shoes round." But then the smiths recorded the sale of a half bushel of turnips to David Rowland for $.12½. D. W. Buckley paid them $.17 for "mending Tea kettle & setting shoe," and the same David Rowland gave them $2.00 for "getting one Load of wood off of pine swamp, team work done sometime in the year 1821, some stones for barn, [and] drawing some wood & some timber." The Buckleys charged Silliman Godfrey $.17 for "mending 2 Chains" and Bradley Downs $3.67 for a pair of andirons that weighed twenty-two pounds. Lemuel Lyon paid $1.33 for two hoes and David Godfrey $.70 for one "with handle." But then the smiths would again find themselves out of the smithing business and selling two bushels of rye to Stephen Perry or charging him $.50 for the use of their oxen "to go after Cider."[4]

If working in their shop and on their farm simultaneously became too demanding, they would hire occasional help. They paid Moses Buckley $7.00 for making "Seven dozen Axes." Stephen Perry earned $.75 for "1 day at farming" and a like amount for "plowing corn the last time." The brothers paid John Tillou $14.50 for "work at Machine 14½ days at 1 Dollar a day part to be paid in work and part in cash."

In addition to accepting work for payment of debts, Aaron and Nehemiah Buckley also accepted commodities for payment. Ebenezer Morehouse paid a debt of $.50 with "3 Bushel apples" and later settled his account for $3.00 by delivering "3 Barrels Cider." Joseph Godfrey repaid $.75 that he owed by "sawing our stuff," as the Buckley brothers noted. Their records clearly indicate the primitive nature of Weston's economy and the fact that no concept of a division of labor existed in the small community.

The agriculture that John Noyes and his neighbors practiced was no more sophisticated than their industry, and, as the *Gazetteer of the State of Connecticut* stated in 1819, "agriculture is the principal business of the inhabitants" of Weston. There were several reasons for the primitive state of the town's agriculture. In particular, local farmers had almost no opportunity to sell their products outside Weston. Thus, they were under little pressure to improve farming methods in order to increase production. Weston's isolation meant a lack of markets. The town was not isolated in terms of being dozens of miles from population centers but was isolated in terms of being valuable hours from these markets. Bulky agricultural goods had to be transported in oxcarts, which traveled at an exasperatingly slow pace. This problem was exacerbated by the miserable condition of Weston's roads. Even the coming of the turnpike system did not significantly improve the highways. Farm produce could be moved no more than ten or twenty miles without allowing the costs of transportation to consume the small margin of profit. Samuel Goodrich, who, in the early nineteenth century, prepared a statistical account of Ridgefield, wrote that "potatoes are very much used and increased attempts are [made] to raise them for the market, but the distance from the market is so great that it is not expected the practice will be general." The market he was describing was Norwalk, fourteen miles from Ridgefield. Weston's agriculture remained inefficient and carelessly conducted. In fact, the farming methods used in Weston in 1800 were but little improved over the methods used by Fairfield's early settlers. Although living in the nineteenth century, Weston farmers observed a routine of husbandry that was really based upon seventeenth-century techniques.

John Noyes's farm was too small to be typical. It included less than a hundred acres, and the typical farm was nearly twice that size. These acres were divided into three more or less equal parts: first, mowing fields and cultivated fields; second, pasture; third, woodland and wasteland. Of the fifty or so acres that constituted the mowing and cultivated fields, only ten or twelve acres actually came under the plow during any given year.

Indian corn and rye were the staple grains that Weston farmers cultivated. Corn was hardy and therefore dependable. Furthermore, it required much less labor than did other grain crops. Barley, oats, and buckwheat also occupied the fields of Weston farmers. The former two did not do well but were regarded as necessary crops for the maintenance of livestock. Local farmers planted buckwheat to clear fields of weeds, and then used the grain to feed their poultry.

To a large extent, Noyes and his neighbors neglected the cultivation of root crops. Some potatoes were raised but were used as fodder rather than as human food. Few other root crops were grown. Pumpkins provided another souce of fodder, but neither potatoes nor pumpkins were as important in this respect as hay.

Noyes, like most Weston farmers, did not raise small vegetables, such as beans, peas, onions, and the like as cash crops. Farmers lacked the time to be gardeners, and so kitchen vegetables were grown by the women of the family. This was not the case with tobacco; Weston men found time to grow enough of it to provide for their own needs. Letters written by Noyes and his family describe the crops that he and his neighbors grew. In a letter to his son Samuel, for example, he mentioned that "we have got in our good hay & rye harvest, & the boys finished pulling flax yesterday. We get our oats next week." That letter was written on July 22, 1803. A year and two days later, Noyes wrote that "the boys chiefly ploughed & hoed the corn & have done it well. It looks promising tho' damaged by an unruly ox of Capt. Rowland's," he continued. "We have a fine crop of english hay & had a fine time to cure it. Our rye is good & gotten in good order." Noyes felt his oats and flax were only "pretty good" and the potatoes "promising." Five years later, on July 27, 1809, he reported that "we have been highly favoured in getting our hay & rye harvested. On Saturday last we carried into the barn five load of good hay, in excellent order; and on Tuesday, got in our rye harvest." In other letters written during these years, the minister referred to the same crops over and over again. They varied only slightly, Noyes occasionally mentioning attempts with watermelons and wheat. The resulting dull diet was occasionally altered by the addition of some wild fruit which the family gathered; cherries and currants were favorites.[5]

Not only was Noyes regular in terms of the crops that he planted; he was also regular in terms of his scheme of crop rotation. He, like his neighbors, followed a three-year plan of rotation. In a particular field, he would sow corn in the spring, and after harvesting the corn in the late summer, he would plant rye or oats. After this crop was gathered, he allowed the field to grow up to weeds, which did little to improve the land.

In addition to his inefficient system of crop rotation, Noyes was also wasteful with his farm's manure. In this respect, he was like other Weston farmers. Manure, collected from the barn and barnyard, could have provided a good supply of fertilizer, but this resource was consistently neglected. Animals were pastured during the spring, summer, and autumn and their manure thus lost, and the farmers uniformly wasted the winter's quantity. This extravagant practice was in part the result of ignorance. But even if Weston farmers had known better, they probably would not have acted any differently. Carting and spreading manure meant the expenditure of a great deal of labor, and they would have seen no real advantage in this. The old ways produced enough for the farmer and his family. And, unfortunately, few markets existed for any excess they produced; thus, the farmer's efforts would have been unrewarded. The result, on the other hand, of his failure to use manure and to rotate crops properly was the eventual exhaustion of his soil.

The lack of markets meant not only indifference to the condition of the soil but also an unwillingness to invest large amounts of capital in agriculture. Farmers bought few sophisticated tools and implements. Farmhouses and barns were obviously necessary and were, for the most part, substantially built. Noyes's barn had a threshing floor, stables for horses and cows, and an area for storing hay. A corn cratch or crib, built upon a high foundation to discourage rodents, was also always present on the farm. Within the barn would be found the farmer's few tools. Most were made right on the homestead, and those that were not were made by the local blacksmith. Estate inventories from Weston demonstrate how sparse the farmer's tools were. The most sophisticated tool to be found in the barn would be a plow, but even it was at best a crude affair. It was made more of wood than of metal, and most of the metal involved in its construction was sheet metal used to protect the basic wooden structure. The device was so crude that it required two men or a man and boy to operate, and it had to be pulled by three horses or a yoke of oxen. The plow was capable of turning over only one or two acres in a day.

Most Weston farms, like that of John Noyes, included an apple orchard, and apples were the town's standard fruit. The fruit was used primarily to produce cider, the favorite beverage of persons of all ages. The account books of Gilbert and Bennett are filled with transactions involving the sale or purchase of cider. Farmers stored it in their cellars for future consumption. Apples were also sliced and dried, and, if the crop were especially large, the farmer used it to feed his cattle. Weston farmers did little for their orchards once the trees were planted. This neglect meant that worms annually devoured a large share of the crop.

Weston was, in many respects, better suited for grazing and pasturing than for agriculture. The soil was thin and encumbered by rocks, but nevertheless grass of excellent quality grew well on it. The pasturage was good, and Weston's annual hay crop was also a quality one, especially after local farmers began to plant clover in their mowing fields. The pasture on a typical Weston farm would support ten or fifteen cows, a yoke or two of oxen, one or two horses, ten or twenty sheep, in addition to a dozen or so hogs. The cows produced milk for Weston families and were also a source of meat and of tallow for candles. "We have killed our fat cow," wrote Ebenezer Noyes in 1808; "she had fifty-four weight of tallow & weighed five hundred and fifty with tallow."[6]

Most Weston cattle were not so rotund as the Noyes cow. In fact, because of insufficient fodder and inattention to careful breeding, the mature cattle were more remarkable for their hardiness than for their production of either dairy products or beef. They managed to provide enough milk and cheese for the farmer and his family, and since there was little market for any excess, the cattle were doing all that was expected of them.

Cattle were also important as draft animals, for oxen were the favorite work animals of Weston farmers. Not until near the close of the nineteenth century was such a premium placed on speed by local farmers as to allow the horse to displace the ox. Despite their lack of speed, these draft cattle were preferred. As Timothy Dwight, the president of Yale College, wrote in 1811: "The advantages of employing oxen are, that they will endure more fatigue, draw more steadily, and surely; are purchased for a smaller price; are kept at less expense; are freer from disease; suffer less from labouring on rough ground;

and perform the labour better; and, when by age or accident they become unfit for labour, they are converted into beef. The only advantage of employing horses instead of oxen, is derived from their speed."[7]

Not only did cattle tend to degenerate because of Weston farmers' ignorance and indifference, but so, too, did other types of stock. Modern horsemen would find little to admire in the animals that worked on Weston farms. As Rodolphus Dickinson, an early agricultural reformer, said: "When one casts his eye upon the saddle horses of Virginia, or upon the draft animals of Pennsylvania, he must be strongly impressed with the great improvement of which our comparatively diminutive breed of horses is susceptible." Sheep also suffered from inattention. They were long-legged animals, shallow-chested, and slow to mature. They were regarded only as a source of wool and did not provide any significant amount of meat to the diet of Westoners. After 1800, merino sheep were introduced to Connecticut, and, as a result, there was a gradual improvement in the bloodlines of local animals.[8]

Hogs did better than horses, cows, or sheep. This was not the result of more attention but rather because the animals were so hardy. They required almost no care. In the fall, they were turned out into woodlands and wastelands and allowed to fend for themselves. During the winter, the hogs ate what was available: low-quality hay, chestnuts, apples, potatoes, or refuse from either the kitchen or the milk house. Only during the few months before they faced the butcher did they enjoy the luxury of corn. Virtually every farm kept hogs, and salt pork was an important element in the diet of Weston people. Frequently, during the fall and winter months, the Noyes family would write to one of their many correspondents that "we killed hogs this week."[9]

During Weston's earliest years, local farmers had greatly valued land that was heavily forested, because relatively little labor was required to harvest timber. Incredible energy had to be expended to clear land and to prepare fields for crops. Thus, farmers preferred to cut timber. But as with other resources, woodlands were mismanaged. Trees were felled and not replaced. This meant that the supply of lumber was lost, and also that the principal source of fuel was destroyed. Enormous amounts of fuel were burned in the amazingly inefficient fireplaces of the day. By 1810, little first-growth timber remained in Weston.

Yet despite all that Noyes and his neighbors were doing wrong, they managed to provide for themselves and their families. They

Restored mill on the Aspetuck River at Old Redding Road

produced beef, pork, and—to a lesser degree—mutton from their flocks and herds. November, with its cool, crisp weather, was regarded as the ideal "killing time," and the killing was done by the farmers, with the possible help of a neighbor who was especially handy with his knife. The farm women then faced the task of drying, salting, or pickling most of the meat. But killing time did mean some fresh meat for the family, a rare commodity in the days before refrigeration. The farmers also grew the corn and wheat that local millers ground to form the basis of their bread. They provided most of their other nutritional needs. They made maple sugar and syrup; they kept bees and used the honey instead of cane sugar. During hard times, they used raspberry and blackberry leaves to concoct a drink that vaguely resembled tea; they might even resort to parching chestnuts or bread, pulverizing the charred result, and using it as a substitute for coffee. As the records of Bennett and Gilbert indicate, about the only food items that Weston farmers regularly had to buy were salt, molasses, rum, and tea and coffee when they could afford them.

These early farmers really had little choice but to produce as much as possible right on the farm, for they had little cash with which to buy store goods. John Noyes often complained about the lack of money. Within town, farmers exchanged items or labor for services or goods provided by area craftsmen. The rum they used was usually made right in Weston, for example; so also were their hardware and their tools and their harnesses and boots. They bought goods from outside the immediate area only when they were forced to.

Self-sufficiency extended beyond foodstuffs. Like the other residents of early Weston, John Noyes and his family were clothed in fabrics woven in their own home from wool and flax grown on their own farm. It is not difficult to imagine the garb worn by a Moses Godfrey or a John Noyes or a Joshua Adams. Basically, each had two suits of clothes, one for every day and work and one for the Sabbath. If the modern reader could return to early Weston on a warm July day—in the midst of the haying season, perhaps—he would find Godfrey or Adams wearing a checked homespun linen shirt, a pair of plain tow-cloth trousers, and a vest which during earlier times would have had sleeves but which by 1810 or so would be sleeveless. The early residents of Weston coped with warm weather by wearing loose-fitting clothing rather than, as is done today, wearing fewer clothes. Their shoes were probably badly worn and tied with leather thongs. A felt hat or an old beaver hat stiffened with age probably completed their costume. During the cold winter months, the same visitor would discover a local farmer wearing a blue-and-white-checked woolen shirt, a pair of buckskin breeches, a pair of white, homemade woolen stockings, and a pair of double-soled cowhide shoes. Old stockings minus the feet were worn as leggings over his shoes during cold or snowy weather. A plain cloth vest with sleeves and lined with a cloth called drugget would be worn over the woolen shirt, and over both would be a cloth greatcoat, usually brown. The coat could be wrapped completely around the wearer's body and was fastened with a belt. Atop the farmer's head would be a woolen cap drawn down over his ears. This garb was bulky and uncomfortable by modern standards but did keep the men warm while they performed chores.

Their Sabbath-day costume for winter was much like their work clothes except that they wore blue stockings, their leather breeches were crisply clean, and they added a straight-bodied plain coat and a white holland cap. During summer months, men wore a checked holland shirt, brown linen breeches and stockings, single-soled boots, and a plain cloth vest without sleeves on the Sabbath. They frequently tied their shirt sleeves above the elbow with arm strings of ferreting of various colors.

Women's clothing was generally of the same style as the men's. Mrs. Noyes or Mrs. Adams wore homemade drugget, crepe, plain cloth, and camlet gowns in the winter, and the exterior of their underdress was a garment lined and quilted, extending from the waist to the feet. Women wore high-heeled shoes, made normally of tanned calfskin but occasionally of cloth. In the summer they wore striped linen gowns, linen underdresses, and cloth shoes. Young and fashionable women wore holland aprons on formal visits and certainly on the Sabbath; elderly women usually wore them only on the Sabbath.

The household production of cloth and clothing was a carefully organized industry. In addition to clothing, Noyes and his neighbors produced from wool and linen such items as sheets, towels, blankets, and rugs. Imagine the men of the family shearing and washing the wool and breaking and hackling the flax to prepare the fiber for spinning. The young women and girls spun the fibers and prepared the yarn or thread on spinning wheels. They even did the bleaching and dyeing, using materials that they could collect locally—pokeberries, goldenrod, hickory bark, and various flowers. They also used indigo, which was less common because it had to be purchased. The family might do its own weaving at home, or, in some cases, weavers, usually men, would take the yarn or thread into their homes and weave it. The final step in the process, the actual construction of garments, certainly took place in the home. In 1814, John Noyes wrote to his son Charles, then at Yale: "We hope to make you a vest from cloth which we have made for pantaloons, & a pattern of which we send you for your pantaloons. If the cloth should not hold out we shall provide in some other way."[10]

Weston farmers, like Noyes, were involved in a whole range of industries. They could be found helping to build, with the assistance of a local or itinerant carpenter, their own homes and barns, using timber they had cut on their own lands. They used as little hardware as possible; what they did use was produced by a local blacksmith. Glass, of course, had to be purchased from outside the area. Even the Reverend Noyes oversaw the construction of his home. Local cabinetmakers or even skilled carpenters made most of the furniture used in Weston. In 1812, James Johnson charged three shillings for building a small desk; by 1828, the price was $11.75 for one that was not only larger but more elaborate. Farm women made mattresses and pillows and stuffed them with home-grown feathers. Even kitchen utensils were made from wood as often as possible. In Weston estate inventories, wooden and earthenware vessels were much more common than porcelain, glass, or silver. Pewter was, however, mentioned in most inventories. Farm tools were also constructed by the farmer. Plows, shovels, and even harrows were all largely wood. Whatever else was needed to operate a farm came from the local blacksmith. The Buckley brothers, Isaac and Nehemiah, provided axes, chains, pitchforks, and other items that had to be made of metal.

Thus, the farmers of early Weston performed a variety of tasks. They built new buildings and repaired old ones; they butchered hogs and cattle; they made tools and utensils and split shingles and tanned leather; they sheared wool and broke flax. They did all this not by choice. They had to be jacks-of-all-trades. Even minister Noyes repaired the shoes of his family. "If I had thot of it in season, I would have sent a pr. of soles for your shoes," he wrote his son at Yale.[11]

But being a jack-of-all-trades meant that the typical Weston farmer could never become highly skilled at any single task. He had no opportunity to adapt individual talents to particular tasks or to acquire special skills through constant repetition of identical processes. In other words, he was as bad a craftsman as he was a farmer. The result was that his standard of living could be maintained only at the cost of great labor.

To the farmers of early Weston, working the land and nurturing a family were inseparable tasks. They found it as impossible to intellectualize farming as they did cherishing a wife or bringing up a child. Rearing a family and working a farm were but two sides of the same coin, and neither side could be approached in a scientific or detached manner.

One would be mistaken, however, to believe that there were no affluent farmers in Weston—perhaps not affluent by the standards of New York City or even of New Haven, but certainly by the standards of rural Connecticut. This small, prosperous group was not set apart from the rest of the population either by interests or by being wealthy in terms of possessing large amounts of cash. Rather, these men were also farmers whose economic concerns were essentially like those of their neighbors and whose prosperity was reflected in the amount of land they owned instead of the amount of cash they possessed. Because of an especially large inheritance or because of a second occupation that supplemented their farm income or because of their willingness to invest vast quantities of labor to deliver a small cash crop to

New Haven or Norwalk, these men were able to accumulate substantial land holdings. Part of these lands was then farmed by hired men or by tenants, and the prosperous became even more prosperous.

David Coley, when he died in 1819, left an estate valued at almost $50,000. Obviously, he was not a typical subsistence farmer. But a careful examination of his estate inventory demonstrates that what he owned was essentially like what other, less well-to-do Weston farmers owned, only he owned more of it. His wealth did not take the form of bank accounts or stock holdings; it took the form of land, livestock, and farm and household items. He owned more silver utensils than his neighbors; he even owned a magnificent grandfather clock that was the envy of the town. But fully seventy percent of his wealth was in the form of real estate and twenty percent consisted of farm implements—hay forks and crosscut saws and the like—and farm products, 300 pounds of cheese and 400 bushels of oats and endless loads of hay. This percentage breakdown was essentially like that for the estates of his less prosperous neighbors.

While some of Weston's residents were richer, others were poorer. John Higgins, in 1797, owned no land at all. He was obviously one of those hired men or tenants who worked the land of men like David Coley. As the nineteenth century progressed, more and more Weston men discovered they were in Higgins's predicament.

Families grew, and farms were divided and subdivided to provide for sons and grandsons. Residents had to use more marginal lands, lands that produced even less than those earlier in use. As the first phase of Weston's history drew to a close, many people in town faced the unattractive alternative of either pulling up roots, as several Noyes children did, and moving to a different part of the country, where agricultural opportunities were greater, or of finding some alternative form of livelihood—possibly in industry, which was already becoming the way of life in such population centers as New Haven. But in 1820, what the future held was hardly clear.

The Inventory of the Estate of Squire Adams, Esqr. late of Weston, 22 of January 1827. (Fairfield County Probate Records, Connecticut State Library.)

Namely–

1 Whitefaced steer $16, 1 Do [ditto] Brown $16	*$32.00*
1 old Stag $20, 1 hors best $40, 1 Do Small $30	*90.00*
1 pr. Young Oxen $37, 1 pr Stags $25	*62.00*
1 Whitefaced cow $11, 1 Do $10	*21.00*
1 Do old $8, 1 Black 2 Year old Steer $8	*16.00*

1 Yearling Heffer $6, 1 Do whitefaced $5	*11.00*
1 Calf $3, 1 Great Chain $1.25	*4.25*
1 Do $1, two old Yokes with Irons $1.50	*2.50*
1 one Horse Waggon with Harness $10	*10.00*
1 Ox Cart with Gears $18	*18.00*
1 two horse wagon with Harness $7	*7.00*
1 pr. hors Gears with Harness 50c	*00.50*
1 Drawing Knife 25c	*00.25*
1 Plow & Clovis and pin $1, 1 pr. adds 12c	*1.12*
1 Bitte & 1 wedge 25c, 1 one Horse Sleigh $8	*8.25*
1 fanning mill $8, 1 Corn Shedder $3	*11.00*
1 Crobar $1, 1 Grinston 50c, 1 Sythe & Snath 50c	*2.00*
1 pitchfork 34c, two old rakes 16c	*00.50*
1 Small Ax 25c, 9 Sheep $9	*9.25*
3 Store hogs $6.50, 1 pr Small Andirons 34c	*6.84*
2 old candlesticks 10c, 1 nale hamer 20c	*00.30*
1 Great Bible $1, 1 Set Scotts Bibles $10	*11.00*
1 time pies $5, trumble on revelations 25c	*5.25*
1 tea table $1.75, 1 old chest with drawers $1	*2.75*
1 Small looking glass 25c, 1 old kitchen table 25c	*00.50*
1 Great Chain 75c, 3 old fiddleback Chairs $1	*1.75*
2 Black Chairs with Slats 60c	*00.60*
8 old kitchen Chairs 12 Cents each	*00.96*
2 two Qt. bottles 50c, 1 butter tub 25c	*00.75*
1 Cider pale 25c, 1 tin Churn 40c	*00.65*
1 Black teapot 17c, 1 old case & 5 bottles 75c	*00.92*
2 pr. Brown linning Sheats $1.50 each	*3.00*
1 pr. Cotten $1.25; 4½ pr. old $1.50	*2.75*
15 old pillow cases 8c each	*1.20*
1 old diaper table Cloth 12½c, 1 Do 12½c	*00.25*
7 old towels 6c each, 1 pr. Small bellows 6c	*00.48*
2 large Silver Spoons $2, 6 knives & forks 25c	*2.25*
7 pewter Spoons 18c, 1 Set knives & forks 40c	*00.58*
1 pr. Shovels with tongs 75c	*00.75*
1 pr. Small Andirons 50c	*00.50*
1 porrig pot 34c, 1 Do. small 17c	*00.51*
1 Small tramel 12c, 6 winsor Chairs $1.25	*1.37*
1 old table 75c, 1 old Chest with draws $1.25	*2.00*
1 Squire Stand 25c, 1 looking glass 50c	*00.75*
1 pr. Small brass andirons $1, 1 pr Small tongs 12c	*1.12*
2 Brass Candlesticks 40c, 5 old Silver tea Spoons $1.25	*1.65*
7 yd. Drab fuled flanel 50c pr. yd.	*3.50*
5 pr. linning Sheats 75c pr. pair	*3.75*
4½ pr. Do. 34c pr. pare	*1.53*
1 old diaper table Cloth 25c	*00.25*

2 towels diaper 25c	00.25
3 Pillow cases 24c	00.24
lot Crockery in west room $1.50	1.50
1 Bedsted & under Bed in west room 50c	00.50
Bed & Bolsters & Pillows to the Same $4	4.00
1 old Callico bedquilt & pr. old woollen Sheets $1	1.00
1 old low Chest 12c, 1 Stand 25c, warming pan $1	1.37
1 Bedsted & cord in bedroom 75c	00.75
1 Bed & bolster & Pillows to the same $2.50	2.50
1 linning sheat 1 Cotten & 2 Chect Blankets and Bedquilt to the Same $1	1.00
1 old Calico bedquilt 34c	00.34
1 pr. Sad Irons 25c, 1 Stove 25c, 2 tramels 75c	1.25
1 Gridiron & tostiron 25c, frying pan 25c	00.50
1 peal 25c, 1 Small Dishkettle 12c	00.37
1 Iron teakettle 25c, 1 old pr. andirons 25c	00.50
1 Spider 25c, 1 Griddle 25c, 6 tin pans 75c	1.25
2 old tin pales 30c, 1 long pewter platter 34c	00.64
2 Do. small 24c, 1 two Qt. bason 24c, 1 Do one Qt. 12c	00.60
4 pewter plates 24c, 1 old Churn 8c	00.32
1 lantern 8c, 1 Stew Cup 12c, 1 Chopping knife 8c	00.28
1 Woodden bole 8c, kitchen table 50c	00.58
1 Small Morter 8c, Crockery in kitchen 25c	00.33
1 old long brass kettle $1.50, 1 Do. Small $1.25	2.75
2 Washing tubs 25c, 2 old Chect Blankets $1	1.25
1 old round table 25c, 1 low chest 34c	00.59
1 old Bedsted with cord in Chamber 25c	00.25
1 Small looking glass 12c	00.12
1 old Bedsted with under Bed 50c	00.50
1 Bed bolster & pillow $6.50	6.50
1 pr. Woollen Sheets $1, 3 Blankets $1.50	2.50
1 old Bedquilt 75c, 2 Do. old 50c	1.25
1 Calico Bedquilt $2, 1 Woollen Sheet $1	3.00
2 old Saddles with one Bridle $1.75	1.75
the bed in the Kitchen chamber with bedding as it Stands $2, 1 Great wheel & real 75c	2.75
1 Coffe mill 12c, 1 Cutting knife 12c	00.24
11 Bags $1.75, 1 chees press 50c, 2 bushels salt $1.40	3.65
About 3 bushels flaxseed $3	3.00
1 old Sidesaddle $1.25, 2 Meat Casts $1	2.25
6 Hogsheads with Sider $18, 1 good keg 50c	18.50
old lumber such as old hogshead &	2.00
1 old rope 25c	00.25
the husks & Sedge & Storcks in the Barn $3	3.00
1 Stack of Storcks with some Sedge $6	6.00

About 5 tuns hay in the Barn $50	*50.00*
About 5 bushels potatoes in seller $1.25	*1.25*
About 100 bushels of Corn in the Crib $50	*50.00*
About 125 bushels oats in the Sheaf at 34c pr.	*42.50*
the old Sider mill	*5.00*
About 16 Bushels Rye at 65c pr. bushel	*11.40*
1 Beever Hatt $2, 2 pr. old Boots 34c	*2.34*
1 Great Coat Drab $1, 1 pr. old panterloons 25c	*1.25*
1 old under vest 34c, 1 old strate bodied coat $1.25	*1.59*
1 old Black Do. 75c, Under vest woollen 34c	*1.09*
1 Do. Black velvet 25c, 1 Do. black woollen 25c	*00.50*
1 Black pr. woollen panterloons 75c	*00.75*
8 old Shirts $2, 5 pr. stockings 34c	*2.34*
3 old neck handkerchief 18c, old hat 17c	*00.35*
Several notes held by Adams	*625.82*
The Dwelling House $150	*150.00*
Barn $30, Waggonn House $15	*45.00*
Dwelling House & Shop where Joseph Downs lives $50	*50.00*
25+Acres of Land in the Homestead $50	*1272.81*
13+Acres of Land by Dikemans $50	*697.50*
19+Acres of Land by the Branch $35	*698.46*
6 Acres of Wood Land farm hill $40	*240.00*
11+ Acres of Burn land $40	*447.50*
3+ Acres Lacy lot $40	*156.25*
4+ Acres Land by Trobridge Crossman $25	*106.25*
15+ Acres land claimed by Silliman Adams $35	*558.80*
Grand Total	*$4183.37*

Present-day collectors of antiques—and real property—may enjoy trying to calculate the value of this estate in today's market.

NOTES TO CHAPTER 9

1. This chapter benefited from my reading of Peter Laslett's *The World We Have Lost* (New York, 1965); Percy W. Bidwell, *Rural Economy in New England at the Beginning of the 19th Century* (New Haven, 1916); and Albert Laverne Olson, *Agricultural Economy and the Population in Eighteenth-Century Connecticut* (New Haven, 1935).

2. The account books of Gilbert and Bennett for the years 1792-1796 are in the Connecticut State Library, Hartford.

3. Mary Noyes to Samuel Noyes, February 2, 1807, in the Noyes Collection, New Canaan Historical Society.

4. The account books of the Buckley brothers are in the possession of Mr. and Mrs. Eugene F. O'Hare of Weston.

5. John Noyes to Samuel Noyes, July 22, 1803; John Noyes to Samuel Noyes, July 24, 1804; John Noyes to Benjamin Noyes, July 27, 1809, in Noyes Collection.

6. Ebenezer Noyes to Benjamin Noyes, December 5, 1808, ibid.

7. Timothy Dwight, *A Statistical Account of the City of New Haven* (New Haven, 1911), p. 22.

8. Rodolphus Dickinson, *A Geographical and Statistical View* (Greenfield, Massachusetts, 1813), p. 11.

9. Mary Noyes to Benjamin Noyes, December 29, 1811, Noyes Collection.

10. John Noyes to Charles Noyes, October 26, 1814, Noyes Collection.

11. Ibid.

THE FABRIC OF SOCIETY IN EARLY WESTON

"Instructors of the schools shall be able to read the english language"

For the residents of early Weston, life was more than just earning a living. The town was the scene of their childhood and education, of their courtships and marriages, of their recreations, of their disputes and crimes, and of their illnesses and ultimately of their deaths. In fact, virtually all of their existence took place within their community, something that could be said of few late-twentieth-century Weston people.

No institution was more important to the society of early Weston than the family. While it certainly performed an important economic function, its greatest contribution was through its role as nurturer of the community's children. In earlier years, when future Weston was little more than a scattering of crude houses in the wilderness, the family was responsible for a whole range of tasks, tasks that were gradually assumed by the parish and then by the town. For example, the family had once provided all the education that was to be obtained by local children. Fairfield was too distant to allow even the most ambitious student to commute there for school. But by the time the town of Weston came into existence, the community had developed to

Banks onion barn, built about 1830

the point where it could relieve the family of this as well as certain other social burdens and concentrate on raising its own children. Thus the role of the family had gone through a significant change even during the first seventy-five years of the community's life.

The families of early Weston were extended families in that the town was full of persons who were related in one way or another—by blood, by marriage, by both. Fantons were related to Sherwoods, who were related to Bradleys, who felt a tie to the Fantons by virtue of their shared cousins, the Sherwoods. John Noyes, it will be recalled, was the son-in-law of the parish's first minister, Samuel Sherwood, and because of this connection was related, either directly or indirectly, to many of the members of his church, as well as to a variety of other local families. Of the twelve persons who lived in Weston in 1797 and whose last names began with the letter *A*, all but one were named either Andrews or Adams. During that same year, sixteen town residents had names beginning with *F;* of these, ten shared the surname Fanton. There were sixteen Coley families in Weston and fourteen Sherwood families and thirteen Godfrey families in that year. Children growing up during the town's first decades had access to seemingly endless numbers of uncles, aunts, and cousins, as well as grandparents, great-uncles, and great-aunts.

But while the families of early Weston were extended families, the households were not. Once children married, they normally lived separately from their parents. In other words, grandparents, parents, and children seldom shared a dwelling. Neither did uncles and aunts live with nieces and nephews. They were available nearby but rarely resided under the same roof. Most Weston households—the vast majority, in fact—consisted of two parents and their children. While the size of the family varied greatly, the typical family included about five children. John and Mary Noyes had a much larger family—ten sons and daughters—but for every large family like the Noyeses there was one like that of Joshua and Sarah Adams that included only two children. Thus, the twentieth century's stereotype of multitudinous children and endless relatives sharing the same home during the late eighteenth or early nineteenth century does not hold true for early Weston.

Another stereotype that the early town refuses to confirm is the idea of the austere patriarch who dominated his offspring until well into their adult lives. Such a situation might well have existed in Fairfield during the seventeenth century, when sons depended upon their fathers for land, but in early Weston, sons established their independence sooner by buying and farming marginal lands, by learning a trade to supplement their farm income, or occasionally by departing the community for richer economic opportunities. One result of earlier filial independence was to break down many of the barriers between fathers and sons and to encourage a more intimate and affectionate relationship between them. Thus, the families of early Weston managed to avoid the stiffness that characterized the century before in Connecticut. No more convincing evidence of this could be found than the correspondence between John Noyes and his sons. By twentieth-century standards, his sons were dutiful to a fault; but by the standards that had existed only a few years before, the atmosphere within the Noyes family, and Weston families generally, was close and affectionate. When boys and girls reached their teens, they felt themselves "very near upon a level" with their parents. In an age when privacy was a scarce commodity and when children and adults shared the same tasks, the same entertainments, and the same friends, this familiarity made life much more tolerable.[1]

The familiarity that existed within Weston families did not mean that permissiveness was the rule, for at about age seven or eight, Weston children became accountable to adult expectations and standards. At that point in their lives, they were expected to begin slowly abandoning childish things and to become miniature models of their parents. By the time they reached the age of fourteen or fifteen, they had become adults. The process was clearly gradual, but the whole concept of adolescence, a concept so dear to the twentieth century,

Building at junction of Georgetown Road and Newtown Turnpike served as Weston's post office until the late nineteenth century.

was outside the awareness of the residents of early Weston; where there was a continuum between generations, the idea of adolescence was superfluous.

John Noyes, the occasional spiritual leader of a significant part of Weston, prepared a list of rules for bringing up children. Within his list can be seen the tension between the old, severe attitudes toward child rearing and the more relaxed atmosphere that was then developing in communities like Weston. Noyes, remembering the example he had known as a child, began by suggesting that "the first thing which can be done for [children] in a moral point of view is to teach them submission to parental authority." This process, he argued, should begin as soon as a child can "distinguish between a smile & a frown," and its object was to check the "turbulent & rebellious spirit" in the child. "Let a child be once made to bow to the parent," he continued, "it will be comparatively easy to keep him in subjection for the future."[2]

But Noyes, whose dour countenance concealed a warm personality,

Ebenezer Fitch and his oxcart, in the late 1800s

refused to emphasize only submission. He urged that children should be taught early "to be generous,—to give a part of what they have to some one else." He also warned that if a parent deceives his children, "he will lose their confidence & learn them to practise deception." While Noyes endorsed the idea of corporal punishment, he warned against using the rod "in a passion" and argued that "by frequent beating, a child becomes hardened & set against his parents. Children therefore should be governed as much as possible by reason."

Much of his advice must have made good sense to his neighbors. He warned against one parent's interfering "with the government of the other," and he urged that parents grant "the reasonable requests of their children" and that they "scold them only when there is absolute need of it. By too much scolding children's tempers are soured," he warned. He also argued that children be taught truthfulness and faithfulness and that they be warned against pride and covetousness.

Their religious education was of great importance to Noyes. "When a child is capable of being taught that there is a God, he ought to be told who made him, & what his Maker requires of him. He should be taught," he continued, "that he is a sinner, & the way of salvation should be opened to his mind." Children, he believed, should be regularly reminded of their dependence on God, of his all-surrounding power, of their accountability to him, and "of the uncertainty of life, as also of the importance of being ready to meet death."

The harshness of part of Noyes's statement should not be taken as proof that relations between parents and children were harsh. Rather, the inconsistencies in his statement reflect the uncertainties that existed at the time about how to bring up children. The old ideas were slow to give way, but they were, nevertheless, losing ground. The result was probably as much variety in styles of parenting in early Weston as there is in modern Weston. Parents then expected more obedience from their children than do late-twentieth-century parents, but today's reader would do the Noyeses and Sherwoods and Fantons a great disservice if he were to conclude that love and familiarity could not play as large a part in relations between children and parents then as they can today.

There is no evidence to indicate that children were desperately eager to leave their parents' homes. The typical male did not marry until he was between his twenty-second and twenty-third birthdays, and his bride was only slightly younger. The first generation of persons to live in the Weston area, the generation that moved into the region well before the town was established, had married later, possibly because of the delay in transferring property from fathers to sons and the prolongation of parental controls over lands conveyed to sons, but the first generation to live in the town itself married in its early twenties. Marriages between teenagers were rare.

Few relationships are more intimate than those between husbands and wives, and few are more difficult for historians to understand. Occasional references to his wife in the correspondence of John Noyes would indicate that this marriage was especially strong, but certainly Noyes never opened his heart on this subject in his letters. Likewise, from a strictly legal point of view, the women of early Weston had virtually no political rights and little control over the family's property. But whether this was really true in the day-to-day functioning of the family is another question. Without doubt, some wives had as much control over family finances as wives do today. But the reality of that situation is lost to history.

The fact that divorce was almost unknown in early Weston also tells little about the success of marriages. As far as the public records indicate, the General Assembly received only one petition for divorce from a resident of early Weston. Sarah Gorham petitioned the legislature for a divorce from her husband, Stephen. The couple had originally lived in Weston but in 1767 moved to New York City. Sarah claimed that she had lived with her husband and had performed "all the duties of the marriage covenant on her part—and faithfully discharged all the Duties and Obligations of a wife unto the said Stephen

Coley barn, built after earlier barn burned in 1882, is now the museum of the Weston Historical Society.

until on or about the 1st day of January 1796." At this time, she claimed, Stephen began to beat her "in the most Cruel and Abusive Manner" and to make threats on her life. He continued his abuse of her until she finally left his home and took "Refuge in the open Streets, and the said Stephen then and there, declared, in the Most Solemn Manner to your Petitioner that she never should again return to his House, and that if she attempted a return, he was determined on Acts of intolerable Cruelty to her." Thus, she returned to Weston.[3]

Sarah described in graphic detail her efforts to reconcile with Stephen; but, she stated, "he has been Obstinately determined on Acts of Cruelty, and has threatened the Life of your Petitioner in the Most determined Manner; and has declared he would make a Sacrifice of her your Petitioner to the Gratification of his Inveterate hatred." She said that since her return to Weston, she had continued her attempts at reconciliation and had asked for some explanation of his cruel conduct. But Stephen refused an "Explanation there of but that a Master has a right to Correct his Servant in what way & manner he thought proper."

The David Dimon Coley house on the Weston Road, built in 1841

Thus stating her case, Sarah requested a bill of divorce. The legislature ordered John Gray, a Weston constable, to present a copy of the petition to Stephen and to ask him "to appear if he see cause before the General Assembly . . . at their Next Session." Whether Stephen appeared or not is unclear, but at its October, 1797, session the Assembly turned down the petition. What became of Sarah and Stephen Gorham is unknown.

That only one petition for divorce ever reached the Assembly from Weston does not mean that marital problems were unknown within the community. Most of these problems were hidden from contemporary friends and neighbors, and hidden even more deeply from historians operating nearly two hundred years later. But occasionally these secrets were preserved and then inadvertently shared with posterity. For example, one of John Noyes's sons—which one is uncertain—apparently planned to leave his wife for another woman. The son asked his father's opinion on his plan, and his father wrote back a long letter. The elder Noyes concluded his letter with these words: "I entreat you therefore my dear Son with all the tenderness of a kind parent to hearken to my advice, and as you value your own honor, interest & happiness, as you value the welfare of your children, as you value the answer of a good conscience, as you value the solemn vows & obligations of the marriage bond, as you value your soul's everlasting welfare, have no further connection with the woman who hath drawn you away from your duty & cleave only to her who is your lawful wife." That a single such letter survived for nearly two hundred years is most remarkable. Similar advice was undoubtedly given by other fathers to other sons and daughters.[4]

The reasons that there were so few divorces in early Weston are fairly obvious. The economic and social realities of this era made life for a single person extremely difficult, and the laws of the time and the predisposition of the General Assembly made obtaining a divorce nearly impossible. This was an age of uncertainty; the family was something enduring, something stable. It had to be preserved. With these social, economic, and legal forces working to maintain marriages, it is hardly surprising that divorce was so rare. Whether marriages were happier is a question no one can answer.

Because of the finality of marriage, courtship in that earlier age was much less haphazard than today. In most instances, both sets of parents were involved in the selection. When John Noyes, Jr., decided that he might have found his heart's desire, he first asked his parents for permission to court the woman in question and then asked her parents' consent to propose to her. Legally, neither set of parents could exercise an absolute veto, but both certainly had an opportunity for their say. Other aspects of courtship were also fastidiously attended to. The custom of "tarrying" was widely practiced in early Weston. In 1760, Andrew Burnaby, who had spent considerable time in New England, described the practice: "When a man is enamoured of a young woman, and wishes to marry her, he proposes the affair to her parents," Burnaby wrote; "if they have no objection, they allow him to tarry with her one night, in order to make his court to her." As bedtime approached, the older couple would discreetly disappear, "leaving the younger ones to settle matters as they can; who, after having sate up as long as they think proper, get into bed together also, but without pulling off their undergarments, in order to prevent scandal." If the young man and woman agreed that all went well, they proceeded with plans for marriage. If not, the couple parted, "unless, which is an accident that seldom happens, the forsaken fair-one prove pregnant, and then the man is obliged to marry her." Burnaby was correct in asserting that the practice resulted in few unwanted pregnancies, for in early Weston only about one in fifteen first pregnancies came before marriage, and certainly not all of them could be blamed upon the custom of tarrying. William Wheeler, who for a time taught school in Weston, made the following entry in his diary under the date December 12, 1787: "Died at Weston Z.H.—his Death was occasioned by sleeping on the ground (after spending the night with a beloved female) where a shower fell upon him." Clearly not all premarital sex took place under the protective cover of the tarrying custom.[5]

One of the functions that the family had delegated to the town was responsibility for formal education. As was noted earlier, there were, from 1795 to 1856, eight school districts within what is presently the town of Weston. These districts were the Southern, Kettle Creek, Middle, Upper Parish, Osborn Town, Den, Lyons Plains, and Good Hill. The districts were arranged in a circular fashion, beginning with the Southern District in the southwestern part of town. The first five districts ran from south to north on the west side of Weston, and the remaining three from north to south along the present eastern boundary.

Unlike modern Weston, the early town took little pride in its school system. This was indicated by teachers' salaries. When William Wheeler first taught in the town, he earned forty-five shillings (about $7.50) per month for the three months—January through March—that school was in session; at the same time, a common laborer could demand six shillings (about a dollar) a day. In 1812, John Noyes, Jr., was paid ten dollars per month; fifty cents a day was then the rate for common labor. The tightfisted policy was also evident in the curriculum. Reading, writing, spelling, and common arithmetic were the extent of the school's offerings. If a student wanted to study such esoteric subjects as grammar, composition, or mathematics, he would have to go to the Staples Academy in North Fairfield or to some private school.

The Weston schools relied largely on tax money to pay for their operation; additionally, the scholars themselves were expected to pay a share of their own expenses, and Samuel Staples's estate provided funds to help those in town who were too poor to pay their own way.

Blacksmith shop on upper Lyons Plains Road, in 1896

But the dependence upon taxes made the schools responsive to the intellectual needs of the society which they served. The intellectual needs of early Weston were minimal, and the schools provided the minimum.

Even the school buildings bespoke the town's lack of enthusiasm. The typical Weston schoolhouse was about twenty by twenty feet, of frame construction, and endowed with a small entrance foyer. The classroom was sheathed with rough boards as high as the windows and was plastered above this point to the ceiling. Only two or three windows provided light; this was supplemented by the flames from a large fireplace. Three walls were lined with long plank desks, and along the fourth stood the schoolmaster's table. During the cold months, when school was in session, the building's large fireplace provided just enough heat to roast half the students while those at the opposite end of the room froze. The huge fireplace also devoured vast amounts of wood—wood which was supplied by the parents of the scholars. When the supply of wood ran out, school had to be dismissed.

School attendance was at best haphazard. John Noyes, Jr., who taught at the Den School during 1812, recorded the number of days that his pupils had attended school. He noted that during Job Lockwood's scholarly career, he had been present 129 days and Silliman Andrews had been in school 127 days. But during the same length of time, Seth Osborn attended only five days and John Griffin was present only ten days. Parents seem to have been even more casual about the attendance of girls; if they got to school or not was of no great moment. More important was their parents' desire to keep them away from a variety of pernicious influences that were all too readily available. Mary Noyes, for example, had been taught the evils of novels, which she regarded as "very injurious to young Ladies, especially to those who make a practise of reading them, for I consider that they have a tendency to corrupt the mind." Like most of her fellow students and like those who determined policy for the schools of early Weston, Mary Noyes valued rote memorization more than the analysis of works of fiction.[6]

School administration was accomplished by a group of men known as the "Visitors." They met annually to select teachers. From the minutes of their meetings, it seems they paid little attention to school policy. Apparently, the Visitors felt that if they could locate adequate faculty, the faculty would take charge of the specifics of the curriculum. At the Visitors' meeting of February 4, 1801, for example, they decided that "those whom we shall approve as Instructors of the schools under our inspection shall be able to read the english language with readiness & propriety, that they shall spell correctly, that they shall write a good fair hand, and be well versed in Arithmetic." Teachers were also to be of good character and manners and able to teach English grammar. The specifics of how they would deal with the pupils were left largely to their discretion; of course, they had to accomplish only the most rudimentary aspects of education.[7]

The faculty of the Weston schools was expected to provide lessons in manners and breeding as well as in reading and spelling. John Noyes, himself one of the school Visitors, made a list of the rules with which he believed every young man and woman should be familiar. He contended that young persons, whenever walking or riding with superiors, should "give them the right hand." In similar situations on stairs, youth should give up the banister side to superiors. Young people were warned that they should "always use moderation in laughter; for a wise man is never known to laugh loud." As much deference as the young were expected to show their betters, they were also admonished, when with inferiors, never to say or do "anything that shall make them feel their inferiority." If Weston placed little premium on things intellectual, the town did value decorum.[8]

Fortunately, a picture of what school was like in those earlier days has been preserved in a manuscript written by J. Dimon Bradley. Born in 1819, Bradley attended school during the 1820s in North Fairfield. His experiences there were undoubtedly like those of his contemporaries in Norfield. "When I was old enough," he wrote, "my parents began to send me to school, to lay the future foundations of my school education. The first day I went I was rather shy, but the teacher spoke to me and took me to the table and to what they called a spelling book and opening it took a pen knife and pointed to *A*. We said the line down and then I took my seat." The teacher then told Bradley that he must not disturb the class, "for if I made a noise I would scare his foxes in the table drawer, but afterwards some of the large children looked in the drawer but the foxes had gone."[9]

Eventually, Bradley learned to spell, and "in a year or two," he continued, "I learned to read and had the 'Easy Lessons' and also to write a little." His first writing book contained only a single sheet of paper with a cover sewn over it. "In those days the paper had to be ruled with a ruler and a lead plummet as they had no lead pencils at that time." The teacher ruled Bradley's book for him. "In those days," he went on, "they had no metal pens, but good goose quills to make pens. I had one and the teacher made me a pen with a pen knife and if it did not write well he mended it. My father obtained a lead inkstand and filled it with ink for me."

After learning to read and write, Bradley was ready to begin exploring the world of arithmetic. Thus, he needed a copy of *Duboll's Arithmetic,* the standard text of that era. To raise the money to buy the book, he went into the woods and gathered chestnuts, which he then sold at Gregory's store. He received thirty-six cents for the nine quarts of nuts he collected. The arithmetic book was three "bits," thirty-seven and a half cents, but the generous proprietor gave him the book for the nuts.

Bradley attended school during both the summer and winter until he was eight or nine. "After that," he explained, "I went in the winter and not so much in the summer until I was ten or twelve years old. After that three or four months in the winter to common district schools working on the farm for my father until I was sixteen years old." He concluded his education at the Staples Academy, which he

Old Weston town hall and Norfield Grange, destroyed by fire in 1951

attended "for five or six winters, working the farm in summer." Dozens of other Weston children followed the same pattern that Bradley did.

It would be pleasant to be able to believe that early Weston was free from unsavory aspects of American life. As far as slavery was concerned, this was hardly the case. In 1800, there were twenty-one slaves in Weston. Andrew Lyon owned four slaves, Ebenezer Coley and Samuel Wakeman three each, and several men, including the Reverend Noyes, owned single slaves. Eventually emancipated during the beginning of the nineteenth century, these blacks joined the small free-black population already in Weston and lived out their lives in town.

Crime, too, was part of early Weston's existence. For example, between January 1, 1809, and April 9, 1810, complaints were made against fifty-one residents for gaming, seven for breaking Thanksgiving Day, eight for breaking the Sabbath, nine for retailing liquor without a license, four for profane swearing, five for breaking the fast day, one for perjury, five for breach of peace, two for adultery, and three for horse racing. While none of these was a major crime—or even a crime at all, by today's standards—and while none involved violence, there were regular violations of the law during the town's early years. The most notorious crime committed during those years was perpetrated by Squire Oysterbanks. "Subject to turns of mental derrangement" and "strong nervous afflictions," Oysterbanks, in September, 1810, set fire to the meetinghouse in North Fairfield. He was convicted and sentenced to two years in prison. He served four months in New-Gate prison at Granby, but then, because of his delicate mental health, was transferred to the more hospitable confines of the Fairfield jail, where he completed his sentence.[10]

Squire Oysterbanks's mental illness took the form of violence against the community. More frequently, those of his contemporaries who were mentally ill inflicted violence upon themselves rather than on their neighbors. The records of the Norfield Church listed the deaths of church members and the causes of those deaths. While those records are too haphazard to provide the basis for a statistical analysis, they do demonstrate that suicide was not an extraordinary occurrence in early Weston. Neither was suicide an escape sought only by those who were alone or ill or old. Benjamin Noyes, third son of the second minister, was eighteen and a student at Yale when he drowned himself in the Saugatuck River. Convinced that he could never know Christ as his father did, young Benjamin left the following note, dated

April, 1815: "Pa & Ma do not grieve—be extremely careful to instruct your children in the great concerns of eternity. . . . I know my case is distressing. My ruin was owing to my great negligence in the great matters of the soul. I feared when I ought to have loved. . . . Be careful that you come not to this world of torment. I do not realize my own situation."[11]

The health of the residents of early Weston, whether physical or mental, is difficult to assess. Only a very crude estimate of longevity can be obtained from cemetery and genealogical records. If these obviously imperfect records can be relied upon at all, the residents of early Weston, both male and female, could, on the average, count on living into their sixties, assuming that they survived childhood. Childhood was clearly a dangerous age, the greatest killers of children being dysentery, smallpox, diphtheria, and scarlet fever. When illness struck the community, children were the principal sufferers. "It is a very melancholy time with us & with the people of our land generally," wrote John Noyes in 1813. "The fever is among us. Numbers have died of it. . . . Beebe Gray has lost his daughter Eunice by the disorder & has another child sick with it." Even the childbearing years for women were less dangerous. Apparently, Weston's women endured these years in fairly good health for—based again on scanty records—women tended to live longer than their husbands. Perhaps the most persistent and painful health problem that Weston's people faced was poor teeth. For one to lose all of his teeth at an early age was by no means unusual. John Noyes wrote to his son Benjamin, when Benjamin first went to Yale, advising him to wait to have all his teeth removed until he was able to return home. In the letter, the elder Noyes reminded his son that his brother William had already had his out. At the time, Benjamin was thirteen and William seventeen.[12]

Accidents were a great hazard. In a single letter written in 1813, John Noyes described the death of a two-year-old who had been inadvertently struck by an adz and of an adult who was killed by a falling tree. Less than a month later, mishap struck his own family. "Last Thursday fortnight your brother Ebenr. getting down from the mow, stuck the pitch fork into his body near the passage about 2½ inches deep," Noyes informed his son Benjamin, "and as he sallied on the fork it tore the wound within to a much greater width than the orifice. The fork turned with him on it till he came to the floor." Ebenezer collapsed as he tried to make his way to the family house and was found by his brother William. Eventually, the boy recovered, but only after a long convalescence.[13]

Although Weston included among its population several physicians, including Thomas Davis, who lived in Norfield, home remedies were heavily relied upon. Many of these have been lost to time, but a favorite Weston cure for boils, then called cancers, has survived. It called for the juice of sheep sorrel "expressed, and exposed in a pewter plate, in the Sun until somewhat jellied." The result was to be applied to the skin over and around the sore. "As soon as the pain of the first drawing subsides, renew the application, and continue repeating it until the cancer, with the roots attached, loosens and drops out." In an age when disease came and went outside all human control, a home remedy did not need to produce miracles to maintain the confidence of simple people.[14]

One vitally important aspect of Weston's life is the part that religion played. It is easily overlooked because it was so basic an ingredient, so much an assumed part of life, that the people of the time were completely unpretentious about it. They regarded its underlying presence as part of the environment in which they functioned. The declining fortunes of the Norfield church or of the churches in North Fairfield were no index to the importance of religion. Evidence of its importance is better found in the Bibles that were frequently the only books in Weston homes, in the meetinghouse's dominant place in the village, in the reverence with which the Sabbath was observed, even when its observation meant that essential work was left undone. Events, painful and pleasant, small and large, were understood in terms of religion; the death of a child, a bountiful harvest, an early spring, an especially bleak winter were all "explained" in terms of God's all-powerful and mysterious ways. Religion determined the conduct of Weston's population, and while church and state would remain connected only until 1818, and while enthusiasm for the Norfield church had begun to decline much earlier, religion remained a vital, if frequently unmentioned, condition of Weston's life.

A variety of amusements was available to the town's residents. Much social life revolved around the church, where dinner, women's circles, and Bible classes provided opportunities for the parishioners to socialize. The Ark Lodge of Masons was revived in 1797, after several lean years. Work and recreation were frequently combined; barn and house raisings were important events, as were quilting bees. Athletics were completely without organization. Boys ran races or wrestled or kicked a ball, but they did so according to their own rules and their own schedules. During the warm months, there were plenty of opportunities to swim. Favorite games for girls were hopscotch,

Middle District School behind the Norfield church, with shed added for a fire station. The fire truck is a 1934 Mack.

maypole dancing, hoop and hide, and thread-the-needle. Adult sports were largely limited to hunting, fishing, clamming, and the officially condemned and fiercely hated sport of kings, horse racing. During the cold months, sleighing was a popular pastime for all, male and female, young and old.

The center of the town's social life was the Banks Tavern at Lyons Plains, at this time operated by Thomas Banks. He hosted meetings, auctions, and dances, and also provided a place for residents to gather and enjoy a pint or two of cider or a glass of rum. In 1794, William Priest described the lighthearted gaiety of a late winter evening. "The chief amusement of the country girls in winter," he wrote, "is sleighing, of which they are passionately fond, as indeed are the whole sex in this country. I never heard a woman speak of this diversion but with rapture. Every moment that will admit of sleighing is seized on with avidity." Priest said that on a night when the sleighing was particularly good, women, early in the evening, began heating sand in their kitchen fireplaces. The hot sand was then put in bags and deposited in the bottoms of the sleighs, from whence it radiated heat up under the robes that covered the riders' legs. As the sleighs arrived at a tavern, the riders would "alight and have a dance." Tom Banks would be up all night, serving customers. The favorite dance of Weston folks at this time was called "Setting to Partners." Exactly how the dance proceeded is unknown, but it did involve much twirling of female partners, in some cases so much twirling that the gentle damsels became dizzy and were prone to swooning. Such light-headedness was encouraged by both a desire to attract male attention and by the Madeira that the women imbibed. Whatever the cause, the desired effect was more often than not produced in the hearts of the rough-edged Weston farm lads.[15]

The favorite beverage of Weston men on such occasions was a drink called "flip." Fortunately, Tom Banks's recipe for flip has survived and might be tried by a brave twentieth-century connoisseur. "To make a quart of flip: Put the ale on the fire to warm and beat up three or four eggs with four ounces of moist sugar, a teaspoonful of grated nutmeg or ginger, and a quartern of good old rum or brandy," the recipe began. "When the ale is near to boil, put it into one pitcher and the rum and eggs, etc. into another; turn it from one pitcher to another till it is smooth as cream." This concoction was heated by plunging into it a red-hot poker. Flip in this amount was called "one yard of flannel." Without much difficulty, one can picture four or five young couples, fresh from the cold and flushed with excitement, striding into the

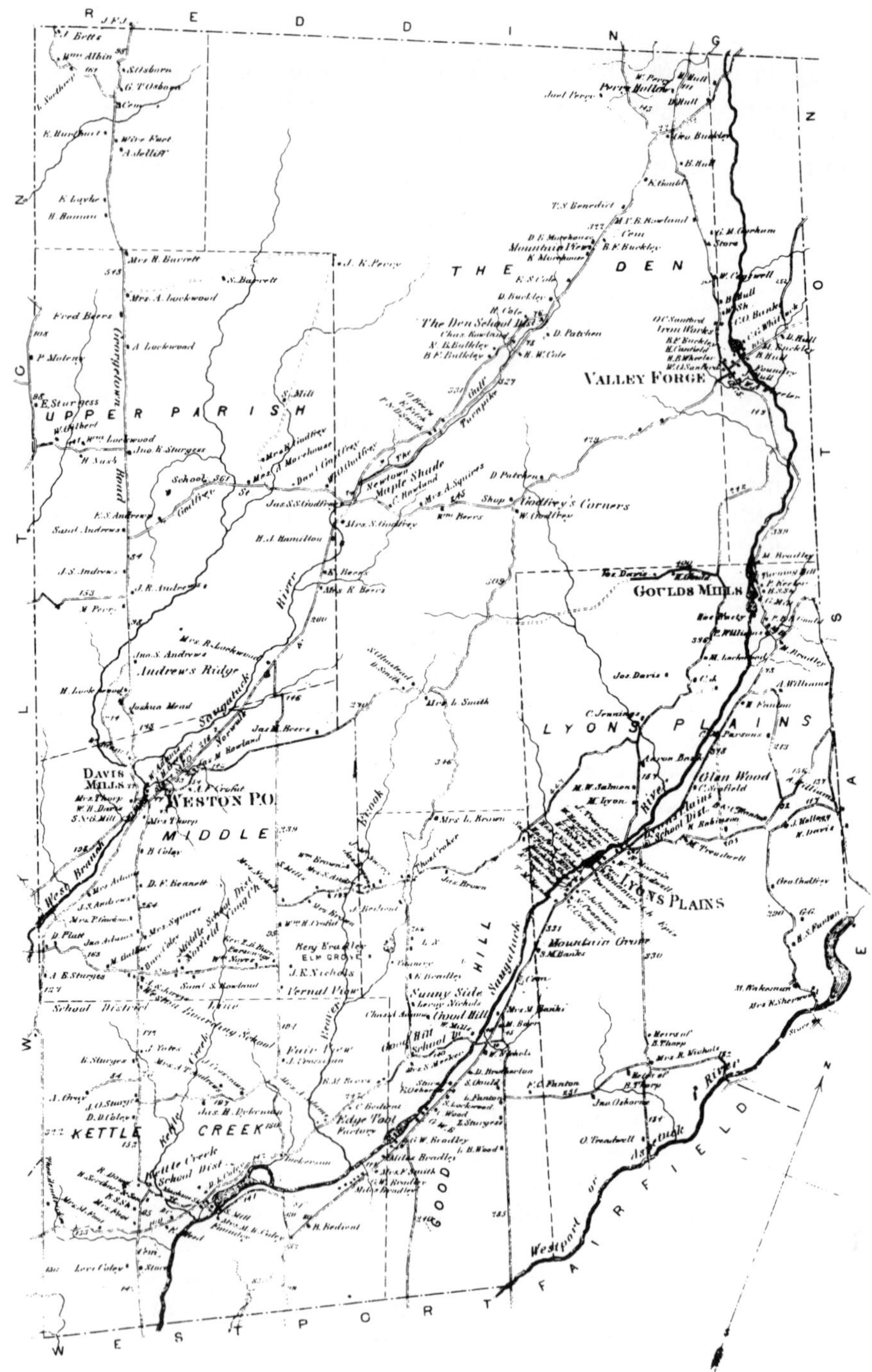
R E D D I N G
E A S T O N
W E S T P O R T
F A I R F I E L D
Perry Hollow
Mountain View
THE DEN
The Den School Dist.
VALLEY FORGE
UPPER PARISH
Georgetown Road
Newtown Turnpike
Maple Shade
Godfrey's Corners
Andrews Ridge
Saugatuck River
GOULDS MILLS
LYONS PLAINS
Lyons Plains
Glen Wood
DAVIS MILLS
WESTON P.O.
MIDDLE
Middle School Dist.
West Branch
ELM GROVE
Vernal View
Fair View
Mountain Grove
Sunny Side
Good Hill
Good Hill School Dist.
GOOD HILL
Edge Tool Factory
KETTLE CREEK
Kettle Creek School Dist.
Westport or Aspetuck River

TOWN OF

WESTON

Fairfield Co. Conn

Scale 2 Inches to the Mile

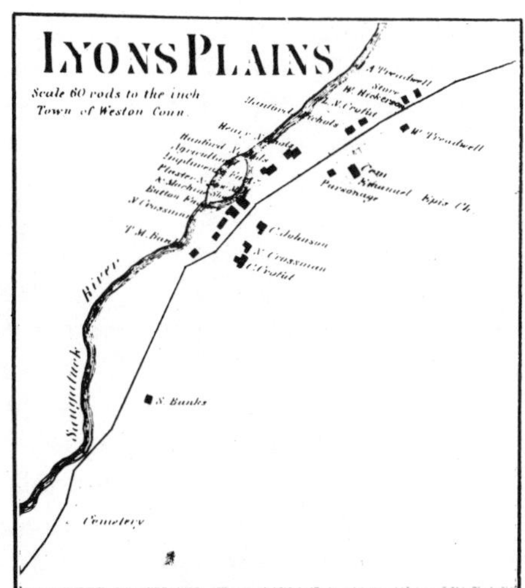

LYONS PLAINS BUSINESS ADVERTISING DIRECTORY.

Crossman & Wells, Proprietors Button Factory.
C. Crofut, Maker of Hay Cutters and other improved Agricultural Implements.
W. Hickerson, Dry Goods and Groceries.
E. Osborne, " "
Hanford Nichols, Proprietor of Plaster Mill.
P. B. B. Gould. " Grist "
Platt Keeler, Turner of Irregular Forms.

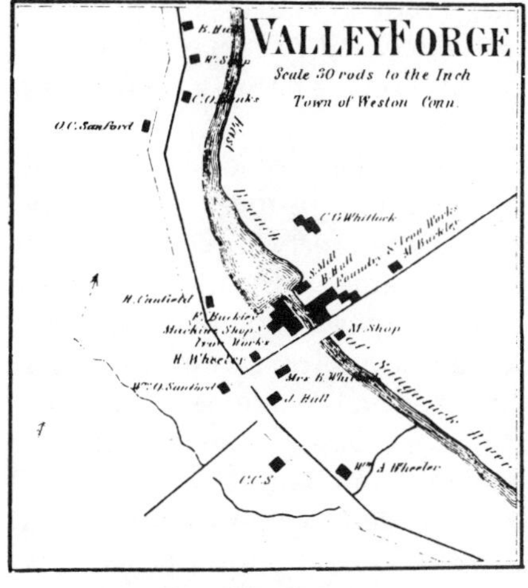

VALLEY FORGE BUSINESS DIRECTORY.

B. Hull, Proprietor of Foundry & Machine Shop.
B. F. Buckley, " Iron Works and "
C. G. Whitlock, Dealer in Groceries & Provisions.

Map of Weston from Atlas of Fairfield County, Connecticut, *compiled by F. W. Beers and published in 1867* warmth of Banks's tavern and ordering up Madeiras for the women and "one yard of flannel" for their beaux. On such an evening, life in Weston was as good as it could be.[16]

Other aspects of Weston's society were more complex. It is pleasant to believe that early Weston was a community of equals—one in which there was no great wealth, no true upper class, and few landless laborers. Unfortunately, this picture bears little resemblance to reality. What happened, instead, was that as Weston's population grew, the gap between the richest and the poorest grew; good land became increasingly scarce, the wealthier families grew in power, and the younger sons of other families had to endure a declining standard of living or, reluctantly, leave town to seek a livelihood elsewhere.

The men and women who originally settled Norfield did so because of reduced opportunities in Fairfield. By coming to Norfield, they became generally substantial, middle-class settlers. They accumulated more land than they could use. Their sons created estates that were nearly as large from their patrimony and from the purchase of additional lands. By the time of the third generation—that is, by the time the town of Weston was established—some families saw their economic power grow as they were able to acquire even more lands, but others saw their power decline as modest estates had to be divided several ways to provide for numerous sons. These sons, who faced dim economic prospects, occasionally made the decision to leave Weston. Only one of John Noyes's sons decided to remain in town, and even he refused to try to eke out a living on his father's small farm; he became a merchant.

The result, by the end of the century, was that a small minority of taxpayers owned a large percentage of the town's property. In fact, by 1797 the top ten percent of the taxpayers owned forty-three percent of the town's property. Furthermore, in that same year, the ten largest individual taxpayers, out of a total of 486 taxpayers, owned eighteen percent of the taxable property. These men were, in descending order of their assessments, Ebenezer Coley, Samuel Wakeman, Thomas Sherwood, John Sherwood, David Coley, Jr., Daniel Glover, Zachary Lyon, William Prince, Samuel B. Sherwood, and Samuel Thorpe. The total grand list of Weston at the time amounted to about $170,000; of that amount, these men owned about $30,000 worth of property. The median value of taxable property for this group was $2,542, while it was only $130 for the town as a whole. Clearly, economic equality was not a reality of early Weston.

But while a relatively wealthy class had developed in Weston, and while this class controlled an amazingly disproportionate percentage of the town's wealth, there did not develop on the opposite end of the spectrum a large class of landless laborers. Only about eight percent of the heads of household in Weston owned no land—significantly fewer than were to be found in most other Connecticut towns. In Simsbury, for example, twenty-one percent of the heads of household did not own land.

The picture that emerges of Weston society shows, at the top, a small wealthy class—wealthy by Weston standards, at least; an even smaller poor class, and a large group of people who farmed their own modest holdings, who provided reasonably well for themselves despite the fact that they rarely saw any cash money, but whose progeny would face grave economic problems as small estates were even further divided. But that problem lay in the future. At the end of the eighteenth century, Weston was still something of a land of promise, for a son still had the opportunity to take up land and become another subsistence farmer.

NOTES TO CHAPTER 10

1. This chapter has been enriched by my reading of James Axtell's *The School Upon a Hill: Education and Society in Colonial New England* (New Haven, 1974).

2. John Noyes, Rules for Bringing up Children, in the Noyes Collection, New Canaan Historical Society.

3. Petition of Sarah Gorham, October, 1797, Lotteries and Divorces, Series II, Connecticut Archives, I, 67, Connecticut State Library, Hartford.

4. John Noyes to (unknown), undated, in the Noyes Collection.

5. Andrew Burnaby, *Travels through the Middle Settlements in North-America* (Ithaca, 1960), pp. 102-103; entry of December 12, 1787, William Wheeler Journal, Connecticut State Library.

6. Mary Noyes to Benjamin Silliman, August 19, 1806, in the Noyes Collection.

7. John Noyes, Regulations for the Schools, 1801, in ibid.

8. John Noyes, A Compendium of Rules Necessary to be Observed in Good Breeding, in ibid.

9. J. Dimon Bradley, Memoirs, Fairfield Historical Society.

10. Petition of Ezekiel Oysterbanks, October 15, 1810, Crimes and Misdemeanors, Connecticut Archives, II, 76-79, Connecticut State Library.

11. Benjamin Noyes to John Noyes, April 1815, in Noyes Collection.

12. John Noyes to Benjamin Noyes, April 22, 1813, in ibid.

13. John Noyes to Benjamin Noyes, March 20, 1818, in ibid.

14. John Noyes, Cure for Cancer, in ibid.

15. William Priest to (unknown), March 18, 1794, in Weston Historical Society Collection.

16. Tom Banks, Receipt for Flip, in ibid.

A CENTURY OF CHANGE
the 1800s

"Old Weston is no longer one.
The town has been divided.
The people asked–the deed was done.
The law has so decided."

Weston's population remained stable from the time of the American Revolution until the Civil War, when it began a gradual decline that lasted almost until World War II. In 1860, 1,117 people lived in Weston,* approximately the same number as in 1790. By 1880, this number had fallen to 918, and by 1900 to 840. In 1930, only 670 individuals resided in town.

One might assume that these numbers indicate that Weston made no attempt to cope with the great economic changes of the nineteenth century, that Weston's agriculture surrendered to the far more efficient agriculture of the Middle West, and that Weston never sought to adapt to the brave new world of industry. Such an assumption would be incorrect. As the nineteenth century unfolded, as industry replaced

*Before Weston and Easton were divided, the town was obviously larger than this.

Davis's saw- and gristmill, later Cobb's, is thought to have operated as early as the eighteenth century.

agriculture as the backbone of New England's economic life, Weston, and towns like it, fought desperately to readjust their agriculture to new demands and to create an industrial base. If Weston could maintain its standard of living only by modernizing, then Weston would modernize.

Eventually, the town's effort was a failure, as its declining population strikingly illustrates. But the failure was clearly not the result of Weston's indolence or indifference. Rather, the effort failed because of factors over which Weston had no control, factors like the inaccessibility of raw materials, the limited sources of power to operate industrial machinery, and the problems of transporting finished products to market.

That Weston failed to accommodate to the nineteenth century does not mean that those decades did not bring significant change to the town. As Weston tried to adjust, many of the basic patterns of life were so altered that the Weston of 1900 became a community very different from the Weston of 1830 or 1840. Certainly, many aspects of Weston's existence remained stable, but much also changed. By 1900, the homogeneity that had typified Weston's early years was replaced by diversity, and by 1900 the ideological uniformity that had once characterized the town had become ideological pluralism, as new ideas came to challenge old ones.

Weston's attempt to cope with the nineteenth century can be seen in the changing employment patterns that developed in town. As impersonal as statistics are, they do graphically point up what was happening in town. In 1840, most of the people working in Weston made their living in agriculture. Seventy-two percent of all working people were either farmers or farm laborers in that year. Nineteen percent were craftsmen, most of whom served the needs of local farmers. These were blacksmiths, millers, carpenters, and the like. Fewer than 6 percent of the town's workers were involved in the manufacture of goods that were sold outside Weston. The remaining 2 or 3 percent were merchants, teachers, or other professionals.[1]

By 1860, this picture had changed. In that year, only 54 percent of the town's work force was composed of farmers or farm laborers. The percentage of local craftsmen fell from 19 percent to 16 percent, and the number involved in industrial production had risen from 6 percent to 22 percent. The remaining 9 percent of workers in 1860 were servants, teachers, merchants, or professionals. One additional difference between the labor force of 1860 and that of 1840 ought to be noted: Whereas in 1840 almost no women were gainfully employed, by 1860 fully 10 percent of the workers were female.

Clearly, Weston attempted to industrialize. Local men abandoned the farm for the factory, and their wives and daughters, no longer occupied with farm chores, were now able to seek employment to supplement the family income. The days when nearly everyone in Weston was a member of a subsistence-farm family had—for the time being, at least—passed by 1860.

But an examination of employment patterns twenty years later, in 1880, shows that Weston's flirtation with industry did not permanently change the ways that Weston men and women supported themselves. By 1880, the percentage of farmers and farm workers had returned to the 1840 level; in 1880, 71 percent of Weston's laborers fell into this category. On the other hand, only 15 percent were involved in industry. The remaining 14 percent were craftsmen, professionals, or merchants. Weston's inability to compete with large industrial centers like Bridgeport is seen in the declining numbers of industrial workers in town and in the increasing percentage of workers forced to return to the farm. The rise of cities also meant that fewer craftsmen

The Miles Bradley house, built about 1859, on Lyons Plains Road, then known as Bradley Street

could survive in Weston, for items that had previously been produced in town—items as diverse as boots and chains and even clothing—were now being mass-produced in industrial cities and delivered to Weston to meet local needs. By 1880, Weston's attempt to industrialize had collapsed; the fate of that attempt was probably sealed much earlier.

Statistics tell only part of the story. They say little about how the town's attempt at industry influenced the lives of individuals. This can better be seen by looking at the histories of some Weston families.

The Nichols family was prominent in Lyons Plains. In fact, Hanford Nichols not only had the largest farm in that area, he had the biggest and most productive farm in town. Born in 1797, he vastly increased the holdings that he had inherited from his father. During the 1850s, as the spirit of industrialization came to Weston, Nichols converted a saw- and gristmill on his farm to allow for the production of plaster. This operation was continued by his son, Henry, who was also a prosperous farmer. By the 1870s, both the Nichols farm and the Nichols plaster mill had fallen on hard times. Weston farmers were finding it more and more difficult to compete with Middle Western agriculture, and the local plaster mill could not keep up with comparable mills in larger towns. Thus, when Henry's son, Henry H., born in 1856, decided upon a career, he gave up both the family farm and the family mill. He moved to Danbury, where the future seemed brighter, and became a hatter.

One branch of the Gilbert family tells a similar story. Although Nathan Gilbert had been a farmer, his son, also named Nathan, decided that his skill as a shoemaker would provide a more substantial living, and so, during the early 1800s, learned that trade. His son, William, born in 1822, also took up the trade. Like his father, he additionally operated a small farm. But as more and more industrially produced shoes appeared in Weston, William saw his prospects wither. Finally, he decided that he had no future in town and moved to another part of Connecticut to find employment in a wire factory.

The shrinking opportunities that Weston offered can also be seen in the rise and then the fall of wages paid to laborers. In 1850, the average farmhand in town received about forty cents a day in addition to his board. Factory workers earned seventy-five cents a day with board and a dollar a day without. By contrast, a skilled craftsman, such as a carpenter or mason, could make a dollar and a half a day. At that time, the price of board in Weston was about $2.25 per week.

By 1860, the cost of board in Weston had increased only to $2.50, a jump of 11 percent. Yet the average farmhand saw his wages increase between 20 and 33 percent during those years. Factory workers experienced an increase of about 25 percent. Both farm and factory hands were clearly in demand, yet skilled craftsmen saw their wages remain constant. This would lead one to believe that there was little building in Weston about the time of the Civil War. With a stable population, this is hardly surprising.

The increase in wages that occurred during the 1850s evaporated during the 1860s and 1870s. By 1880, Weston workers were earning what they had in 1850, and prices had increased substantially since that earlier time. In fact, the declining demand for labor in Weston meant that Weston wage-earners were making fewer real dollars in 1880 than they had in 1850.

From the perspective of the 1970s, the prices that the residents of nineteenth-century Weston paid for goods and services seem ridiculously low. Nathan B. Johnson, who was a carpenter in Weston between 1840 and 1867, charged a customer only $3.50 for a bedstead and only $42 for twenty-four window frames. Daniel Wheeler, one of the town's blacksmiths during this period, asked only $7 for a brass-top fire shovel and a set of brass-top tongs. David Silliman, who lived in the part of Weston that eventually became Easton, paid $3.12 for a pair of boots in 1840.

But as attractive as these prices seem, the cost of various necessities was not similarly appealing. In 1848, the stores in Weston charged a dollar for a pound of sugar and 88 cents for a pound of tea. Rice was 25 cents a pound and molasses 34 cents a gallon. In other words, a pound of sugar was worth a day's labor and a pound of tea almost that much. A man had to toil for one quarter of a day for a pound of rice and a third of a day for a gallon of molasses. From this perspective, bargains were much less common in nineteenth-century Weston than later generations might like to think. The town's attempt to attract industry brought some temporary increases in wages to the town's workingmen, but those increases were less dramatic than they seem at first and certainly were short-lived.[2]

What increase did occur, occurred because industry did, in fact, come briefly to Weston. Actually, some industry had existed in town since before the American Revolution. As early as that time, Oliver Sanford had begun operating a forge in Valley Forge. No significant industrial development occurred from that time until the 1830s. By then, people in Weston, as in most parts of Connecticut, were aware that they possessed few physical resources and even less capital. Only people were in abundance. The choices that faced Weston residents were to move west and hope to succeed in agriculture in a land where the topsoil was thicker and not choked with rocks; to accept a declining standard of living; or to try to introduce manufacturing and hope that the match took. Weston had an advantage over many Connecticut towns in that it was close to New York City, and from that center Weston's goods could be easily distributed to the southern and interior parts of the United States. Marketing was a general problem for budding manufacturers in Connecticut, but this problem was less severe for manufacturers located near New York.

A tremendous variety of manufactured goods was produced in nineteenth-century Connecticut in general and in Weston in particular. One might argue that Weston specialized in goods produced of iron and steel, but to contend this is to overlook the cigars, horn buttons, shirts, and hats that were also produced in town.

Weston's industry was as flexible as it was varied. The waterpower that was used to produce one item could be used to manufacture a variety of others. Also, the skills necessary to operate one kind of mill were not vastly different from those needed to operate another. The result was that products and owners changed with amazing frequency.

The changes in ownership were also encouraged by the intense competition that existed in American industry at the time. Little capital was required to duplicate the industry that existed in Weston, so only skillful manufacturing methods and intelligent marketing schemes could prevent a competitior from entering the field and gobbling up the market.

These generalizations are borne out by examining Weston's industry and its changes during the mid-nineteenth century. One can also see how quickly industry began to desert Weston for the superior facilities offered by larger towns.

In 1850, there were nine manufacturing establishments in Weston. But to avoid confusing these small nineteenth-century businesses with modern industrial giants, one must keep in mind that all nine of these concerns together employed only forty-three workers. William Bradley and Son, a tanning company, was the town's largest employer in that year. Bradley employed fifteen workers; his average monthly payroll was $270, almost twice as large as that of the second-largest employer. Bradley's capital investment was $6,000, and the business annually produced about $7,000 worth of leather hides. Gershom Bradley, William's cousin, was the town's second-largest employer. Eight men worked for him, and together they earned about $150 a month. Bradley's business, which produced edged tools, was as efficient as any in Weston. With a capital investment of $3,000 in 1850, he was producing $9,000 worth of tools each year.

Charles Crofut manufactured portable mills which could be used to grind a variety of grains. He employed six men and paid them a total of $100 a month. The Bradley and Sanford Forge and the Oliver Sanford Foundry were the largest plants in town. Each involved a capital investment of about $5,000. The forge made bar iron, and the foundry made castings of various types.

The other industries were even smaller affairs, each employing only two workers. These businesses were the Abraham Bradley Company, makers of edged tools; the Charles Whitlock Company, producers of wagon axletrees; Gorham and Winton, spring makers; and David L. Coley, who built planing mills which he sold to local lumber companies. All of these nine businesses relied upon water power except William Bradley and Son, whose tanning business utilized only hand power.

By 1860, the only businesses that were still owned by their 1850

The Bradley Edge Tool Company on the Saugatuck River, about 1910

owners were the edge-tool company of Gershom Bradley and the machine business operated by Charles Crofut, and Crofut had branched out to build shingle machines and straw cutters as well as portable mills. Bradley Hull was now running the forge that Oliver Sanford had headed. All the other 1850 industries had either been absorbed by Gershom Bradley, as in the case of the Abraham Bradley Company, or had collapsed.

In 1860, only five manufacturers existed in Weston, but these five were larger than their fifteen predecessors in terms of total capital invested, total wages paid, and total value of products. In addition to Gershom Bradley, Charles Crofut, and Bradley Hull, Aaron Jelliff and Hanford Nichols operated manufacturing businesses. Jelliff's company produced riddles, sieves, and ox baskets; Nichols ran a plaster mill, as was mentioned earlier. Gershom Bradley's business dominated all others, as is shown by the fact that he employed forty of the fifty-three industrial workers residing in Weston in 1860. The value of goods produced by Bradley in that year was about $45,000; the combined value of the goods produced by the other concerns was only $14,000.

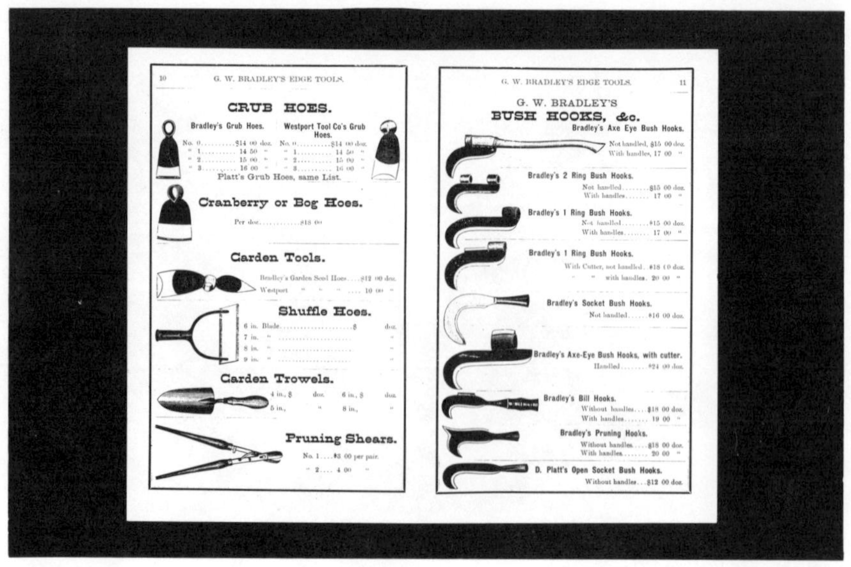

10 G. W. BRADLEY'S EDGE TOOLS.

CRUB HOES.

Bradley's Grub Hoes.

No. 0..........$14 00 doz.
" 1.......... 14 50 "
" 2.......... 15 00 "
" 3.......... 16 00 "

Westport Tool Co's Grub Hoes.

No. 0..........$14 00 doz.
" 1.......... 14 50 "
" 2.......... 15 00 "
" 3.......... 16 00 "

Platt's Grub Hoes, same List.

Cranberry or Bog Hoes.

Per doz............$18 00

Garden Tools.

Bradley's Garden Seed Hoes....$12 00 doz.
Westport " " " .... 10 00 "

Shuffle Hoes.

6 in. Blade......................$ doz.
7 in. " .... "
8 in. " .... "
9 in. " .... "

Garden Trowels.

4 in., $ doz. 6 in., $ doz.
5 in., " 8 in., "

Pruning Shears.

No. 1....$3 00 per pair.
" 2.... 4 00 "

G. W. BRADLEY'S EDGE TOOLS. 11

G. W. BRADLEY'S
BUSH HOOKS, &c.

Bradley's Axe Eye Bush Hooks.

Not handled, $15 00 doz.
With handles, 17 00 "

Bradley's 2 Ring Bush Hooks.

Not handled........$15 00 doz.
With handles........ 17 00 "

Bradley's 1 Ring Bush Hooks.

Not handled........$15 00 doz.
With handles........ 17 00 "

Bradley's 1 Ring Bush Hooks.

With Cutter, not handled..$18 00 doz.
" " with handles. 20 00 "

Bradley's Socket Bush Hooks.

Not handled......$16 00 doz.

Bradley's Axe-Eye Bush Hooks, with cutter.

Handled........$24 00 doz.

Bradley's Bill Hooks.

Without handles....$18 00 doz.
With handles....... 19 00 "

Bradley's Pruning Hooks.

Without handles.....$18 00 doz.
With handles....... 20 00 "

D. Platt's Open Socket Bush Hooks.

Without handles...$12 00 doz.

Merchandise offered for sale in Bradley's catalogue of 1876

In 1870, the Bradley company was still in operation. Miles Bradley now controlled the business, which by this time employed seventy of the eighty-five industrial workers in town. Bradley Hull still ran an iron foundry, and Charles Crofut still produced a variety of small machines. But A. B. Sherwood had taken over the plaster mill from the Nichols family, and Aaron Jelliff's riddle-and-sieve company had moved out of Weston. By 1870, however, two new industries had come to Weston, and an old one had been revived. In that year, T. J. Bennett was producing cigars in town and M. W. Salmon was making horn buttons, while Bennett Bradley had re-established his father's tanning business. These new concerns were not large; Salmon employed four workers, Bennett two, and Bradley only one. For that matter, however, Charles Crofut was down to a single employee, and Bradley Hull and A. B. Sherwood employed only seven workers between them. By 1870, the only Weston concern that could be called thriving was the Bradley Edge Tool Company.

Weston's industry began to shrink drastically after 1870. By 1880, the Bradley company employed only forty men, as opposed to seventy only ten years before. The value of the plant had declined even more rapidly, from $70,000 in 1870 to only $25,000 by 1880. Furthermore, it was now operating only eight months a year instead of

Workers at the Bradley tool factory, in photograph taken about 1910

twelve. Henry B. Wheeler had taken over Bradley Hull's foundry; Platt Keeler was now operating Charles Crofut's business; and Amos G. Judson headed the cigar company that T. J. Bennett had begun. Even the Bradley company had changed hands again. Henry Ogden now ran it. Only Morris W. Salmon, of the leaders of Weston's industry, remained in the position he had held ten years earlier. Fluidity and decline seemed a way of life for Weston's manufacturers.

The extent of the gloom that hung over Weston's industry by 1880 was probably difficult for town residents to perceive. Some figures will vividly point up the dim prospects. In 1850, the capital invested in Weston industry amounted to $26,500. By 1860, this figure had risen to $41,300, and by 1870 to $93,000. But by 1880, it had already fallen to $38,500. The number of persons employed in industry in town followed a similar pattern. Forty-three worked in manufacturing in 1850, fifty-three in 1860, and eighty-five in 1870. But by 1880, the employment figure was back to the 1850 level; only forty-six worked in industry in 1880. Weston's industry did not totally disappear in the next decade, but it would continue to become weaker and weaker until 1900, when it had virtually vanished.

In 1911, a fire destroyed what was left of the Bradley Edge Tool Company. This event signaled the final demise of Weston industry. That the Bradley factory should have persisted to the very end was particularly appropriate in that the Bradley company was the strongest and longest-lived of Weston's industrial concerns. The company was so important that it deserves special attention.

The business was started by Gershom W. Bradley. His father, Wakeman Bradley, had learned the trade of axe-making from David Wakeman of Southport. In 1812, the elder Bradley established a shop in Valley Forge. He was attracted to the region by the fact that the Sanford forge was already there and by the water power that the Saugatuck River provided. Young Gershom was only eight at the time, but he was already expected to assist his father in whatever ways he could. In the process, he learned how axes and other edged tools were made.

In 1834, when he was thirty years old, he bought out a comb factory farther down the Saugatuck and there established a small plant. The tools he made became renowned for their quality, and Bradley prospered. By 1850, his was the most important business in town.

A handsome, clean-shaven man with an intensity about him that demanded the best from his workers, Bradley was an active member of the Methodist church in Westport and a strong supporter of the Whig Party. A craftsman as well as a businessman, he set a high standard of workmanship which he expected his employees to emulate.

When his plant was destroyed by a flood in 1854, Bradley transferred most of his rights in the company to Miles Bradley, his eldest son, and to Miles fell the task of trying to reconstruct the factory. Once it was back in operation, Miles hired his brother-in-law, Henry Ogden, to help run the business. Ogden, whose large frame and enormous sideburns attracted great attention in town, eventually became the manager of the company, running it until 1882, when DeWitt and Gershom W. Bradley took over the company. DeWitt died in 1905; and the following year, Gershom sold out to the Adams and Staples Company. That firm owned the factory at the time it burned, May 1, 1911.

Using steel imported from Norway and England, the company fabricated and ground edged tools. The axes produced there had to run a gantlet of eight series of grindstones. These stones, imported from Nova Scotia, were each eight feet in diameter, and each weighed about two tons. The stones and the imported steel were shipped by boat to Saugatuck and then hauled by oxen to Weston. Obviously, this necessary step cut deeply into the firm's profits. Nevertheless, the

Remains of tool factory in 1911 after disastrous fire which destroyed Weston's largest industry

factory continued to prosper and to expand.

During its heyday, the axe company produced a variety of specialized tools—tools that were used all over the United States. Axes and hatchets were its most important products, and it made a variety of each. It produced seven different patterns of woodcutters' axes, as well as post axes, ice axes, and four patterns of broadaxes. It made shingling hatchets, claw hatchets, broad hatchets, axe hatchets, and lath hatchets. Many of the tools produced by the Bradley company were highly specialized tools that appealed to special markets. They sold a variety of tools used to collect and process turpentine and other such products. They also sold ship carpenters' tools, as well as dozens of specialized devices used by coopers, box makers, and butchers. The company produced a variety of knives and machetes used in sugarcane production and gimlets, samplers, and hooks used by cotton planters. Given the fact that cotton, sugar, and turpentine were all southern products, it is not hard to understand why the Civil War had such disastrous consequences for the edged-tool concern. Fortunately, farm and garden tools remained in demand during the years of the war. Ultimately, the costs of shipping both raw materials and finished products between Saugatuck and Weston put the business at a great disadvantage relative to factories built near railroads. Only

Coley iron foundry, built in the 1880s on the Saugatuck River near the present River Road Bridge, with David and Maren Laura Coley in the foreground

those willing to pay more for a clearly superior product bothered to seek out the Bradley brand. The company's market became smaller and smaller, and its fortunes dwindled.

Gershom Bradley, although the most successful, was not the only industrial innovator in Weston. Morris Salmon spent his early years learning the carpenter's trade, but he did not remain a carpenter long. He bought a horn-button factory in the Lyons Plains section of Weston in the 1860s. The factory had originally been started by Charles Crossman, but it was Salmon who made a success of the venture. Equally successful was David L. Coley. Born of Weston parents who had migrated to Lansingburg, New York, Coley returned to his parents' birthplace and went to work in a sawmill operated by his grandfather, David Coley. (David Coley was actually his maternal grandfather, because David L. Coley's parents were both Coleys, his father being the son of Levi Coley and his mother the daughter of David Coley.) Eventually, David L. opened a machine shop at the site of his grandfather's mill. Here he made a substantial living manufac-

Irving Lockwood with his hay baler – a practical invention but not a commercial success

turing parts for firearms and iron stoves.

At the end of the nineteenth century, I. J. Lockwood of the Upper Parish began producing a hay press that he had invented. The design of the machine was such that "two men, of average weight and strength, with this press can press a 200-lb. bale in less than one minute, exerting a pressure of twelve tons upon the same." The secret of the machine's success was, according to its inventor, "that by a changeable cam when the bale is begun to be pressed a long fulcrum (bait) and notch is used, and when the bale is half pressed then a short fulcrum and short notch is used, by which operation the lifting power of the press is doubled." As convincing as the argument sounded, Lockwood attained neither fame nor fortune by his invention.

Another aspect of Weston's industry deserves mention. William Noyes, son of the town's second minister, organized a small shirt business in town. This particular industry was a cottage industry, the women who made the shirts doing the work in their own homes. These women, like Eunice Coley, for example, bought their supplies from Noyes and then sold to him the finished products. A typical seamstress might make six or eight shirts a month. Some of these were simple cotton or muslin shirts, but others were elaborate, ruffled linen shirts. How much a woman would receive for making a shirt is difficult to determine, because Noyes, who remained in business until the middle of the century, insisted on keeping his books in pounds, shillings, and pence.

But one must be careful not to overstate the importance of industry to Weston. Even when industry was at its height, twice as many Weston workers made their living on the farm as in the factory. In 1878, a visitor to town described Weston as "strictly an agricultural town." Weston's agriculture was always of greater importance than its industry.[3]

Looking back at the history of farming in Weston, one can discern three distinct periods. From the beginnings of settlement down until about 1820 or 1830, the lack of markets forced Weston and its households to be self-sufficient. This period was followed by an era of perhaps two or three decades during which the new manufacturing centers in Connecticut began demanding food from nearby farmers. This caused a brief movement in the direction of commercial farming. Unfortunately, Weston's farmers soon faced intense competition from western agriculture. After the Civil War, railroads had developed to the point where farm goods produced in Ohio and shipped to Bridgeport or New Haven could undersell Weston farm produce. Commercial farming then died in Weston, and the town's farms returned once more to subsistence agriculture, although many farmers continued to produce a small surplus of various items which they then peddled in Bridgeport or Norwalk. Generally, agriculture had returned by 1880 to what it had been in 1800.

Weston's agricultural statistics point up these general trends. For example, in 1850, Weston was just emerging from years of subsistence agriculture. In that year, Weston farmers were still producing a wide range of items that were consumed right on the farm, but some specialization had begun to appear. Hanford Nichols, the plaster-mill owner, was the biggest farmer in town. He owned three hundred acres of improved land, and his farm was estimated to be worth $10,000. Nichols produced a variety of farm goods, but he placed special emphasis on livestock and dairy production. Although he owned only fourteen dairy cows, these animals were of the best bloodlines, were especially valuable, and produced a thousand pounds of butter and 250 pounds of cheese annually. Nichols also slaughtered animals worth $350 in 1850. To accomplish all this, he produced on his farm 400 bushels of corn and 800 bushels of oats, as well as 75 tons of hay. No other farmer in town could match his production in these areas. William O. Sanford of Valley Forge produced a ton of butter, but his production of cheese and meat was considerably smaller than Nichols's. Other important dairy farmers in Weston were David B. Godfrey, David W. Buckley, and Samuel Andrews. These men all sold at least 300 pounds of cheese and between 300 and 700 pounds of butter. Thus, in 1850, there remained the diversification that was typical of subsistence farming, but some farmers at least partially specialized in the production of butter and cheese, both of which could be transported easily to nearby urban centers.

Although figures for 1870 are incomplete, they reveal a continued emphasis on dairy farming and a further tendency toward specialization. In 1870, Gregory Osborn produced 8,500 pounds of milk, while John Sturges and Harry Lockwood each produced more than 5,000 pounds. At the same time, sheep and swine production in the town dropped way off. Weston families were no longer making cloth and were buying pork or doing without rather than producing their own. Between 1860 and 1870, Weston's agriculture became as commercial as it ever would.

By 1880, the trend back in the direction of subsistence farming had clearly begun. Exceptions existed, of course. Eunice Buckley, who operated the most efficient farm in town, produced 600 pounds of butter in 1880, as well as 2,700 pounds of tobacco. Henry Nichols and Gregory Osborn each produced 400 bushels of potatoes, and Joel Terry sold 500 bushels of apples. But even in the case of these last four individuals, Weston farmers were coming to rely more and more on subsistence agriculture and to obtain small amounts of cash by peddling products in the immediate vicinity. Nichols and Osborn peddled potatoes; Terry peddled apples; Horace Fanton peddled eggs and chickens. Others peddled onions.*

What was happening to Weston agriculture can best be seen by looking at the changing size of Weston farms. In 1850, the average farm included 63 acres of improved land; by 1860, this number had increased to almost 75 acres; but by 1880, the number was down to 34 acres. The same thing is obvious in terms of the cash value of Weston farms. In 1850, the average farm was worth about $4,500, in 1860 about $7,200, but in 1880 only about $2,950. Given the inflation that occurred during this period, the decline in value was much greater than it

*Unfortunately, statistics on onion production in nineteenth-century Weston are not available. At one time, onions were a major market crop in Fairfield County. The variety called Southport Globe is still among the most widely cultivated in the country.

appears. Weston farms were getting smaller and poorer. Buildings were less well tended and livestock leaner. Obviously, the outlook for Weston's agriculture was no brighter than that for Weston's industry. It is little wonder, then, that Weston's population began to drop significantly after 1870. Between that date and 1900, the population fell by nearly twenty-five percent while the population of the state generally almost doubled.

The dilemma facing Weston's farmers did not mean, however, that Weston's life was one of want and suffering. Most of those who remained in town led simple but satisfying lives. Farmers of the late nineteenth century resorted to a style of life not vastly different from what their grandparents had known sixty or so years earlier.

Horace B. Coley's life points this up. Although a resident of Westport, he owned a farm that was partially in Weston. Coley had been born in 1839 and had spent many years away from farming before returning to the family homestead in 1874. Much is known about Coley's life, because for years he kept a thorough diary in which he spoke of his farm, his social life, and his convictions.[4]

The diary reveals how much a Weston farmer's life in 1890 or 1895 was like a similar man's life in 1810 or 1820. On November 12, 1895, for example, Coley noted: "got up early & I started for the cider mill 20 minutes past 8 & when I got there 9 teams were ahead of me. I made 162 gallons of cider to day." The same statement could have been made by a Coley a hundred years before. "I had my hogs killed to day by Dykeman & Beers. I paid them $1.50. They done everything," he wrote, as his grandfather might have. Even more common to the late eighteenth century or early nineteenth century was Coley's statement that he "cut up ½ of one hog in the forenoon. In the evening Fred Gray helped me cut up the rest of my pork." In January, 1895, Coley wrote: "In the forenoon I hung up my hams and kept a smoke under them." Also like his ancestors, Coley seemed forever to be taking his oxen to be shod and seemed always eager to be off to the coast for a little fishing: "I & Edgar [his hired man] went down to Cedar point clamming. We had good luck. I got ½ bushel long clams & Edgar got most a ½ bushel of fine round clams. We caught about 7 or 8 fish & got home about 4 oclock." Coley was considerably less enthusiastic about his periodic trips to the sawmill. "After breakfast I went up to Smith's Saw Mill with 3 small logs," he wrote; "I brought home some ash lumber I had at the mill."

But if much that Horace Coley did fell into the old patterns of Weston life, he also did things that his ancestors had never thought of.

James Coley, Jr., with his team of young oxen in the early 1920s

For example, he raised pears, cherries, grapes, cabbage, tomatoes, and onions on his farm. These were crops in which his grandparents had shown almost no interest. In his orchard he grew as many plum trees as he did apple trees; again, this was an idea alien to his forebears.

Much of what Horace Coley did differently he did because of changes in agricultural technology. He baled his straw and hay; his grandfather had never heard of a hay press. Coley's son, Henry, had a windmill that he used to bring water to his home and barn; windmills—at least, prefabricated, steel ones—were new to Connecticut. Horace Coley even insured some of his livestock. He insured his oxen for $80 each. Certainly, insurance for stock was part of the new world in which he lived.

Many of the changes in his life came about because he was a peddler as well as a farmer. This role was a new one for the residents of the Weston area. In 1800 or 1820, Weston farmers did not peddle goods to Norwalk or Bridgeport, because both towns were then themselves self-sufficient. This was not true in 1895 or 1900. Thus, on June 13, 1895, Coley took to Norwalk 50 gallons of cider, which he sold for fifteen cents a gallon. Usually the items he sold were more varied. On January 4 of that year, he sold one fowl, a dozen bunches of celery, two bushels of potatoes, two dozen pickles, a half-bushel of onions, three-fourths of a bushel of apples, and two dozen eggs. For all these items and for a day spent in traveling to and from Norwalk, he received $5.34. This was a typical peddling day for Coley. On September 19, 1895, he managed to sell three and a half bushels of potatoes, four quarts of canned white onions, three heads of cabbage, one half-bushel of pears, nineteen pounds of grapes, a half-bushel each of apples and corn, five pounds of butter, and six dozen eggs. From this he brought home $6.60. Obviously, what Coley and his neighbors were doing was operating subsistence farms and selling what they did not consume at home.

A Weston farmer's life was not without pain and pleasure, and sometimes the two ingredients were so thoroughly mixed as to make it impossible to determine where one ended and the other began. David Silliman did not know whether to laugh or cry over a certain "broken horn cow" which seemed the object of his constant attention. The cow apparently had a sexual appetite that knew no limits. "Took broken horn cow to E. Sanford's Bull," he noted in his diary. "She came back hotter than ever." Several years later, Silliman was doing all that he could to satiate her needs: "drove the broken horn cow to bull, but expect to drive her again."[5]

Like Weston's agriculture, the institution of the family as it existed in town went through some important changes around the middle of the century but then returned to familiar patterns. The most important changes resulted from the town's brief flirtation with industry. During this period, the demand for factory labor increased and the obligations that had traditionally fallen on farm women were relieved. The coincidence of these two events brought relatively large numbers of women into the work force. George Fitch was a craftsman; this allowed his daughter, Phoebe, who was nineteen in 1860, to make shirts for William Noyes rather than devote her time to farm chores. Stephen Olmsted was a laborer at the Bradley factory. His two daughters, Sarah and Mary, both worked for Noyes. Morris Bradley was a skilled worker, but his daughter, Julia, made shirts. Whitmore Nichols worked as a skilled factory hand, and his daughter also made shirts. The idea of having women gainfully employed was new to Weston. But when employment opportunities began to dry up toward the latter third of the century, women returned to their traditional roles within the home.

With the exception of this brief aberration, the structure of the family changed little during the nineteenth century. Households within the town remained nuclear; that is: consisted of husband, wife, and offspring. Family size also remained constant, each family including five or six children. Men and women were marrying slightly earlier, the typical first marriage occurring when the groom was twenty-one and the bride nineteen. But even this change was subtle, and the family remained a healthy institution.

Physically, the community also enjoyed health. The chances that an individual would survive childhood greatly increased, and among those who reached adulthood, most men could count on living well into their sixties and most women until nearly seventy. Consumption and old age seemed to be the biggest causes of death.

During the half-century that began in 1876 and ended in 1926, Dr. Frank Gorham looked after the health of Weston residents. The son of George M. Gorham, who operated a general store just north of Valley Forge, Frank Gorham was born in 1852 and graduated from Yale Medical School in 1876. He remained in Weston throughout his life. His wife, Fannie Salmon Gorham, was the daughter of Morris Salmon, the button manufacturer.

As conscientious as Gorham was, town residents continued to rely upon a variety of home remedies. David Silliman believed that one of the best antidotes for a cold consisted of one tablespoon of molasses, two teaspoons of castor oil, one teaspoon of paregoric, and one of spirits of camphor. These ingredients were to be mixed together, and Silliman urged that the concoction be "taken often." Silliman also had a solution to a problem more common than the common cold. He designed a device "to allow an old man to pass water without getting out of bed in the dead of winter." He recommended his invention to a friend and suggested that, if he would start manufacturing it, he "would oblige a number of old people."[6]

But despite Silliman's ingenuity and Dr. Gorham's skills, Weston residents of the nineteenth century had to live in a world where medicine was a much less precise science than it is today, and they more frequently had to face situations over which physicians and medicine had no control. Horace Coley, in his diary, told the story of the passing of an elderly aunt. She had been ill for several days when, on August 25, 1895, he noted that she "is much the same yesterday-is failing." Three days later, Coley recorded that his aunt "had a poor turn ½ past 10 last night. This morning is very much worse. She hardly knows us this morning. I think she is struck with death. 1 p.m.

She is failing. 4 p.m. She cannot swallow & can take no medicine. I got up ½ past 10 & was with her until 4 a.m. next morning. It does seem as if she could not live but a short time."[7]

The following day, she was still alive, much to the amazement of her nephew. "It seems as if every hour would end her sufferings, but she is breathing yet," he wrote. At eleven that morning, Dr. Gorham arrived and announced that "she cannot live long." She died at two that same afternoon. On the day of her burial, Coley wrote: "This is a sad day with us. How lonesome we shall be. Death enters and there's no defense." In those days, there were many fewer defenses against unexpected death than there are today. Yet medical practice had made significant advances since the time Weston had become a town.

The same could not be said about the educational system in Weston. It remained a system that offered, at best, only the very basic elements of culture. The school districts, which had replaced the original school societies, managed the individual schools even after 1856, when the town assumed general responsibility for the education system. At that time, six schools existed in town; in 1857, a seventh was added, the Valley Forge School. But as the town's population declined, the school population fell correspondingly. In 1870, the Kettle Creek School, which had an enrollment of five, closed. The town closed the Den School in 1889. The other five schools remained in existence for many years, although all lost population except the Upper Parish School, which had as many students in 1890 as it had had in 1858. The Valley Forge School was so much smaller than the others that its appropriation was each year smaller than the other four. In 1909, the school districts were abolished, and the town took over direct responsibility for the schools.

All of these administrative changes made no difference in the type of education that Weston gave its children. One-room schoolhouses were still the order of the day, and a single teacher had responsibility for students of all ages. The education system continued to place little emphasis on things intellectual. The rules which governed the schools' operations certainly demanded that more time and consideration be given other matters. For example, these rules insisted that the Bible be read twice each day by students, the teacher to correct "pronunciation, emphasis, and pauses." Spelling exercises were held daily, and instruction in catechism came at least once a week. Teachers were to give their charges frequent moral lessons and "to inspect the conduct of the children in all their behavior & teach them to conduct properly in every respect." The teachers, who had to be at least eighteen, were to conclude each day with a prayer. The major function of the schools seemed to be to teach godliness and obedience.[8]

The schools received funds from several sources; from tuitions before 1856, from the state, from town taxes, from federal funds deposited with the town, and from the Staples endowment. This fund had been established, the reader will recall, in accordance with the will of Samuel Staples, a resident of North Fairfield (later Easton). The trust fund which he established was to be used to pay the school tuitions of poor children from North Fairfield and Norfield. When, in 1856, tuition charges were abandoned, the fund came to be used as a general school fund, and the income was divided between Weston and Easton in proportion to the number of schoolchildren in each town.

Weston's indifference to education was reflected in the salaries paid to its teachers. In 1880, the average salary paid to a male teacher in town was $21.96 a month; the average female teacher received only $18.61 a month. What these figures meant can be seen by looking at the average salaries paid in nearby Norwalk. There the average male teacher made $77.25 a month and the average female $41.77. Yet surprisingly, Weston attracted able and dedicated teachers. Among the most able was Vanderbilt Godfrey. Born in town in 1853 and educated at the local schools and at the Staples Academy, Godfrey taught for twenty years in Weston before retiring to a life of farming. His relaxed manner and his devotion to education made him a favorite with Weston scholars.

In addition to the town schools, there existed a private academy in Weston. This was the Weston Boarding School, founded in 1835 by Matthew Bulkley but operated for many years by his son-in-law, Andrew Sanford Jarvis. Most of the school's students came from New York; they pursued either a classical or a business curriculum. Jarvis claimed that "special attention is given to English Composition," and he was equally proud of the school library, which, he maintained, was "designed to allure boys from idleness and useless reading, by presenting books which shall be at once valuable and entertaining." The school was "military in organization and regulations." The state of Connecticut provided the students "with regulation muskets, drums, and other appurtenances." Uniforms, however, "which are required of all for dress suit, may be obtained at Brooks Bros., Catherine and Cherry Streets, New York City."

The school accepted fifty students a year, each of whom paid $200 for tuition, board, laundry, fuel, and lights. These fifty students rose

The Weston Boarding School, seen here in an 1880 engraving, offered military training from 1835 to 1888.

each morning at 5:30, were at breakfast at 6:00, studied from 7:00 until 8:00, and then drilled and prepared for inspection. School hours were from 9:00 until noon and from 1:15 until 4:15. After dinner came battalion drill, study time, and taps.

The school prospered until after the Civil War, but by 1875 had fallen on hard times and by 1888 had closed. The reasons for the academy's sudden decline and collapse are unclear, but apparently Andrew Jarvis's fondness for alcohol was a major factor. The buildings—which consisted of a dwelling house,* dormitory, school building "fitted up with Paton's Patent School Furniture," and gymnasium complete with bowling alleys—sat empty in the center of Weston, a haven for youngsters in search of places to play.[9]

During the nineteenth century, the Norfield church also knew hard times. Church membership and church attendance were both down. This resulted from a trend that had begun many years before, when,

*This building, now restored, is a cornerstone of Weston's first historic district, the Norfield District. A second historic district, the Kettle Creek District, includes houses on the Weston Road, River Road, and Broad Street.

Original section of the boarding school, at Norfield Corners, is in Weston's first historic district.

during the era of the American Revolution, Weston men and women had begun to lose interest in church affairs. By the time of the Civil War, probably a third of Weston's population never bothered to attend church and another significant group was attending a church of another denomination, the Methodist church in Westport or perhaps the new Episcopal church in Lyons Plains. The decline of the Norfield church was apparent in the rapid turnover in pastors. Between 1841 and 1915, nineteen different men served that pulpit, each averaging fewer than four years at the post. This contrasts with the fact that two men held that same position during the first eighty years of the church's history.

The church's weakness was also seen in the frequent disputes that racked the congregation. The most important of these came in 1898, when the Norfield church summoned a Mutual Council, a group made up of pastors and delegates of area Congregational churches. "Differences and disagreements having arisen within this Church . . . which difficulties and disagreements disturb our peace and harmony . . ." began the summons to the Council. After long deliber-

The Treadwell homestead in Lyons Plains, seen in 1896 photograph

ation, the Council recommended that the pastor, C. M. Arthur, be discharged, "that the Church amend its Standing Rules so far as to make them conform to . . . approved Congregational usage," and that "all the members lay aside all bitterness and strife, and seek, from this time on, to live in all charity and mutual helpfulness, as becomes the Gospel of Christ." Obviously, the kind of rancor that forced the calling of such a council could not be legislated out of existence.

A dispute in the Episcopal Society resulted in the establishment of the Emmanuel church at Lyons Plains. This dispute, which began back before the separation of Easton and Weston, was over the location of the new church building which the Episcopalians planned to construct. Everyone in the church agreed upon the need for a new building, but some members of the congregation from the Lyons Plains area were determined to see the church moved there. Hanford Nichols and Walter Treadwell, two of Weston's most prosperous and—as it turned out—most determined residents, led the faction that hoped to move the church. North Fairfield church members bitterly opposed the move, claiming that the church was an integral part of that community.

Nichols and Treadwell refused to await the outcome of long-winded debates and on their own initiative began the construction of a church building on Nichols's property. By 1846, the year after North Fairfield became Easton, the church was completed, David P. Tomlinson had accepted the post of minister, and the Lyons Plains group had brought suit in Superior Court against the Easton group, requesting to be recognized as the legitimate descendant of the older church and to be granted the records and a share of the treasury of the Easton church. Church members from Easton resisted Nichols, Treadwell, and their supporters, refusing to surrender without a fight.

Finally, the dispute was heard by three impartial arbiters, Joshua B. Ferris, Cyrus H. Beardsley, and Henry Dutton. The arbiters decided that Emmanuel church should be recognized as a legitimate offspring of the older congregation and ordered that half the parish money and two-fifths of the building subscriptions be paid to the Lyons Plains group. Thus, Weston's second church came into being, thanks in large measure to the tenacity of Hanford Nichols and Walter Treadwell.

Much of the social life of nineteenth-century Weston centered around the two churches. Church socials and dinners as well as Sunday-school picnics and temperance meetings provided diversion from the routine of life. Whereas Christmas had been ignored during Weston's early history, when the Protestant townspeople thought the celebration of that holiday smacked too much of Catholicism, by the time of the Civil War, Weston did honor that day.* Typically, the families from each of the churches would gather at their church, where a Christmas tree was raised. It was here that small gifts would be given and received, the congregation as a whole providing for those unable to participate themselves. After the gifts were distributed, the families would return home to entertain friends and relatives.

Fortunately, many of the details of nineteenth-century Weston's social life are known because of a diary kept by a young lady during that period. Owned by the Weston Historical Society, the diary tells of the activities of a young woman from a well-to-do family in town; her name was Fanny H. Coley.[10]

Parties were a regular part of her life. On September 10, 1866, she attended a "maskerade party" in Weston. It must have been a grand affair, for musicians were hired from Bridgeport, and the party lasted

---

*The observance of Christmas had been outlawed by the Puritan government of England in 1643, and the early colonists of New England incorporated this restriction in their own statutes. The New Haven Colony even forbade the making of mince pies.

until 2:00 A.M. Her party-going was not limited to town. During the previous February, she went to Greenfield Hill to attend a party at Carrie Milbank's. She wrote that she "had a very nice time, had babelows & Sherrades & Music & Dancing. Got home about 3 oclock in the morning."

Other activities also occupied her time. During the spring of 1866, she mentioned going to Norfield to a band concert. From the context of her remarks, it seems that these must have been regular events. She and her sister took music lessons, and her whole family took dancing lessons. Apparently, the dancing school was an itinerant school which spent a month or so in town before moving on. On May 8, 1866, she wrote that "Father & Mother & I & Ella have been down to the Dancing School. . . . Had a gay Time I can tell you." At the end of the month, she noted that she went to the last dancing class. "We had a splendid time nice refreshments a grate many there."

For the women of prosperous families, life seemed to be a constant round of visits. The young diarist noted daily calls at friends' homes. At times, the visits were strictly social, but on other occasions, the visits also involved work for some charitable organizations. Women gathered together to make items for church fairs, for missionaries serving abroad, and, during the Civil War, for soldiers in the field. Especially active with such charitable organizations was Delia A. Jelliff, who lived in Georgetown. The daughter of Elijah Gregory, a shoemaker and farmer, Mrs. Jelliff was married to Aaron Jelliff, who operated the sieve-and-riddle factory. From this enterprise he went into the wire business. While her husband pursued his business interests, she busied herself with work with the town's benevolent societies.

Jury duty appears to have been a pleasant diversion for the town's male population. H. B. Coley considered it an honor, although an inconvenience, to be summoned for jury duty in Bridgeport. He took his work on the jury seriously. In 1893, he served on a murder jury. "I feel as if I was in a very responsible position," he confessed to his diary. After the evidence was in, Coley decided the defendant, one Florence Hawley of Bridgeport, was innocent. His fellow jurors agreed, and the prisoner was acquitted.[11]

The population of nineteenth-century Weston was more mobile than the generations that preceded it. The Danbury Fair was an event that many Weston people anticipated. "There was lots of things to be seen & there was 2 good races in the afternoon," noted Coley. Phineas T. Barnum made circus day in Bridgeport another important day on

Weston calendars,* and at least one Weston resident, Henry Coley, traveled all the way to Chicago for the 1893 World's Fair and another, Fanny H. Coley, to the Philadelphia Centennial 1876.[12]

But for the most part, entertainment had to be found nearer home. The Weston Grange, which was founded in 1896, was established both to educate local farmers to deal with their economic problems and to provide recreation for local families. Many of the old pastimes continued to delight Weston's population. Sleighing was as popular in 1895 as it had been in 1795, and it was as popular with men as with women. Fishing and clamming also continued to be popular pastimes. In these, as in so many other respects, life in Weston remained little changed.

The structure of Weston's society was also stable. No one in town was extraordinarily wealthy, although during the mid-nineteenth century a prosperous group of small industrialists and efficient farmers lived in town. In 1860, John Crossman of Lyons Plains owned between six and seven times as much property as did the typical town resident. David D. Coley owned about three times as much as an average neighbor. Samuel Rowland, who lived across the road from the Norfield church, was the wealthiest man in town; he owned about ten times as much property as his fellow townsmen. Most of the wealthy men in town, even during the height of the industrial period, were farmers. The important exceptions would be Gershom and Miles Bradley. Weston's well-to-do could afford substantial homes, fashionable if not elegant furnishings, and in many cases servants to help maintain their establishments. The well-to-do were not, however, a special class. They were a more prosperous version of their neighbors; they shared the same economic interests as their neighbors; their existence did not disrupt the economic homogeneity that existed in Weston.

But as the century progressed and as the town's prosperity declined, so also did the fortunes of this group. By 1900, few Weston families could be described as prosperous. Throughout the town's history, a disproportionately small element of the population had controlled a disproportionately large part of the property in town. As Weston's economic fortunes sank, this situation changed, and the more prosperous either moved on or settled into the great mass of the population

*During the early twentieth century, the Barnum circus wintered horses on the Weston farm of Andrew Gustafson, the grandfather of town clerk Gertrude Walker. The farm was at the corner of Whippoorwill Lane and the Georgetown Road.

that lacked few essentials but which rarely enjoyed the feeling of having either cash on hand or money in the bank.

At either end of the nineteenth century, few Weston residents owned no property at all. But during the middle of the century, when industry was at its strongest, many industrial workers owned little or no property; they lived in rented houses or in company dormitories. Wages were high, and these workers lived on their wages. When industry collapsed, these men left, thus never becoming charges of the town. The town never supported more than eight paupers at any one time; thus, the propertyless clearly found work elsewhere.

There had always been some poor in Weston, but not many. In 1831, the town abandoned the poorhouse that it had operated with Fairfield and Wilton and adopted a policy of "letting out" its poor; that is: boarding the paupers with some town resident. Because there were so few indigent persons in town, this was not a complicated or expensive process. In 1880, for example, there were only five persons living "on the town." They were a widow and her three children and the town drunk.

By the close of the nineteenth century, Weston had become a single-class society. Poor and rich persons were almost unknown. Almost everyone belonged to a propertied class that was wealthier in land than in money.

Concern over the poor, although there were few of them, occupied a great deal of the town's time. Weston was less concerned over other social issues. Temperance was such a question. It attracted only passing attention. On January 15, 1840, the town voted "that no one be allowed to retail spirituous liquors within this town for the year ensuing." Apparently, this motion passed in the heat of the moment, for cooler heads prevailed at the next town meeting. On January 16, 1841, the town decided "that all persons living within this town have the privilege of retailing wine or spirituous liquors—provided they keep no disorderly houses or shops wherein said liquors may be sold by any person or persons, so as not to violate the peace and be of evil example."[13]

The town's indifference to the temperance movement was matched by its lack of concern over the antislavery question. There was no early abolitionist society in Weston and no abolitionist leader there comparable to William Wakeman of Wilton. The small black population in Weston lived in an area called Little Egypt, a section along the Easton-Weston border. At the time of the Civil War, about fifty blacks resided there, about half of whom were residents of Weston.

The town's indifference to the slavery question is made clear by the way the town voted in the presidential election of 1860. In that year, the voters could select from four candidates: Abraham Lincoln, the Republican candidate and an opponent of slavery; Stephen A. Douglas, the northern Democratic candidate; John C. Breckinridge, a southern Democrat sympathetic to slavery; and John Bell, the Constitutional Party candidate. Weston gave fifty-five votes to Lincoln, two votes to Bell, one vote to Douglas, and ninety-nine votes to Breckinridge. Clearly, Weston was hardly a bastion of abolitionist feeling.

But the town's indifference to slavery did not mean that the town was unwilling to support the Civil War when it came in 1861. During the early months of the war, Weston men enlisted eagerly. If they were not enlisting to fight against slavery, then one must wonder what explained their enthusiasm. What made them willing to endure horrendous food, terrifying hospital conditions, and incompetent officers? What prompted them to opt for exhausting marches and camp conditions that defied even the most fundamental rules of hygiene?

Apparently, the service offered the young men of Weston the opportunity to escape the drudgery of the farm and the mill. Life in the mill meant long hours and small wages, and the physical demands and physical dangers of the army were greater than those found in the mill—but not significantly greater. Factory work was hard work, and industrial accidents were as common as flywheels in nineteenth-century mills. Farm work was hardly more attractive. Spring, summer, and fall were times of unending labor, and life in the winter was bleak and uncomfortable.[14]

In addition to the physical demands of their work, the lives of Weston's young men were also restrictive beyond the imagination of the twentieth century. Travel to the outside world was rare. The social life provided by the church was designed for the married and the sedate, not the young and the reckless.

The chance to go to war was a chance to escape all this, was a chance to see the world—or, at least, more of it—and to experience some of what that broader world had to offer. Little wonder that Weston men enlisted, and little wonder, as well, that once the war was over, they remembered the glory and excitement and companionship of their experience and forgot the horrors of the years in service.

Weston men served in a variety of units during the Civil War. They served in the First Connecticut Cavalry, the First and Second Connecticut Artillery, and the Fifth, Eighth, Ninth, Eleventh, Twelfth, Thir-

David Dimon Coley (1811-1894) and his wife, Mary E. Andrews Coley

teenth, Fifteenth, Seventeenth, Twenty-third, Twenty-ninth, and Thirtieth Connecticut Regiments, the last two units being units composed of black troops. The vast bulk of Weston's soldiers served in the Fifth, Seventeenth, and Twenty-third Regiments, and far more served in the Twenty-third than in any other.

The history of the Twenty-third was, unfortunately, not very exciting. Numbering twenty-one Weston men among its ranks, the unit was organized in September of 1862 and was recruited from Fairfield and New Haven counties. The regiment rendezvoused at Camp Terry in New Haven, where it remained until November before moving to Camp Buckingham on Long Island. From that post the regiment proceeded to New Orleans, arriving there in late December. In Louisiana, the regiment, at the time commanded by Colonel Charles E. L. Holmes of Waterbury, was assigned the task of guarding the New Orleans and Opelousas Railroad, which connected Algiers and Brashear City, Louisiana. The only significant engagement involving the Twenty-third came on June 2, 1863, when the Confederates attacked the railroad and captured large quantities of supplies stored at Brashear City. The regiment was mustered out on August 31, 1863.

Twelve men from Weston served in the Seventeenth. Commanded by Colonel William H. Noble of Bridgeport, the Seventeenth fought well at Chancellorsville and Gettysburg before being sent to Jacksonville, Florida, to perform picket and fatigue duty. At Gettysburg, the Seventeenth held a stone wall on Cemetery Hill near the entrance of Gettysburg Cemetery. The Connecticut Fifth was also at Chancellorsville and Gettysburg, although only as reserves. Including nine men from Weston, this regiment accompanied General William Tecumseh Sherman on his march through Georgia. Colonel Orris S. Ferry of Norwalk commanded the Fifth.

In all, seventy-eight men claiming Weston as their residence served in the Civil War. Of these, about half were really Weston men and the others were substitutes hired by Weston residents or by the town itself. Most of the Weston men who were enthusiastic about serving enlisted in 1861 or 1862. During the last three years of the war, enthusiasm dwindled, and few Weston men joined.

Actually, in August of 1862, the town began to pay bounties to encourage enlistments. It would pay $125 to a married enlistee and $100 to a single man. The town had to borrow $3,000 to provide these bounties. In 1863, the town voted to offer $300 to each man conscripted, to be used as a bounty for serving, to pay a substitute, or to pay for exemption. This required the town to borrow an additional $8,000 and also to hire an agent to procure substitutes. In 1864, another $14,000 had to be borrowed, thus leaving the town facing bonded indebtness at the end of the war.

The man who spent most of this money and who had the task of finding soldiers to fill the town's quota was David D. Coley. The son of Eliphalet Coley, he was born in Weston in 1811. Coley operated a machine shop in addition to his farm, yet still had time to serve as a town selectman year after year. Probably this dark, heavy-featured man did more than anyone else in Weston to support the Civil War. It was men like Coley, working in hundreds of small towns, who kept the ranks of the Union army filled.

Other Weston civilians were involved in the war effort. Weston women formed themselves into a soldiers' aid society and met to roll bandages, to knit stockings and mittens, and to prepare preserves. At Thanksgiving and Christmas, the women created special delicacies for the men in service. During the winter of 1863-1864, scurvy became epidemic among the Union troops. The Army Medical Corps dispatched desperate pleas for fresh vegetables, and the farmers of Weston responded generously. Within ten days, over 700 barrels of vegetables were shipped from Bridgeport. Much of this stock came from the larders of Weston farmhouses.

But as well as Weston responded to the war, the town was never enthusiastic about President Lincoln. In 1864, Lincoln won Connecticut handily, but Weston voted for his opponent, General George McClellan. Supporting the war was the townspeople's patriotic duty as they saw it; they felt no similar obligation to Lincoln.

The war played havoc with the town's finances, but soon the selectmen had things back to normal. A typical town budget in the late nineteenth century involved the expenditure of about $1,200. (Thus, the debt produced during the war amounted to approximately the cost of operating the town for twenty years; the fact that all these moneys were repaid in slightly more than a decade is a real testimonial to the frugality of the town fathers.) Of this sum, approximately $1,100 went as wages to the town's schoolteachers, about $75 for fuel for the schools, and the remaining $25 for incidental expenses.

Funds came into the town from a variety of sources. The state paid about $500 annually toward the education of Weston children, and a like amount was collected as the town tax. Money also came to the town from the Staples Fund and the Town Deposit Fund. The Town Deposit Fund came from surplus funds in the United States Treasury which had been deposited with the several states in 1836 and which Connecticut passed on to the individual towns. On January 28, 1837, Weston accepted the fund and decided to lend out the money in the form of mortgages. In 1841, the first step toward the dissipation of this fund was taken when the town meeting itself decided to borrow $1,150 from it. When Easton and Weston separated, the fund was divided, Weston receiving about $3,000 and Easton slightly more than $4,000. During the Civil War and the financial crisis produced by it, the town consumed what was left of this money.

As the nineteenth century progressed, Weston became more democratic. This is not to say that many men had been denied the franchise during earlier years, but rather it is to say that more options became available to Weston voters, and they took advantage of these options. Weston was no longer thoroughly Congregational, thoroughly agrarian, nor thoroughly of English stock. Methodists, Episcopalians, even Catholics now lived in Weston. A fairly large group of Irish resided in town, and some men worked as factory hands or as budding industrialists. The result of all this was that differences among the people began to appear. What was good for local farmers was not necessarily good for factory workers; the interests of Episcopalians and Congregationalists did not always coincide. What had been a political system based upon consenus between people of similar interests became a system of pluralistic democracy.

Town meetings became more interesting. Even the method of voting for town officers had to be altered to accommodate the changing circumstances. Whereas town officers had been selected by acclamation during the town's early years, by 1838 enough outspoken differences existed to require that the town clerk and selectmen be chosen by ballot. By 1857, the town decided to choose school Visitors by ballot, and in 1866 agreed to use ballots in the selection of all officers.

The increasing interest in town business prompted the town to hold all its meetings at a single location. Before the 1870s, the town meeting was held at various places, but after that date the meetings were held at the schoolhouse of the Middle School District, which was adjacent to the Norfield Church. In 1883, the town decided to construct a town hall. It was built behind the church on land given the town by Thaddeus Burr nearly a century before. The building was ready for the annual town meeting of 1884. Three years later, the town authorized the Church Society to hold its meeting in the building, and in 1910 agreed to allow the church and Grange to enlarge the hall and to use it for their meetings.

The items that seemed to attract most of the town meeting's attention were roads, boundaries, schools, and regulations governing the grazing of livestock. The schools, then as now, were the largest item in the town budget, so it is hardly surprising that they would receive considerable attention. The only controversy that touched the schools was over the relative appropriation to each school, and even this was fairly easily resolved, because the appropriation was tied to school population. The question of highway maintenance was a problem, because the town still depended upon its citizens to keep the roads passable. Many of Weston's citizens lacked enthusiasm for this work, and so the roads suffered. By 1851, both the Northfield and the Newtown and Norwalk turnpikes, which roughly followed the courses of the Saugatuck River and its West Branch, respectively, had been made public roads. As such, they suffered the same inattention that other town roads endured. Only the threat of a suit by the State Attorney convinced the town it should maintain the former Northfield Turnpike.

At various times during the century, Weston was involved in minor boundary disputes with Redding, Wilton, and the recently established (1836) town of Westport. A great deal of heat was inevitably the result of these disputes, but they certainly did not alter the town's history. Neither did the fact that horses, sheep, swine, and geese were allowed to roam the public highways. But this does point up the essentially rural character of the town throughout these years.

Clearly, the most important political issue faced by nineteenth-century Weston was the separation of Easton and Weston. This issue had been developing for many years before it reached a climax. In fact, as early as February of 1818, the Weston town meeting voted to petition the General Assembly to divide the town, but this decision was reversed by the meeting the following month. In 1824, 1840, and 1844, the question again arose but was rejected. In each of these instances, the voters from what is presently Weston advocated separation and those from what is now Easton opposed the idea. David C. Salmon and Levi Coley were the driving forces behind separation.

Why the former Norfield parish wanted to separate from North Fairfield is obvious. North Fairfield dominated the town government of Weston. Most of the important officeholders were from North Fairfield. Town meetings were normally held in North Fairfield. This had been true from the beginnings of the town. The marriage of the two parishes was hardly a natural one, and the marriage never really took. North Fairfield was more populous and wealthier—although not by much—than Norfield, and by the mid-1840s, Norfield men and women were tired of being dominated by their neighbors to the east.

Weston's move for separation succeeded on April 29, 1845, when the town meeting voted that "the Hon. Legislature be requested to grant the Prayer of the Petitioners for the division of the town of Weston varying the line of the mile of Common at the lower end so as when said line strikes the Aspetuck River to follow the same to Fairfield." The meeting then appointed two agents, Matthew Bulkley and John Edwards, to work for the adoption of the petition and granted to them "full power to employ Counsel, summon witnesses and do all that is necessary and proper to further the prayer of the petitioners."[15]

At its May, 1845, session, the General Assembly agreed to separate Weston into the towns of Weston and Easton and granted both "all the powers, privileges and immunities now enjoyed by the town of Weston" except that the towns were to have the right of sending only one legislator each to the legislature. On June 23, 1845, the first town meeting of the new town of Weston gathered and voted David Patchen, Joseph Rowland, and Hanford Nichols selectmen; Matthew Bulkley town clerk; and William Noyes town treasurer. The meeting having ended, the people of the town marched to a tract of land just below the home of Willis Banks; there a great celebration was held. A

Valley Forge School in the late 1800s

special song had been written for the occasion:

Old Weston is no longer one.
The town has been divided.
The people asked – the deed was done.
The law has so decided.

Once the singing and a series of long-winded speeches ended, the tables were "loaded with the good old style of cooking and plenty of it."[16]

The separation was simple, but not so simple that a few minor difficulties did not develop. Easton, later in 1845, challenged Weston's right to be called Weston and also challenged Weston's control of the town's ancient records. Both challenges were denied, and the break was finally complete; two towns existed where there had been one.

The years between 1830 and 1900 were years of both change and stability. Change took many forms. New ideas and new people came to Weston; the old town was divided; industry arrived; agriculture went through several changes. But despite all of this, Weston, in 1900, retained many of its old ways. Industry had all but died; agriculture was back to the subsistence level; the family, the basic institution of Weston society, functioned essentially as it had; and the rural innocence and narrow convention that had been so evident during earlier times remained an integral part of Weston's life.

If a time warp would allow twentieth-century people to go back to the Weston of seventy or eighty years ago, these modern men and women might well encounter H. B. Coley driving his team to Gould's Mill on a cold December day with a wagon full of corn and rye. At the mill, he would line up to have his meal ground and then make his way back to his farm to finish his chores. And if a further miracle took these twentieth-century visitors back another century, they could not help but see how much Coley's existence was like that of Weston men and women of that earlier age.

NOTES TO CHAPTER 11

1. The statistics used in this chapter were derived from the United States censuses of 1840, 1850, 1860, 1870, and 1880. The census returns for Connecticut are located in the Connecticut State Library, Hartford.

2. The price of goods and services in nineteenth-century Weston were obtained from the account books of Nathan B. Johnson, 1840-1867; Daniel Wheeler, 1817-1839; David Silliman, 1834-1853, all in the Connecticut State Library; and of William Noyes, 1846-1873, in the New Canaan Historical Society.

3. Duane H. Hurd, *History of Fairfield County* (New York, 1878), p. 805.

4. The diaries of H. B. Coley are in the possession of the Weston Historical Society. Because of Coley's irregular pagination, citations are indicated by date of entry, and the date is indicated in the text when possible. See entries of January 5, 12, May 28, 30, 1895. Mrs. Cleora Coley of Weston also owns an H. B. Coley diary.

5. Entries of June, 1834, and June 18, 1836, David Silliman Day Books, Connecticut State Library.

6. Entries of November 3, 1851, and September 4, 1853, in ibid.

7. Entries of August 25, 28, 29, 30, 31, 1895, in H. B. Coley diary.

8. Rules for Schools, Noyes Collection, Box 50, New Canaan Historical Society.

9. *Annual Catalogue of the Officers and Scholars of the Weston Boarding School* (Hudson, New York, 1869). In Weston Historical Society.

10. Fanny H. Coley's diary is owned by the Weston Historical Society. Citations are by date. See February 28, April 26, and May 8, 1866. Other Fanny H. Coley papers are in the hands of Mrs. Cleora Coley of Weston.

11. Entry of October 25, 1893, in H. B. Coley Diary.

12. Entry of October 10, 1895, in ibid.

13. Weston Town Records, Town Meeting Minutes, II, 74.

14. John Niven developed these ideas in his thoughtful book *Connecticut for the Union: The Role of the State in the Civil War* (New Haven, 1965).

15. Weston Town Records, Town Meeting Minutes, II, 94, 95.

16. Ibid., 107-110; Carrie Bradley Manuscript, Weston Historical Society.

NEW FACES, NEW VOICES IN THE TWENTIETH CENTURY 1900 to World War II

"A haven for artists, writers, and musicians"

The twentieth century was late in arriving in Weston. The ways of the nineteenth century maintained their hold nearly three decades beyond 1900 but then suddenly disappeared in the flurry of change that came in the 1930s.[1]

The persistence of the nineteenth century could be seen in virtually all areas of life. Weston farmers still plowed with oxen; they still grew rye, which they took to local mills, like Gould's on Ford Road in Westport, to be ground into meal to form the basis of their bread. Morton Lyon and Irving Patchen were local carpenters who continued to build barns as their ancestors had, from hand-hewed timbers. The fact that they used machine-made nails to fasten their barns' sheathing was almost their only concession to modernity.

The children of Weston still attended one-room schools, still contended with their drafty floors and the voracious appetite of the box stoves that attempted to keep them warm. The dangers of falling stovepipes were as great in 1925 as they had been in 1825. During the

Class of 1911, Middle District School, poses with teacher Willis Banks. From left to right, the pupils are Richard Coleman, Andrew Dexter, Rollin Gifford, James Coley, W. McClintock, Lewis Wirth, William Reeves, Willis Wilcox, Vernon Gifford, Herbert Gifford, William Wilcox, Christine Wirth, Frank Reeves, and Albert Dexter.

winter months, the students could depend upon their lunches to freeze unless they were kept close by the stove. As in the years before, older children, who knew the luxury of school only when work on the farm eased, sat at desks while younger scholars struggled to maintain their interest and their balance on hard and narrow benches. But all could look forward to a picnic at the end of the school year, perhaps at their school or, if the students had been especially good that year, at Compo Beach.

Social life in Weston also changed little with the coming of the new century's first decades. Households continued to be nuclear, and families continued to form the basic ingredient of Weston's society. The townspeople continued to enjoy old-fashioned dances held at John Lockwood's on Godfrey Road, to look forward to the sleighing that winter brought, and to go clamming at the shore in early summer. Coon hunting was a favorite fall pastime; Weston men usually hunted fox in the winter. Trapping was both a form of recreation and a means of accumulating small amounts of money. Well into the twentieth century, deadfalls called "figure fours" remained more popular than steel traps. Because the land was much more open that it is today, few deer lived in town. When all other forms of entertainment failed, there was always corn, grown right on the farm, to be popped.

Membership in Weston's two churches continued to be small; but for those who did belong, the churches offered suppers, picnics, and religious classes. Both churches still had woodcutting bees to provide fuel for the box stoves that heated them. Hardly less important than the church as a social organization was the Grange. Until 1905, it met in the old Jarvis Academy and then, when the Academy burned, began gathering at the town hall.

Perhaps the town's continued dependence upon traditional medical techniques best points up the tardiness of the twentieth century in arriving. Surely, Dr. Gorham still made his rounds and would until the 1920s, when he himself lost his health, but the town's population, in many cases, still did things the old way. As late as World War I, some mothers in town were still vaccinating their children against smallpox by scratching each child's arm with a needle that had been rubbed on the scab from a cow infected with cowpox. This procedure dated back not merely to the nineteenth century but back even to the time before the Norfield Society existed.

Barter continued to be the basic medium of exchange. Farmers traded with one another as they had for decades. One family that had an abundance of apples but was short of potatoes could probably find

The class of 1911 poses for the camera.

another whose predicament was the opposite. The old store that had been located just above Davis's (later Cobb's) Mill had gone out of business before the turn of the century. For a time, the post office had remained in operation there, but now it, too, was gone. So was Gorham's Store in Valley Forge. The nearest stores were in Wilton and Georgetown, and much of their business involved the exchange of goods without the exchange of money. In other words, those stores still operated in essentially the same way that William Noyes had operated his seventy-five years before.

Fred Bennett, also of Wilton, peddled meat in Weston, meat that he butchered himself from animals that he bought from local farmers. He also did a brisk business in calfskin coats, Bennett providing the skins, which were then made into coats by a firm in New Jersey. John Fanton, who bought much of his meat in South Norwalk, replaced Bennett as the town butcher, but even Fanton bought and killed some local animals.

Like H. B. Coley, many Weston farmers continued to peddle produce in Bridgeport and Norwalk. Apples, potatoes, onions, eggs, chickens, and cider were all likely to be found on Weston farmers' wagons as they made their way to those urban centers. Weston's dairy farmers were now selling more milk than cheese and butter. In fact, one notable concession to the twentieth century was the trucks that came from Fairfield to collect Weston's milk. Wade's Dairy bought much of the town's output.

When the twentieth century first began, the hammers of the Bradley axe factory could be heard around town, but they were heard less often than they had been twenty or thirty years before. After the 1911 fire, the hammers were silent, for not only had most of the plant been destroyed, but what remained of the company's assets—in particular, its patents—had been sold to the Collins Tool Company and removed to Collinsville, in the northeastern part of the state.

The rest of Weston's industries were also dead by then. Some of the last to disappear were those owned by Franklin Bulkley, who made various types of castings and whose plant was in Valley Forge; by Henry Wheeler, who operated a forge and blacksmith shop; and by Ward Nichols, who had a hat factory on Good Hill Road. The button factory at Lyons Plains had long operated irregularly, thus occasionally providing small amounts of cash for local children who collected bones to be made into buttons. By World War I, only the empty shells of these small factories remained. In this respect, nineteenth-century Weston was more modern than the town of the early twentieth.

The one industry in town that flourished in the early twentieth century was the lumber-and-charcoal industry. In part, the industry remained traditional, relying on the same methods that had been used for decades. Will Osmond, for example, still ran an up-and-down sawmill as late as the war period. But other aspects of the industry were modern. Two steam-powered sawmills existed in town—one in the Upper Parish, owned by Eugene Lockwood, and one on Lyons Plains Road, owned by James Smith. These were modern machines that were capable of producing large amounts of lumber.

Lumbermen in Weston cut many varieties of trees. They cut chestnut, which was struck by a devastating blight in the years just before World War I, to be used as railroad ties. Weston had long been known for its magnificent stands of chestnut, a wood that is amazingly resistant to the elements as well as being easily worked, and Weston lumbermen generally believed that these trees deserved a better fate than to be used as ties. But the railroads paid well, and the ties were delivered. Black walnut also made rugged ties. Oak was used principally for sills and stairs, although oak planks were cut to provide flooring for area bridges. Many of these planks also found their way into the hands of the Barnum & Bailey Circus; at the time, Barnum & Bailey built its own circus wagons. Later in the twentieth century, during the 1930s, Weston oaks provided the guard rails for the new Merritt Parkway.

The logs that were too small to be cut into lumber often ended up as charcoal. Woodsmen had long ago learned that the limbs and tops of the trees need not be wasted. Weston men made charcoal as they had for years. With a horse and scraper, a man would dig out the bottom of the charcoal pit. Then he would drive four long stakes into the four corners of the pit and bring their tops together to form a tepee-like structure. Up the sides of this structure would be placed four-foot logs, four layers of which would make a pit sixteen feet high. Between twenty and thirty-two cords of wood were required to complete the pit.

On top of the wood, the men placed leaves or low-quality hay, onto which they shoveled earth. At various places around the bottom of the pit, they constructed vents which could be opened and closed as needed. Then the workers fired the pit from the top, using a kerosene-soaked rag, and began the long and tedious task of seeing that the pit burned slowly and evenly. If they allowed too much air to enter the pit, it would burst into flames and become a wild bonfire.

Too little air would encourage gases to form in the pit and could result in its exploding. Either situation meant the loss of many hours of brutal labor.

The colliers—the men who watched over the burning—lived in tar-paper shacks built adjacent to the pits. Usually, two men shared a shack and its crude accommodations. Frequently, their diets were even less appealing than their quarters, their only meat being an occasional rabbit or squirrel they managed to trap.

Once the pit had burned down, the colliers raked out the charcoal and loaded it by the basketful in heavy wagons capable of carrying two hundred bushels for the trip to market. Almost all the Weston charcoal was sold to the brass and bronze companies in Bridgeport. About the time of World War I, the going rate for charcoal was eighty cents a bushel. Once the load arrived in Bridgeport, the colliers had to shovel it off by hand. Normally, ten or eleven hours were required to complete the round trip to Bridgeport.

John Morton of Weston and the Stone Brothers Lumber Company of Monroe were both big charcoal producers in Weston. During the First World War, the Stone brothers delivered four hundred bushels of charcoal a day to Bridgeport. This company did not necessarily own the land that it lumbered but often only bought the timber from Weston landowners. At times, the Stone brothers also bought wood already cut. They paid sixty-five cents a cord, a stack four feet by four feet by eight feet. The charcoal industry lasted until the manufacturing processes of the brass companies changed. Then it, like the rest of Weston's industries, disappeared.

As Weston's industries declined, so did its population. In 1900, the town included 840 persons; by 1930, this number was all the way down to 670. Individuals were obviously leaving Weston at a rapid rate, as they had begun to do in the late nineteenth century and which they continued to do in increasing numbers during the first three decades of the twentieth century. There simply were too few ways to make a living in the little town to support any substantial population. The town could not even support its own store.

But the decline in the town's population did not mean that Weston had lost its identity. Rather, the people of Weston insisted upon maintaining their uniqueness. For example, as urban centers with their large immigrant populations became bastions of the Democratic Party, Weston, which had been strongly Democratic since the days of Andrew Jackson, switched its political allegiance. Those strong-

Class of 1932 at the old town hall: From left: Back row–Betty James, Mary Gjuresko, Edith LaMotte, Helen Rowland, Marion Lockwood, Helen Wessels Front row–David Coley, William James, Anson Keene, Joseph Webber, Clayton Broch, Carol Rafa.

willed Yankees who remained in Weston had no desire to be confused with the urban masses of Bridgeport and New Haven. By 1900, the town was clearly Republican.

Although the decade that ended in 1930 showed a marked decline in Weston's population, the same was not true of the towns around it. Even by that early date, a population shift away from the cities was beginning to take place. Large numbers of men and women employed in New York City had already decided to make their homes in small towns outside the city. This was reflected in the rapid growth of the Fairfield County towns near New York. For example, between 1920 and 1930, Greenwich grew from 22,123 to 33,112 and Stamford from 40,067 to 56,765. Darien's population increased from 4,184 to 6,951, while New Canaan's went from 3,895 to 5,456. Both Norwalk and Wilton also experienced significant growth, the former from 27,743 to 36,019 and the latter from 1,284 to 2,133. Relatively, Westport grew

Local artists painted murals, such as these in the seventh-grade classroom throughout the original Hurlbutt school.

more slowly, from 5,114 in 1920 to 6,073 in 1930. Fairfield's population increased, not so much because of New York commuters as because of the spillover from Bridgeport's expanding population; Fairfield increased from 11,475 to 17,218.

On the other hand, Weston's population was falling. Still located slightly too far for all except the most adventurous New York commuter, the town had yet to feel the influx of large numbers of newcomers. But to any thoughtful observer, it was clear that Weston's day was not far off. Railroad service to the Saugatuck station in Westport was outstanding, and the advent of the automobile made the journey from Weston to Westport easier than previous generations had ever thought possible, despite the unpaved roads.

The first half of the 1930s brought no real change in Weston's population. Housing was still hard to find, because there had been almost no new construction in town for many years. And commuting from Weston was still not for the faint of heart. Those commuters who chose Weston as their home were either absolutely determined to live in the country or else enjoyed the luxury of having to travel to business only once or twice each week.

After 1935, Weston's population began to increase abruptly. Several factors accounted for this. In the first place, while housing was not plentiful in Weston, it came to appear relatively so as large numbers of people crowded into neighboring towns. Furthermore, the complete paving of Route 57, the Weston Road, in 1937 made the trip to Westport even less bothersome. And finally, in November of 1938, the Merritt Parkway was completed as far as Weston, thus providing an alternative means of reaching New York as well as easy access to the large towns of southwestern Fairfield County. The result was that Weston suddenly fell within commuting range of people working in towns from New York to Norwalk, and the population began to rise. By 1940, it exceeded 1,000, a figure that had last been seen in 1870.

Those venturesome souls who were the very first outsiders to move to Weston before it was either convenient or fashionable were an unusual lot. They began to arrive in the 1920s and came in increasing numbers during the 1930s. If they had any characteristic in common, it was their creativity. Many, but certainly not all, were artists—writers, musicians, illustrators, sculptors, actors. But among the business people who arrived early was also to be found this same creative bent.

Franklin P. Adams, more commonly known as F.P.A., moved to Weston in 1930. The author of several books, including *Tobagganing on Parnassus* and *Half a Loaf,* Adams was in 1930 affiliated with the New York *World;* his column, "The Conning Tower," appeared there until 1931, when he moved to the New York *Herald Tribune* and then to the New York *Post.* Adams's social life was as exciting as his professional life. Intimately involved with the most important writers of the era, Adams was a respected critic and an admired wit. He was among the first to recognize Sinclair Lewis as a great novelist, but when Lewis insisted on boring F.P.A.'s party guests by inflicting upon them the plots of yet unwritten novels, Adams excused himself, returned with a huge volume of his "Conning Tower" columns, placed it in the midst of the company, and announced "Next!"

Van Wyck Brooks did not arrive in Weston until 1938. A more important writer than Adams and certainly more of an intellectual, Brooks never possessed the humor that Adams did. But his books, among them *The Flowering of New England* (which won a Pulitzer Prize for history in 1937) and *The World of Washington Irving,* won popular as well as scholarly acclaim. Between 1909 and 1955, he was the author of

Actress Eva Le Gallienne with one of her pet goats in the early 1920s

more than twenty major works.*

James Daugherty was a muralist and illustrator. Coming to Weston in 1923, Daugherty was a man of many accomplishments. In 1928, he illustrated Edward White's biography of Daniel Boone. This encouraged the artist to write and illustrate a children's life of that famous frontiersman, a book which won the Newbery Medal in 1940. A reviewer of children's books wrote that "Mr. Daugherty's pictures stand out as the richest imaginative contribution to the reading and study of American history which has been made in my time." Jimmie, as most Westonites knew him, was described by a friend as "tall, muscular, straggling, possessed of arms and legs that defy all dancing school theories of grace but that never appear awkward, alive with a vitality and a rhythm that color and shade his personality. . . ." He was the husband of Sonia V. Daugherty, the writer, and the father of Charles Daugherty, the painter.[2]

Lawrence Langner moved to Weston in 1928. He was a man of many

*The house Brooks built off Old Weston Road was later owned by John Hersey, who also won a Pulitzer Prize (in 1945, for his novel *A Bell for Adano*). It seems unlikely that any other single house—and certainly no other in Weston—has sheltered two men of letters thus honored.

talents, for he was a patent agent, a playwright, and a theatrical producer and director. While he pursued a career as a patent agent, he served as director and co-administrator of the Theatre Guild, which he founded. It was Langner who arranged with George Bernard Shaw for the Guild to produce *St. Joan* and with Eugene O'Neill to produce *Strange Interlude* and *Mourning Becomes Electra*. With his wife, Armina Marshall, he owned the Westport Country Playhouse, and he also founded the American Shakespeare Festival Theater. Additionally, he wrote several plays and books, both on the theater and on international patent law. Few Weston figures had more diverse careers.

Musicians were also among the town's population. Nicolai Sokoloff moved to Weston in 1930. Born in Kiev, Russia, he was the conductor of the Cleveland Orchestra from 1918 until 1933. From 1935 until 1938 he headed the Federal Music Project of the Works Progress Administration and later became the conductor of the Musical Arts Society of La Jolla, California. The tenor James Melton made his concert debut in New York in 1932, five years before moving to Weston. He was a popular radio and concert singer, eventually joining the Metropolitan Opera in 1942, an affiliation that lasted until 1950.

In 1926, Eva Le Gallienne bought a home in Weston. Actress, director, producer, author, and translator, Miss Le Gallienne's demands for excellence in the theater were supported by both her theatrical example and her outspoken advocacy, and have resulted in her selection as the woman of the year in 1947 by the Women's National Press Club, as recipient of Norway's Cross of the Royal Order of St. Olav, and as the recipient of honorary degrees from Tufts, Smith, Russell Sage, Brown, Mt. Holyoke, Ohio Wesleyan, Goucher, and the University of North Carolina.

In her autobiographical work *With a Quiet Heart*, she wrote of her Weston home. "In giving up the Fourteenth Street building [in New York City] I naturally also gave up my apartment there, and from that time on my only home has been in Weston, Connecticut—a small township a few miles inland from Westport.

"This home has meant so much to me for so many years, and has brought me such comfort, serenity, and peace, that I should like to dwell on it for a few moments and try to express some of the gratitude that fills my heart when I think of how greatly blessed I have been in the enjoyment of it.

"I have always loved the country. I love trees, plants, flowers, animals, the earth, the stars, the quiet, the solitude; I am happiest in such surroundings. It has often seemed strange to me that I should

Mrs. Bayard Waring of Weston, as Miss America of 1948

have become an actress, for by temperament I am not in the least theatrical. . . .

"In line with my love of the land, I always planned to have a little place in the country that was my very own. During the days of my Broadway successes, culminating with *The Swan*, I managed to put by a small sum of money for this purpose. Several good friends of mine, engaged in big business, tried to persuade me to invest this money in gilt-edged securities, but they might as well have tried to get a French peasant to give up his little hoard of gold.

"With this money I bought a tiny little house in Weston in 1926. The house was well over two hundred years old, and about four acres of rocky woodland went along with it. To this haven I fled every week end—rain, shine, or snow—and those few hours of peace helped me immeasurably to sustain my physical and spiritual energy. Shortly after I bought the house, five acres of land adjoining mine came up for sale, and, to insure my solitude, I raised a loan on my little house and added them to my "estate." So, through the years, the place grew.

"I built a small house on the new land. . . . I myself lived in the tiny old house, which was a couple of hundred yards down the lane, but when I moved out of New York for good I had no room for my books and furniture from Fourteenth Street. These were all things I loved, and I didn't want to part with them. On the other hand, I was afraid of spoiling the old cottage, which in its way is perfect, by adding onto it. So, instead, I decided to add onto the new building and make that my permanent home.

"Originally the house was a small box-shaped three-room structure, and it was easy to throw out wings on either side, as well as to add a large room upstairs. Building then, compared with the fantastic prices of today, was unbelievably cheap. . . . When the alterations were finished I moved all my worldly belongings to the country and settled down. . . .

"The large window by my desk looks out over part of the rose garden and beyond the rose-bed a mass of lilies blooms in a glory of white and gold. At night their heavy fragrance creeps into the room to rekindle the image of their beauty.

"From early spring, when the first snowdrops so delicately and valiantly fight their way up through ice and snow, to the first days of November when Michaelmas daisies, hardy chrysanthemums and a few late-blooming roses still hold their own against frosts, and the woods are a flaming riot of color, there is not a day when one is not overwhelmed by the beauty of the world. One stands in silent awe before the exquisite perfection of some tiny blossom, some spray of foliage, the gemlike brilliance of some insect, the free joyous rhythm of a bird in flight. One or another of the myriad miracles of nature, at every moment, fills one with amazement and humility."[3]

Many of Weston's early notables were businessmen. John Orr Young, who lived for many years across from the Norfield Church, came to Weston in 1930. An advertising executive, Young was as creative in his profession as Weston's artists were in theirs. In 1923, he and Raymond Rubicam established the firm of Young & Rubicam. The firm was literally built on a shoestring, because its first account involved advertising a contraption for making shoestrings at home. Despite that dubious beginning, the firm became one of the first $100 million agencies and Young one of the pioneers in the field.

These people hardly represent the sum of Weston's talent during the 1920s and 1930s. Stuart Benson, the sculptor, and John Benson, the painter, were both established in town by 1930. The illustrator Earl Blossom came in 1933, and Frank Cobb, editor of the New York *World*, owned property in Weston before 1920. Wood Cowan, the cartoonist, came in 1928, and was one of the first "outsiders" to be elected first selectman; and Clifton Fadiman, then book editor of *The New Yorker* and master of ceremonies of the *Information Please* radio pro-

Artist James Daugherty, 1889-1974

gram, moved in during 1939. The sculptor James Earle Fraser, who had created "The End of the Trail" and designed the buffalo nickel, came to town in 1913, and his fellow artist, John Held, Jr., who immortalized the "Flapper" of the Roaring Twenties, came in 1919. Illustrator Robert Lambden was in Weston in 1921, and Joseph Lyford came almost as early as Lambden, as did sculptor Charles Prendergast. The eminent conductor Fritz Reiner moved to Weston in 1939, the same year as writer and editor John Selby and radio commentator Paul Wing. Webb Waldron, the writer and editor, and Rosamond Tudor, the etcher, and William M. Prince, the illustrator, were in town early in the decade.

The point of mentioning all those names is not to pretend that everyone who made his home in Weston was a genius. Rather, the point is that suddenly an immensely talented group of people were residents of the town. Attracted by the town's isolation, by the beauty of the countryside, and by each other, these people brought to Weston a variety of backgrounds, of vocational interests, and of cultural attainments. They were highly educated and, in many cases, nationally prominent. Their arrival meant that new demands were placed upon the town's services and new pressures fell upon its existing social patterns. In other words, these new residents meant change.

But to attribute to the new residents all the credit for the changes that came in the 1930s would be to overlook the vital role played by the old families of town. The families that had been in town for decades had begun, during the era of World War I, to recognize the need to come to grips with the twentieth century. It was at that time that several of these longtime residents had come together, at the urging of Charles Benedict, to form the Weston Improvement Society. This group, which met for years in the town hall, sought to make Weston a more attractive community. The group built a dining room (where community activities could be held) onto the town hall. It recognized the problems created by poor roads, and the men of the society worked together to straighten roads and to cut down steep hills.

The work of the Improvement Society was no isolated phenomenon. The Grange had been working for similar objectives for years. Meeting in the town hall during the same years that the Improvement Society did, the Grange was especially interested in bringing paved roads and rural free delivery mail service to Weston. Improvement of the schools was also a perennial concern of the Grange. So if the creative talents of the newcomers were a force for change, so also were the pride, energy, and enthusiasm of the town's old families. The mixture of old and new transformed many aspects of life in Weston before the outbreak of World War II.*

The town's education system desperately needed change. As early as 1922, the Board of Education had considered a system of graded education to replace the old one-room schools. The town meeting, however, took no action on the proposal, so not until late in that decade did the town have a plan to replace the old schools. In 1927, Horace C. Hurlbutt, Jr.—at the urging of Ella Brady Treadwell, a member of the Board of Education—offered the town ten acres near the Norfield Church as a site for a new school. In 1929, the town meeting accepted the gift and appropriated $50,000 to build the new school and auditorium.

Begun that same year, the new school was a single-story brick colonial building containing four classrooms, a library room, a principal's office and teachers' room, a nurse's room, and a small kitchen. The building also had an auditorium that doubled as a gymnasium.

*The one area of town life that saw almost no change before 1950 was town government. Before 1950, whatever changes in government occurred, occurred because the General Assembly mandated them.

Theater luminaries Lawrence Langner and Armina Marshall

But to describe the original Hurlbutt school, completed in 1932, in terms of its facilities would be to ignore the personal commitment that the people of Weston made to the new school. Local artists and craftsmen gave the school an individuality that is found in few public buildings. Several of Weston's talented illustrators painted brilliant murals on the schoolroom walls. Handcrafted wall hangings served as drapes in the buildings. The effect was a warm atmosphere, one that encouraged both the students' curiosity and their esthetic taste. In sum, it was a building that reflected both the town's commitment to education and the town's character.

Unfortunately, the school population soon outgrew the school. By 1937, enrollment had increased 32 percent over what it had been in 1930, and the town began planning an addition to the original structure. In May of 1938, the town meeting voted $30,000 to construct the addition, and the following October the Public Works Administration agreed to grant to the town an amount equal to 45 percent of the sum expended on the project. With this federal encouragement, the town pushed the addition forward, and the enlarged school was ready to receive pupils in 1939. Again townspeople contributed their special touches to the school, and an anonymous gift of $500 made possible a modern playground.

Hurlbutt school in flames, 1963

The school provided for education only through the eighth grade; Weston had no secondary education system. In the nineteenth century, children who went beyond the local one-room schools attended the Staples Academy. This continued to be the practice until into the twentieth century. But with the closing of the Staples Academy in 1905, Weston was forced to make other provisions. In 1906, the school board agreed to pay the tuition of those students wishing to attend high school in a neighboring town, but the students themselves had to bear the costs of either transportation or board. In 1928, Weston began paying for the transportation of Weston students attending Staples High School in Westport and of Georgetown students going to Norwalk High School. Eventually, the board altered this plan to require that all Weston students attending high school—including those from Georgetown—do so at the Westport school if they hoped to have their tuition and transportation paid. In 1908, only five Weston youngsters attended out-of-town high schools. By 1939, this number had risen to almost fifty.

Since 1852, Georgetown had been treated as a special school district, one that included students from Weston, Wilton, and Redding. In

1911, the General Assembly belatedly recognized the district's existence. Wilton directed the educational program of Georgetown, and all three towns contributed to the district's expenses in proportion to the number of students from each town. In 1933, after Weston had opened its new school, the town petitioned the General Assembly to allow all Weston students, including those from Georgetown, to attend the Hurlbutt School, and the Assembly, in 1934, authorized the withdrawal of all Weston children from the Georgetown District.

The forward steps made in Weston education were the result of the combined efforts of the Board of Education, led by farsighted individuals like Mrs. Treadwell, Willis Banks, and Raymond Fitch, and of the Parent-Teacher Association. One of the most important organizations in town and one that encouraged a spirit of town betterment, as the Improvement Society once had, the P.T.A. brought old families and new families together to the advantage of all. Alice Leopold, who would one day be Assistant Secretary of Labor during the Eisenhower administration, was the first head of the P.T.A. Between the P.T.A. and the Board, between the Treadwells and the Fitches and the Leopolds, Weston's school system was becoming the envy of its neighbors, not because of the vast numbers of dollars expended on it, but because of the town's commitment to it.

The town's roads provided less reason for pride, but even Weston's roads were beginning to improve. The Norfield Grange deserved much of the credit for this, for the local members enthusiastically supported a statewide Grange effort to "Get Connecticut Out of the Mud." J. Arthur Sherwood, a Grange leader and an official of the Connecticut Dirt Road Association, urged local Grangers to push their towns for action. Weston responded. In 1930, the town meeting authorized the selectmen to issue bonds amounting to $67,000 to provide funds to improve the roads. In 1931, the town approved the borrowing of an additional $90,000 for roads. With these funds, the town generally improved many roads and even paved some, such as Norfield Road. These improvements, coming shortly after the wide-scale arrival of the automobile, put Weston into the mainstream of Connecticut life as never before. Its isolation had been broken; and after the completion of the Merritt Parkway as far as Route 57, the influx of commuters into town proved this point.

The Grange's demand for improved roads was similar to the P.T.A.'s encouragement of a town library. A library had once existed, encouraged into being by John Noyes, but it had long since been defunct. In October, 1935, the P.T.A. donated $200 toward the crea-

tion of the Weston Public Library, and this gift was matched by a grant from the town. The state also provided $100 for the purchase of books. For nearly twenty years, the Hurlbutt School Library and the Weston Public Library shared the same facility in the school, although each was operated separately, the public library by the Library Board and the school library by the Board of Education.

Fire protection began for Weston in this same period. Until 1931, the Westport department covered Weston. But on February 14 of that year, the Weston Volunteer Fire Department came into being. It was the creation of local citizens; Frank Amis, A. H. DeWitt, Willis Banks, Charles Benedict, and George Gifford signed the incorporation papers. Others—like Ray Fitch, Anson Morton, Irving Patchen, Rollin

Weston's volunteer fire department before Memorial Day parade, 1976

Gifford, and Levi Squires—pledged their own property to guarantee a loan needed to acquire fire-fighting equipment. A variety of techniques was used to raise money with which to repay this loan and buy other items, but none was more successful than the annual Weston Firemen's Frolic, a show produced by the town's men and women. Local artists, most of whom were recent arrivals, drew posters advertising the event; Rollin Kirby, Scott Evans, James Daugherty, Christopher Rule, and Ray Strang all participated. Old families and new hawked tickets: Mrs. Willis Banks, Miss Mabel Patchen, and Mrs. James S. Coley representing some of the old families, and Mrs. John O. Young, Mrs. Nicolai Sokoloff, and Mrs. Wood Cowan the new. Wood Cowan was often the master of ceremonies, Henry La Motte the stage director, and William M. Prince the program chairman. With the money raised, the fire department, in 1934, purchased a Mack Motors pumping engine. The frolic, in particular, and the department, in general, were examples of how longtime residents and newcomers could work together.

But if concern for schools and roads, demands for a library, and the establishment of the fire department were instances of how the old and the new could co-operate, there were also cases of tension between the two groups. One such situation would be the question of the Saugatuck Reservoir. The story of this issue is a complicated one.

About 1920, the Bridgeport Hydraulic Company began to acquire land on both branches of the Saugatuck River for the purpose of constructing one or two reservoirs. The Connecticut General Assembly, in 1927, empowered the company to condemn property when "necessary or expedient for its corporate purpose." Using this weapon, the company, by 1936, had already acquired 4,500 acres of the 5,000 necessary for the Saugatuck Reservoir. Hard hit by the Depression, many Weston families were glad to sell to the hydraulic company. Most of those who held out were recent arrivals in town, people who were sufficiently affluent to ignore the company's offers.

Newcomers were also the leaders of the drive to stop the reservoir. Among the founders of the Saugatuck Valley Association, the organization that led the battle against Bridgeport Hydraulic, were John Orr Young, Webb Waldron, and F.P.A. The association hired Kenneth Bradley to represent it as counsel; Raymond Baldwin, later to be governor of Connecticut, worked closely with Bradley. The association raised money by calling upon the talents of its members and their friends. James Melton sang and the great violinist Jascha Heifetz played at a benefit concert given at Norwalk High School.

The issue became the cause of real conflict in town. On November 26, 1937, the town meeting appointed a committee of seven to work with the selectmen in investigating the dam project and its impact on the town. This committee was formed in the wake of an earlier town meeting decision, September 14, to block, if possible, the construction of the dam. But on March 10, 1938, by a vote of 103 to 75, the town rescinded the September resolution and directed the selectmen and a committee of eight to meet with the hydraulic company to discuss the closing of town roads which the flooding of land would necessitate. The Saugatuck Valley Association protested that the meeting had been held at a time when association members could not attend, yet

The Weston town hall, which was completed in 1953

clearly most of the old-time residents refused to see the dam as a great disaster.[4]

On May 25, 1938, the town meeting voted against a settlement with the company as worked out by this committee and decided, once again, to fight the dam. The Saugatuck Valley Association provided $5,000 to the town to take its case to court. But in June, 1938, the Connecticut Supreme Court of Errors decided in favor of the hydraulic company. In December, 1938, the company and the town reached an agreement; Bridgeport Hydraulic paid the town $40,000 in damages for the roads the dam would interrupt, agreed to build certain new roads, guaranteed a flow of 4,000,000 gallons a day in the Saugatuck below the dam for a fifteen-year period, and announced that it would not dam the West Branch of the Saugatuck until the courts had decided on the necessity of it. Weston residents received limited fishing and hunting privileges on hydraulic company property. The town meeting of December 29, 1938, approved the agreement, and the issue was closed. The Association had lost; the dam was built, and the former settlement of Valley Forge, home of Oliver Sanford and Dr. Frank Gorham, disappeared beneath the waters of the Saugatuck Reservoir.

No less tragic were the divisions the fight had caused in Weston. (Today, of course, the reservoir is considered a scenic asset.)

Less celebrated but hardly less divisive was the question of zoning. The town meeting first considered the subject on September 28, 1928, when it agreed to adopt the provisions of the general state statutes relative to zoning and to appoint a zoning commission. The meeting of September 15 authorized the appointment of a specific commission of five members, its function to draw up zoning regulations and submit them to the meeting for approval. In essence, what the town created was a committee on zoning and not a regular agency of town government.

Newcomers, who had for the most part come to Weston to escape urban congestion, were the movers behind the commission's creation. Their obviously legitimate concerns ran counter to both the traditions and temperament of the town's long-time residents. Unaccustomed to government regulation and by nature fiercely independent, the old families saw little advantage in the scheme, and when the proposed ordinances, which would have made all Weston a residential district, came before the town meeting on July 26, 1934, the voters decided against them by a vote of 135 to 124. In the cases of both the dam and zoning, the newcomers found they could not always have things their way.

But to emphasize the differences between the two groups would be to overlook the spirit of co-operation and of mutual respect that generally existed. Weston was more heterogeneous than it had ever been; more diversity of opinion existed now than ever before. This meant disagreement and heated politics. But it also meant a sense of civic concern that caused the town meetings to outgrow first the town hall and then the Norfield Church and then to fill the auditorium of the Hurlbutt School.

This civic concern—at least as it manifested itself in terms of demands for better schools, improved roads, and a new library—also cost money. In 1900, the total budget of the town amounted to little more than $3,000. By 1930, this figure had increased nine times, and by 1940 nearly twenty-seven times. Similarly, the town's indebtedness grew. In 1900, Weston owed less than $7,000, but by 1940 was in debt nearly $200,000.

As the 1930s were drawing to a close, new residents continued to come to town in increasing numbers. Route 57 and the Parkway made travel to southwestern Fairfield County and New York easy, and the trains were as elegant a way to travel as one could find. By the late

1930s, even businessmen who had to be in New York five days a week no longer thought Weston an impossible distance. Thus, the newest residents in town did not travel to New York once or twice a week, as the writers and artists had; rather, they made the round trip daily. If the age of the business or professional commuter had yet to reach its apogee, it clearly had begun to.

What was happening to the town could be seen in microcosm in what was happening to the old mill now called Cobb's Mill. For decades, the mill had been known as Davis's Mill and had ground the corn and rye and cut the lumber of local farmers. About 1920, Frank Cobb bought it from Simeon Carver, an heir of Timothy Carver, who had operated it as a sawmill. Cobb used it as a weekend and summer retreat. In 1928, his widow sold the property to Moira Wallace and Sydney Dyke. In time, the two women began to accept overnight guests, "mostly artists, writers, or actors." Among the regular guests were explorer-writer Peter Freuchen and journalist Quentin Reynolds. The strains of the Depression proved too great for Mrs. Wallace after Miss Dyke withdrew from the partnership, so, in 1934, she sold the mill to Alice Delamar and Jacques De Wolfe. They converted the inn into an expensive eating and drinking establishment, one which boasted a twenty-six-foot pewter bar imported from France, the finest chefs in the area, and prices beyond the wildest dreams of most old-time Weston residents. But the restaurant was a gigantic success, catering to wealthy Fairfield County residents and New Yorkers.[5]

The town of Weston seemed to be following a similar path. From a small and simple farm town, it had become briefly a haven for artists, writers, and musicians. But then, as word of the town's charms spread, it began to attract wealthy people from New York and from other parts of Fairfield County. By 1940, this final phase had just begun, and World War II was looming on the horizon.

NOTES TO CHAPTER 12

1. This chapter has benefited from my use of the Weston Historical Society oral history collection. This collection and the town records are the major sources of information about early twentieth-century Weston.

2. "James Henry Daugherty," *Current Biography,* 1940, pp. 221-222.

3. Eva Le Gallienne, *With a Quiet Heart* (New York, 1953), pp. 90, 91, 93.

4. Georgia Mansbridge to the Officers of the Weston Watershed Association, August, 1971, a copy of which is in the Weston Historical Society. This letter describes the controversy and contains a list of references to the subject from the New York *Times.*

5. The story of Cobb's Mill was described in an article in the Bridgeport *Sunday Post,* May 30, 1954.

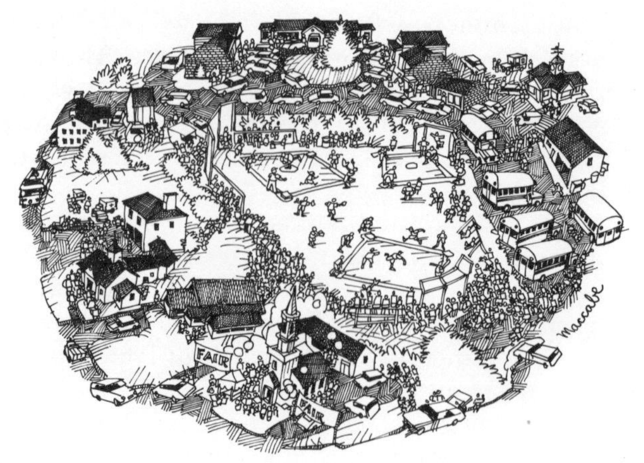

MODERN WESTON: AN OLD HERITAGE, A CHANGING CITIZENRY

"New affluence, new problems, new conflicts, new challenges"

World War II came crashing in on the United States just as Weston's character was beginning to change. In part, the war tended to slow down this change, but ultimately it sped it up, thus helping to complete the town's transformation.[1]

The war brought new difficulties to Weston's population. Many of these problems Westonites shared with the rest of the nation. Commodities were scarce and at times even impossible to find. Rationing became a way of life. The possibility of air raids, as remote as it was, meant that precautions had to be taken in using lights. Weston men and women donated time to the Civil Defense and the Red Cross. Others made greater sacrifices. One hundred and fifty-five persons from Weston served in the armed forces during World War II. Of these, four were killed: Clayton Broch, Samuel Hill, Fred Painton, and Jack Radosevitch.

In certain ways, Weston men and women had to endure fewer hardships than the residents of urban areas. Obtaining food was less

Capsule history of Weston, erected in 1977 by the Connecticut Historical Commission and the Weston Historical Society

difficult, for Westonites generally had room for gardens, and some even began raising cattle and poultry to avoid the consequences of meat rationing. Home-grown vegetables and home-grown beef and poultry not only found their way onto Weston tables, but these locally produced foods also provided a large part of the items used in the hot-lunch program at the Hurlbutt School. Organized by the P.T.A. and directed by Ethel Neuburg, this program both provided balanced hot lunches for Weston children and encouraged the sense of community involvement that had been the secret of the school system's success. Weston parents grew, canned, and helped prepare the lunches, which were then available to all children for five cents a meal.

But if Weston's rural nature simplified some problems, it also complicated others, such as transportation. Being without even a general store, the townspeople had to travel at least as far as Westport to buy the most ordinary items. Likewise, a visit to the doctor or dentist or cleaner also meant a drive to another town. But the scarcity of gasoline, which was sternly rationed, made frequent trips impossible.

Commuters faced the same problems. Gasoline was unavailable for the daily drive to the train in Westport or for the commute to Bridgeport or Norwalk. These problems were solved when local school buses were pressed into service. Buses traveling down both Weston Road

Construction of the Bridgeport Hydraulic Company dam in 1940

and Lyons Plains Road carried commuters to Westport in time for the 7:37 A.M. train to New York and met them on their way home when the 5:25 P.M. train arrived at 6:45. On Saturdays, the same buses made shopping runs to Westport. Because tires and good mechanics were every bit as scarce as gasoline, the buses provided more than a useful service; they provided a necessary one.

Despite these sorts of problems, Weston's population grew during the war years. Defense industries attracted large numbers of workers to the industrial cities of Connecticut, and these workers had to have housing. For those who could cope with the expense and the problems of living a considerable distance from work, Weston, with its pastoral atmosphere and its fine school, provided an attractive solution. The town saw much new construction after 1945, but before that date most of the newcomers bought or rented homes that already existed.

In fact, between 1940 and 1950, Weston's population grew at a fantastic rate. In 1940, 1,053 persons resided in town; by 1950, this number had climbed to 1,988. This represented a growth rate that was four times that of the state as a whole. And this was just the beginning. During the next decade, Weston's population grew to 4,039 individu-

The Saugatuck Reservoir, looking south from the Great Ledge in the Nature Conservancy

als, and by 1970 had reached 7,417. The combined growth rate of the years between 1950 and 1970 was greater than even that of the decade of the 1940s. In 1930, there were thirty-four persons for each square mile within the town; by 1970, there were 372 per square mile, and by 1978 there were 457, the 1978 population being approximately 9,200.

These great increases in population were the result of migration into Weston. In fact, only about 12 percent of the expansion from the 1940 figure of 1,053 to the 1978 figure of 9,200 was the result of natural increase. The other 88 percent came from new families' moving into town. To accommodate this increase, housing had to be constructed at a furious pace. In 1940, there were only about 400 housing units in Weston; by 1975, this number had grown to over 2,500.

Besides its recent arrival in town, there was another characteristic of Weston's new population that ought to be noted. The new residents were almost uniformly affluent. Virtually no lower- and few middle-class families came to Weston. Several factors helped to explain this. Obviously, those who chose to live in Weston had to be able to afford the costs of commuting a relatively great distance. These costs were substantial, whether they involved driving to an urban area in Fairfield County or driving to the train for the trip to New York. Weston's isolation also forced families to own a second automobile, for without one, children could not be transported to organized activities or to the homes of friends, and parents would be free to shop only during weekend and evening hours. In 1970, for example, 80 percent of Weston families owned two or more automobiles, whereas only slightly more than 50 percent of all Connecticut households did.

Living in Weston was also made expensive because the town government depended almost exclusively on the taxes paid by homeowners to finance its operations. Wilton, Weston's neighbor to the west, included both commercial and light-industrial areas, which helped to relieve the tax burden. Aside from the Bridgeport Hydraulic Company, there were no large industrial taxpayers in Weston. Thus, even in the 1940s, when the town was known for frugality, the tax burden was substantial, averaging about 15 mills. The continuously increasing costs of real estate also prevented many families from living in Weston. In many Fairfield County towns, there were areas that were less prestigious and, therefore, less expensive. But for the most part, Weston was generally attractive and, therefore, generally expensive. Once stringent zoning regulations were established in the 1950s, real estate values climbed even more precipitously.

Because it was expensive to live in Weston, few newly married couples or recent parents moved to town. Those who came tended to be families that included children of school age, because these children reached school age before their parents were sufficiently established to afford Weston and because the reputation of Weston's schools attracted families with children. And as the town's reputation for affluence grew, the cost of real estate and of living in Weston increased even further. By the 1950s, Weston was an amazingly prosperous community, prosperous beyond the imaginings of its earlier residents.

Certainly not everyone in Weston was rich, but as early as the 1950s the median family income in Weston exceeded that of all other Connecticut towns except New Canaan and Darien. In 1960, the median family income in Weston was $12,390, while that of Fairfield County, the wealthiest county in the state, was only $7,371. Weston's workers included a disproportionately large group of professional and technical people, of proprietors, and of managers. By 1970, Weston's median family income had reached $23,626 and was exceeded by no other Connecticut town except New Canaan, where the median income was $23,889. The figure for Fairfield County in that year was only $13,086, and that for the state as a whole $11,811. According to a system of socioeconomic index scores devised by the University of Connecticut, Weston ranked highest of all state towns. (Darien, Simsbury, Westport, Wilton, New Canaan, Redding, Ridgefield, Woodbridge, and Orange, respectively, placed second through tenth.)

Measured by any standard, Weston's affluence during the postwar period was phenomenal. In terms of its population, Weston had more dishwashers, freezers, washers, dryers, bathrooms, automobiles, and large houses than virtually any other Connecticut town. In 1970, the median value of owner-occupied houses in Weston was higher than that in any other town except New Canaan; the Weston figure was $54,060 and that for New Canaan, $54,642. Since then, prices have tripled.

Weston's new residents, the affluent commuters who continued to flock into town from the late 1930s on, placed ever-increasing demands on the town's services. One of their greatest concerns was zoning, a question with a long history.

The issue, as the reader will recall, originally came up in 1928, when the town meeting conclusively decided that Weston should have no zoning regulations. The issue remained more or less dormant after that, the selectmen excluding commerce and industry through their power to issue business permits. They held this power by the terms of Section 89c of the Connecticut General Statutes. But in 1943, the Court of Common Pleas declared Section 89c to be unconstitutional, and Weston, like dozens of other small Connecticut towns, was without zoning regulations. Several attempts to create such regulations were defeated.

In 1949, Rogues Ridge Properties, whose president was Weston resident Peter C. Robinson, bought six acres of land near Norfield Corners and began bulldozing operations. A group of interested citizens, led by Willis B. Banks, inquired about the activity and learned that the site was to become a shopping center. This information was presented to the selectmen, Willard Fanton then being the first selectman, and they issued a cease-and-desist order under Connecticut Statute 89c. Robinson's attorney, Harold E. Cable, declared that because 89c had been declared unconstitutional, his client would ignore the order. Then the Weston town attorney, Dwight Fanton,

The shopping center, built in 1950

sought an injunction, but Judge James Murphy refused the request, although he did order Robinson to show cause why the injunction should not be issued.

This crisis produced a special town meeting on January 17, 1950. Charles Wisner, chairman of the Non-Partisan Zoning Committee, introduced a resolution to establish a five-man planning and zoning commission which was to draft zoning regulations for Weston. The committee had been working hard to build up support for the concept of zoning, and Wisner's motion passed by a vote of 290 to 198. This same meeting decided, by a vote of 239 to 98, to discontinue legal action against the Robinson shopping center. Without question, this second vote was influenced by the statement of Mrs. Charles Broch, a member of the Board of Assessors, that the Bridgeport Hydraulic Company was going to court to seek to lower its taxes. If the company won its case, she announced, Weston faced a six-mill increase in taxes. When the meeting adjourned, the town had both a committee to prepare zoning regulations and the prospect of a commercial center.

But the zoning issue remained a lively one. Its opponents, organized by Albert Gerhardt, circulated a petition and forced a special

Public library, completed in 1963

town meeting. Hoping to rescind the zoning resolution, Gerhardt and his allies introduced a motion for repeal. Their efforts failed, and a week later, on April 13, 1950, Weston gave its approval to the code drafted by the five-man committee.

The 1950 zoning regulations established the Planning and Zoning Commission, whose functions were to regulate land use and to plan for the town's future development. The regulations also established a long list of prohibitions on land use. Advertising billboards, hospitals, asylums, correctional institutions, bowling alleys, roller-skating rinks, dance halls, pool parlors, tourist cabins, junk yards, apartments, and roadhouses were all unacceptable. The entire town was "designated by the regulations as a residential and farming district," and one-acre zoning became the rule for all of Weston.

The fight in 1950 was by no means a clear-cut division between old families and newcomers, but to a degree the sides were drawn along these lines. New residents, as in 1928, wanted to hold onto what they had come to Weston to find: a quiet, uncongested existence. Many long-time townspeople recognized that the exclusion of commerce and industry from Weston meant a heavier tax burden for residential

News photograph of the Saugatuck River in flood, October 16, 1955

property holders, and some of these old families could ill afford to pay heavier taxes. The issue of individual liberty was also involved, for many old-timers were jealous of their freedom. The idea of being told how to use their property was totally alien.

During subsequent years, the zoning regulations became even more severe. In 1953, all Weston was zoned as a two-acre residential district. In 1967, the regulations further required that no buildings or structures be built except as single-family dwellings or as "offices of a doctor, dentist, attorney-at-law, engineer, architect, teacher, artist, musician, writer, photographer, real estate agent, insurance agent, or accountant, or services rendered by a dressmaker, milliner, home cook . . . plumber, electrician or home repair or service man. . . ." But these offices were subjected to stringent rules. They had to be operated by resident occupants, could house no more than three employees, had to be located in the same building in which the occupant resided, could involve no more than one commercial vehicle (which could "not exceed one ton in designated capacity"), and could include "no mechanical and structural fabrication or assembly of the products or items." As of 1970, all persons who worked at home,

The Grange on Good Hill Road, moved from New Canaan and erected on its present site by its members in 1954

including doctors and dentists and artists and writers, had to have a special permit from the Zoning Board of Appeals. One would be hard pressed to imagine a stricter system of zoning regulations; its object: to preserve the traditional rural character of Weston.

These regulations frequently faced challenges, most small but some major. In 1961, the Planning and Zoning Commission held a public hearing on the request of Thomas Cartin for the rezoning of a forty-five-acre tract in the Georgetown section of Weston to allow for light industry. Faced with general opposition within town, Cartin withdrew his petition and created a residential subdivision on the property. In 1967, the commission heard an appeal by Edmund Cadoux for permission to construct a ten-store shopping center on Weston Road. Although the commission denied the request, Cadoux continued his fight, eventually taking his case to the Connecticut Supreme Court, which, unfortunately for Cadoux, decided in favor of the town of Weston. A similar proposal made in 1972 by Warren Joblin met a similar fate. Weston's zoning regulations remained intact.

As great a concern as zoning was to Weston's new and growing

In 1965, new elementary-school building replaced the structure destroyed by fire two years earlier.

population, education was an even more important issue. The town's school population expanded after 1940 even more rapidly than did its general population. In 1940, 234 students were attending school in Weston. By 1950, this number had grown to 396, by 1960 to 1,164, and by 1970 to 2,286. In 1976, the enrollment was slightly larger: 2,353.

To accommodate these numbers, Weston had to expand vastly its educational facilities. The old Hurlbutt School remained the only school until 1950, when a new building opened. Containing seven classrooms which were designed to house grades one, two, and three and the kindergarten, the new school cost just under $350,000. Grades four through eight remained in the old school. When, in 1950, the Weston system expanded to include the ninth grade, that grade also went into the Hurlbutt School.

The additional school was but the beginning of an ambitious building program. In 1952, the town appropriated $536,000 for yet another building; it opened in 1954. Four years later, Weston voted, 664 to 262, to spend $900,000 for a junior high school. It accepted its first students

Football practice at middle school

during the 1960-1961 school year and contained a large library, a gymnasium, soundproof classrooms, and a thoughtfully planned science center. During 1971-1972, this building was enlarged to include fifty rooms. At the same time, a swimming pool was added to the school.

Despite these advances, in 1963 the school system encountered a serious setback. On October 30, a fire, urged on by strong winds, destroyed the Hurlbutt School. The Weston Fire Department had to use all its manpower and resources to prevent the flames from spreading to the two adjacent, newer schools. Amazingly, the Hurlbutt students were back in the classroom by November 1, some of them meeting in the Norfield church and others in Temple Israel in Westport. The school systems of Westport and Darien offered to share textbooks, supplies, and even office equipment, and Westonites contributed books, magazines, and other materials that could be used to supplement the curriculum. By November 12, the town had established a School and General Building Committee to investigate the need for a new school building as well as other town building needs. The committee's recommendation for a new school was accepted by

Theater class, high-school courtyard

the town in September of 1964, and $625,000 was appropriated for construction. The second Hurlbutt School was ready for students in 1965.

Throughout its existence, Weston had never had its own high school. The Board of Education had for years discussed the wisdom of continuing to send Weston students to Westport, but by the mid-1960s, sentiment on the board and within the town favored Weston's building its own school. In April of 1965, the town meeting appropriated $6,000 for preliminary engineering for a proposed high school. The following October, the meeting provided $30,000 to obtain preliminary plans, and when these plans were submitted to the town, in May of 1966, it approved them. The meeting then voted to hold a referendum on the question of appropriating $3,297,000 for the school and $175,000 for a pool. Held on May 23, the referendum resulted in the school appropriation's being passed, 789 to 740, and the pool's being defeated, 740 to 468. In September of 1968, the first two wings of the high school opened, the other areas following in stages. By September of 1969, all of the school's facilities were ready for use.

As impressive as Weston's physical plant was, the education the system offered was even more impressive—so impressive, in fact, that

State Senator George Guidera at the town war memorial in the 1970s

many families came to town because of the reputation of the schools. In 1966, the Planning and Zoning Commission conducted a survey of community attitudes in Weston. Of the 1,181 persons responding to the questionnaire, 35 percent listed schools as the thing they liked best about Weston. The willingness of people from neighboring towns to pay tuition to allow their children to attend Weston schools and the consistently high scores that Weston students made on standardized examinations also attested to the schools' quality—quality which was an expression of the community's commitment to a strong educational program. Westonites have been willing to expend not only dollars—more than $4,000,000 for the fiscal year ending in June, 1978—but also time and energy. The P.T.O.'s* presentation of *Weston Union; or, How to Secede Without Really Trying* in April, 1975, was an example of the effort local citizens were willing to make in the cause of good education. The show required nearly six months of planning and rehearsal and involved more than two hundred Westonites.

The commitment to education had been a long-standing one. In

*This organization replaced the P.T.A. in 1970.

Town officials played lead roles in 1975 satiric revue Weston Union; or, How to Secede Without Really Trying.

more recent years, conservation has become a major interest among the town's population. In the Planning and Zoning attitude survey mentioned above, 85 percent of those responding said that they appreciated Weston's "rural character" more than anything else about the town. Westonites' concern about the environment was obviously an aspect of their appreciation of country life. The Aspetuck Land Trust, a private organization established in 1966, sought to preserve open spaces in town. This objective was handsomely served in 1967 when Katherine Ordway gave 1,400 acres to the Nature Conservancy, a national organization whose purpose is the preservation of open

The swimming hole at Cartbridge Road

lands, to be used for scientific and educational research and for aesthetic appreciation. Known as the Lucius Pond Ordway Preserve, in memory of Miss Ordway's father, this huge tract guaranteed that much of northern Weston would remain forever free from building and human habitation.

These two efforts were the work of private citizens and private organizations. In 1968, the town established its own Conservation Commission, and in 1972, the commission began to enforce the Inland Wetlands Act, which meant that it had to oversee all regulated activities affecting Weston's wetlands. The Weston Watershed Association, a citizens' group with a basically educational mission, was formed in 1970 to help preserve the watersheds of the Aspetuck and Saugatuck rivers.

In 1972, the town purchased about nine acres, known as the Lazard property, for open space. This action was followed by Weston's decision to float a $1,000,000 bond issue for open space and recreational land acquisition and then, in 1973, to purchase fifty-four acres, known as the Scribner property, to be used as a recreational and conservation facility. This land became, in 1977, Bisceglie Park.

If zoning, education, and conservation were principal concerns of Weston's recent arrivals, these were certainly not their only areas of interest. The inundation of population, in itself, meant that what had served the town well in the past became inadequate during the postwar years. In 1951, a spectacular night fire destroyed the old town hall and endangered the Norfield church, just to its south. It was decided a new building should provide expanded quarters for the fire department as well as the town offices. On July 5, 1953, the town officers moved into the new building. Equally antiquated was the town's system of finance; therefore, in May of 1952, the meeting empowered the selectmen to establish a committee to act as an advisory board to the selectmen and the Board of Education on questions of finance. This committee, in February of 1953, became the Board of Finance, whose function it was to review budget requests and to prepare the budget to be proposed to the town meeting.

Numerous other such matters had to be attended to in order to keep Weston's government abreast of its growing population. In 1956, the town decided that a more adequate system of law enforcement than part-time constables was needed, and so in that year the first resident state trooper came to Weston. The following year, the town obtained its own post office, a convenience it had been without since before the turn of the century. The fire department began, in 1961, to provide ambulance service—an enormous undertaking for a volunteer department—and in 1962 Weston adopted the state building code. The new public library building opened in 1963.

Change continued through the 1960s and into the 1970s. In 1966, Weston and Westport formed the Aspetuck Valley Health District, which took on responsibility for enforcing the state public health code and local sanitation ordinances. To formalize the system of self-government that already existed in town, Westonites approved, in 1967, their first charter. The Recreation Commission came in 1969, and in 1975 a police department replaced the trooper and constables.

All of these changes cost money. Most expensive, of course, were the costs of education, but all the new agencies, commissions, and boards required funds. The increase in the town budget between 1940 and 1978 was phenomenal—less so, obviously, when considering inflation and the population increase that occurred during these thirty-eight years. But still, the differences were startling. In 1940, the total town budget amounted to about $70,000, with about $33,000 of this going to the school system. The tax rate was then 14.5 mills. By 1950, the budget had grown to $177,000, of which the schools received

Cobb's Mill Inn on the West Branch of the Saugatuck River

$136,000; the taxes were up to 16.8 mills. A decade later, the budget had expanded to $885,000, with $588,000 designated for the schools. The tax rate had reached 44.75 mills. Nineteen seventy saw a budget of $3,704,000, the Board of Education receiving $2,524,000 of this and the tax rate being 59.25 mills. By 1978, the proposed budget had reached $6,245,000, with the Board of Education asking for $4,276,000.

Thus, in those thirty-eight years, while the population increased about nine times, the overall budget increased about ninety-one times and the education budget about 128 times. Obviously, during those years, the size of the government was growing as rapidly as was the population; what had been simple was now complex. If Weston had been lingering on the fringes of the twentieth century in the 1930s, it was, at least in terms of government, clearly in the mainstream by the 1970s.

But despite the change in the size and complexity of Weston's government, much of the old structure remained. The town meeting, the selectmen, and the town clerk continued to fill the functions they had for decades, although since 1968 the selectmen had been assisted by an administrative assistant who directed the town's personnel, worked with planning and budget, and gathered and analyzed data for the selectmen's use. Also, Weston, like other Connecticut towns that have the town-meeting form of government, still had two kinds of voters, as it had in the eighteenth century: property owners, who can vote in town meeting, and registered voters, who can vote in state and federal elections; persons might fall into both catagories but did not necessarily do so.

Weston's residents changed even more dramatically than did its government, but certainly the community maintained many ties with the past. The biggest difference between Weston's postwar population and earlier generations was the affluence of the new Westonites. Whereas in 1970 only 25 percent of the town's families could possibly be considered middle-class or below, during the years before 1920 virtually all of the town's residents would have fallen into this group. This contrast resulted from the differences in occupations between recent and early times; once a land of subsistence farmers, Weston had become the home of professionals, executives, and managers. In 1970, 86 percent of all Weston workers were white-collar workers; in 1870, no more than one percent would have fallen into this category.

The different types of occupations of the new Westonites led to a whole series of other differences from earlier days. In the nineteenth century, all Weston workers were employed in town; in 1970, only about 4 percent worked in Weston, with about 47 percent working elsewhere in Fairfield County, 40 percent in New York City or on Long Island, and the rest elsewhere in New York or Connecticut. The kinds of work done by modern Westonites also made them much more mobile than the town's earlier residents. Those who decided to settle in early Weston and to take up a life of farming were unlikely to move unless forced to. The modern residents moved about at a hectic pace. For example: In 1970, of all the households in Weston, 18 percent had existed in town for a year or less, 29 percent for fewer than two years, 40 percent for fewer than three years, and 55 percent for fewer than five years. Only 26 percent of the families had been in Weston for a decade or longer—hardly the situation when generation after generation of Coleys and Bradleys and Fantons occupied the town.

And the new residents were much better educated than their predecessors. In 1970, 44 percent of Weston's population over the age of twenty-five had attended college for four or more years, and the median education level for this group was 15.3 years. (In the nineteenth century, Weston had been fortunate to have in its midst four or five college-educated men.) This highly educated population

The Norfield Grange fair, 1978

needed to be informed of town happenings, and, in 1970, Patricia Heifetz responded to that need by establishing the Weston *Forum*—the town's first newspaper.

Weston's population during the early years was overwhelmingly of native stock and Protestant. Clearly, this was no longer true in the postwar years. In 1960, about 7 percent of Westonites were foreign born and 19 percent were children of foreign-born parents. The town had substantial numbers of both Jews and Catholics. The construction of St. Francis of Assisi Church in Weston was something that the town's founders would never have predicted. But Weston's black population in 1960 or 1970 was relatively smaller than it had been during the first hundred years of the town's existence. In 1960, only one percent of the population was black, and only .3 percent of the households were black—which indicated that most blacks in town were servants. The days of Little Egypt had clearly passed.

Looking generally at Weston's population, one would be tempted to conclude that the present population was much more heterogeneous than it had been in the days of subsistence farming. But if from an ethnic, religious, and geographic point of view Weston's recent popu-

The Weston post office in 1978

lation is more mixed, in other ways it is as homogeneous as it ever was. In terms of socioeconomic class, occupational status, education, and personal and familiar aspirations, Weston's population in 1960 or 1970 contained little more variety than it did a century earlier. Probably the height of heterogeneity came during the 1920s, 1930s, and 1940s, when enough old-line families remained in town to give the advocates of zoning and the opponents of the Saugatuck Reservoir a fight for their money. This is not to say that politics in Weston during the 1960s and 1970s have been without life, but it is to say that what battles have been fought have been struggles over ways and means and not goals.

The family was the most important institution in early Weston; it probably still remains so. For while it is now less important from an economic and social point of view, it may be more crucial from a psychological one. Clearly, Westonites in recent times have depended upon their families to provide a feeling of connectedness with other aspects of their experience. Eighty-eight percent of Weston households in 1970 were composed of a husband and wife either with or

Actress Bette Davis and artist Blake Hampton, Weston residents both, at the Weston Field Club

without children. This figure indicates the family orientation of the community, an orientation that probably was no stronger in 1770 or 1870.*

This does not mean that the family meant in 1970 what it did in either 1770 or 1870. In 1770, for example, Weston families made no rigid separation between children and parents. Children then learned at an early age that they were miniatures of their parents. Sons were training to be what their fathers were—farmers—and daughters to be farm wives. Modern children face a bewildering array of choices, and so they tend to see themselves as a special category within the family. They become part of the culture created by peers rather than by parents; for within that youth culture, identity, as short-lived as it might be, comes ready-made. In 1970, Westonites recognized the situation by establishing the Youth-Adult Council, which sought to define the needs of Weston's youth and to plan programs to meet

*Only 12 percent of Weston households are headed by widowed, divorced, separated, or unmarried persons.

Aspetuck Country Club, founded 1966

those needs. Such a concept would have been totally superfluous in 1770.

It would be folly to attempt to determine if today's residents are more or less happy than those who came before. All that can be said is that earlier generations enjoyed a quiet sense of order that those of the twentieth century can only long for, but with the order also came a large dose of monotony. Modern Westonites generally can escape that grinding monotony, but the variety of life that many are able to enjoy is laced with large quantities of instability. Fortunately, neither group has had much choice in the matter, for the choice between the two would not be an easy one.

But aspects of the past are all around modern Westonites. The Norfield church, the Emmanuel church, the Grange, and the Staples Fund—which since 1967 has been used to provide college scholarship money to local children—all remain. The same type of local initiative that brought the Grange into being has since resulted in the creation of the Field Club in 1948 and the Aspetuck Valley Country Club in 1966, both home-grown products designed to meet the social needs of the community at some particular time. Furthermore, the same kind of dedication that was found in such public servants as Nathan Wheeler

Weston Field Club, founded in 1948

or John Sherwood can still be found in people like Gertrude Walker, whose tenure in office exceeded even Wheeler's, and Willard Fanton, a local boy who had a successful career in New York and then brought real administrative skills to the office of first selectman for more than a decade.

But other traditions have disappeared or are disappearing. In particular, until recently many of the families that first settled Weston remained deeply rooted to the land and the community. This was important, for they provided a degree of familial and social stability; they provided the continuity that all communities require. But as modern Westonites have attempted to maintain the "character" of Weston, they have created an exclusive community that is simply too rich for those old families that affluence has managed to elude. So there are fewer Coleys, Fantons, Lockwoods, and Bradleys than there once were; a decade hence, there will be fewer yet. And Weston will be a poorer place.

Yet something special of the settlement of 1787 remains in Weston to the present day. There is still, among many modern Westonites, a strong sense of belonging to a unique community, a sense of "us" in the town as against "them" who are out there; who, for whatever reason, do not enjoy being a part of all that Weston is. In 1837, shortly before his death, John Noyes, the second minister of the Norfield Church, wrote of his town: "Surely, for a small and remote town, we have not done very poorly in the past,—the future will look out for itself."[2]

One would be hard put to challenge Noyes's judgment of Weston's past, or his lack of timidity about its future.

NOTES TO CHAPTER 13

1. This chapter was based on material from a variety of sources. Especially useful were the oral history records of the Weston Historical Society; the data provided by the United States Censuses of 1950, 1960, and 1970; *Proposed Development Plan, Town of Weston, Connecticut* (Weston Planning and Zoning Commission, 1968); the annual report of the town of Weston; *This Is Your Town . . . Weston, Connecticut* (Weston League of Women Voters, various editions); *The Weston Forum; The Westport News* and its predecessors; and conversations with a variety of Weston residents.

2. John Noyes, "Famous Residents of Weston," Noyes Collection, Box 34, New Canaan Historical Society.

ANNUAL REPORTS

Appendices

TOWN OFFICIALS

First Selectmen 1879 / 1979

M.V.D. Rowland	1879-1883	Irving J. Lockwood	1924-1927
George A. Sturgis	1883-1885	Samuel Shethar	1927-1929
M.V.D. Rowland	1885-1893	James L. Clarke	1929-1930
James A. Smith	1893-1902	Walter B. Eager	1930-1931
Oscar Budd	1902-1904	Burton P. Merwin	1931-1932
C. E. Lockwood	1904-1905	James S. Coley	1932-1933
George E. Sherwood	1905-1909	George F. Sherwood	1933-1935
Wilbur Sturges	1909-1910	Daniel R. Harvey	1935-1937
Frederick Burritt	1910-1911	Chester G. Coley	1937-1944
Wilbur Sturges	1911-1912	Willard H. Fanton	1944-1955
John P. Kramer	1912-1913	Wood M. Cowan	1955-1957
George F. Sherwood	1913-1914	John Guidera	1957-1961
John M. Lockwood	1914-1915	Paul Coniglio	1961-1967
Burton P. Merwin	1915-1916	James M. Daniel	1967-1969
Oscar Budd	1916-1917	Edward W. Russell	1969-1971
Samuel B. Williamson	1917-1919	David Strassler	1971-1973
Edgar B. Perry	1919-1920	Barbara Wagner	1973-1975
F. Harold Burritt	1920-1924	F. Donald McCormick	1975-1979

Town Clerks 1878 / 1979

David L. Rowland	1878-1893	A. C. Bradley	1906-1932
Iverson C. Fanton	1894-1900	Sarah Treadwell	1932-1945
Charles R. Morehouse	1900-1906	Gertrude Walker	1945-

Town Treasurers 1878 / 1979

Morris W. Salmon	1878-1879	Walter B. Eager	1925-1929
Charles M. Parsons	1880-1883	Willis W. Parker	1930-1937
David D. Coley	1884-1891	Donaldson Strong	1937-1950
David S. Parsons	1891-1892	Charles C. Lunny	1950-1963
G. Warren Bradley	1893-1904	George Stoddard	1963-1968
Burton P. Merwin	1905-1908	Edward J. Gannon	1969-1977
Stephen W. Godfrey	1909-1910	George Sasseen	1977-1979
David M. Andrews	1911-1912	Edward Gomeau	1979-
Eli Wakeman	1913-1924		

*Collectors of Taxes 1924 / 1979**

Willis Banks	1924-1935	Elizabeth Jackson	1976-
John L. Breitwieser	1935-1976		

* Information prior to 1924 not readily available.

*Superintendents of Schools 1919 / 1979**

Frank W. Knight	1919-1948	Dorothy MacLean/Acting	1960-1961
Edward Summerton	1948-1958	Thomas A. Aquila	1961-
Howard D. Wood	1958-1960		

* This position was newly created in 1919.

ILLUSTRATIONS AND CREDITS

The illustrations in *Weston: the Forging of a Connecticut Town* came from varied sources. Many local residents and organizations made available photographs and documents which have been included, and these are acknowledged and identified by page number in the list of Photographic Credits.

The photographs depicting Weston as it is today were, in the main, taken by Scott Hill, who also photographed for reproduction many of the older prints included. Film and prints were processed by Herman Vener, and the map reproduced on page 30 was drawn by Louis F. Bregy.

The Committee is deeply indebted to all those who contributed so generously, most particularly the artists of Weston who created the illustrations which embellish the chapter heads and ends. Their work is identified specifically by page number in the list of Chapter Illustrations.

Photographs and Maps

Photographic Credits

Antique Tools and Trades in Connecticut / page 172
Louis F. Bregy / page 93
Mrs. James Coley / page 194
Charles M. Daugherty / page 215
Clifford Emanuelson / pages 18, 19 and 104
Fairfield Historical Society / pages 120 and 176
Edith Fanton / pages 171, 173 and 175
Raymond Fitch / pages 145, 158 and 181
Ruth Treadwell Fox / pages 151 and 158
Eva Le Gallienne / page 211
Carol Kaliff / page 247
Ruth Lockwood / page 177
Carol Moore / page 45
New York Times / page 234
Norfield church archives / pages 154, 158, 202, 204 and 208
The Theatre Guild / page 217
S. Jo Voigt / page 239
Mrs. Bayard Waring / page 213
Weston Historical Society / pages 13, 144, 165, 186 and 199
Weston Volunteer Fire Department / pages 218 and 220-221

Chapter Illustrations

David Blossom / pages 1 and 35
Monroe Eisenberg / pages 12 and 115
Bill Graveline / page 201
Blake Hampton / pages 47, 78, 121, 122 and 250
Richard Maccabe / page 226
Marilyn Miller / pages 11, 24, 139, 140 and 141
Euclid Shook / page 164
Mary Sowinski / page 25
Lynn Sweat / pages 34, 46 and 98

INDEX

a

b

c

d

e

f

g

m

n

t

u

v

w

y

z

from the front to the rear thereof, there we measured the width of them as of one long lott and the manner of our measuring the width of s^d Lotts and s^d upright highways for the greatest exactness was by a rod pole sixteen feet and a half in length s^d Pole being levelled on all uneven land by a square and plumb line and we found s^d long lotts and s^d upright highways to be in width as here following they are particularly set down, viz, begining next the west side of the Mile of Commons

	Rods	feet	Inches
Isaac Gray / Moses Dimon } thrown into one	26	3	0
John Banks	32	4	2
Jehue Burr	34	3	5
Obadiah Gilbert	24	10	4
Highway	4		
Joseph Wakeman / Thos. Skidmores } now called Hills	44	9	
Part of Sarah Williams / Stephen Hedges now called Willsons	23	5	8
Cornelius Hulls	33	15	4
John Burr	38	8	
Henry Rowlands	42	15	6
John Cable Senr.	30	5	
Highway	4		
Richd. Osborn	34	13	
Joshua Knowles / Nathl. Perry }	31	11	11
Mr. Harveys now called Staples }	31	12	6
Tomkins	9	14	1½
Bradleys	25	15	4½
Highway	4		
Daniel Finches	10	11	4
Thos Sherwood	28	10	2½
Peter Coleys	15	14	9½
old Hide / John Hide } one	40	1	0½
John Thompsons	8	1	6½

	Rods	feet	I
Peter Clapham	27	5	0
Goodwins	5	3	0
John Knowles's	23	12	5
John Sturges	32	6	6
Highway	4		
John Cable Jur.	21	5	1
John Applegates	5	10	3
Thos. Lyons	10	10	9
Samuel Drakes	11	1	9½
James Beers	27	1	11½
Old Barlows	16	10	6
Saml. Smiths	18	15	4
John Barlow Jur.	15	9	3
Eliza Smiths	14	6	
Robert Rumsay	19	6	9
Danl. Lockwood / Saml. Ward / John Smith } into one	51	15	1
Highway	4		
Richd. Ogdens / Daniel Frost now called Applegates }	62	5	6
Jos: Lockwoods	24	15	[illegible]
Robert Beachum	24	2	8½
John Green	27	14	4

Then see